THE OFFICIAL SPORT GUIDE

FORMULA ONE 2012

This edition published in 2012
by Carlton Books Limited
20 Mortimer Street
London W1T 3JW

10 9 8 7 6 5 4 3 2 1

ISBN: 978-1-78097-031-8

Editor: Matthew Lowing
Project Art Editor: Luke Griffin
Designer: Sally Bond
Proofreader: Jane Donovan
Picture Research: Paul Langan
Production: Maria Petalidou

Printed in the UK by Butler Tanner & Dennis Ltd

Sebastian Vettel heads into 2012 in fine form, looking to make it three titles in a row.

THE OFFICIAL BBCSPORT GUIDE
FORMULA ONE 2012

BRUCE JONES

CARLTON
BOOKS

CONTENTS

Jenson Button proved to be the best of the rest behind Sebastian Vettel in 2011, scoring some sensational wins for McLaren.

Red Bull Racing's duo of Sebastian Vettel and Mark Webber are to the fore at the start of the Turkish GP, much as they were all year.

ANALYSIS OF THE 2012 SEASON

We have been spoiled by two seasons of superlative F1 racing and all pointers indicate that 2012 could be better still. The top drivers are spread across the top teams and the chasing pack of McLaren and Ferrari will be looking to mount a greater challenge to the dominant Red Bull Racing. Look, too, to even more exciting action on Saturdays, as Pirelli introduces special qualifying tyres.

The one thing that the teams and drivers do not want this year is a walkover for the World Champion. No one apart from rival drivers would complain if Sebastian Vettel made it three drivers' titles in a row – he is clearly talented enough to merit that – but nobody wants a driver to win by as large a margin as he did in 2011. Indeed, having been spoilt by last-round title shoot-outs in the four of the preceding five seasons, we have rather come to expect them.

What spiced up last year was the see-sawing of team performance between rounds, with McLaren and Ferrari sometimes up and sometimes down, while Red Bull Racing was seemingly always on the pace. As there are no major technical rule changes save for stricter control of the positioning and function of exhaust pipes plus a tougher side-impact chassis test and clearer marking of in-car emergency switches, the designers will have had a clear idea of what they have to play with for 2012, so their cars ought to be closer than before. Otherwise there is always the DRS (Drag Reduction System) wings and KERS (Kinetic Energy Recovery Systems) to boost overtaking.

One of the things that made the racing so exciting last year – and we hope will do so again in 2012 – were the tyres

Pirelli brought along. They certainly added to the show, with drivers being rewarded for making their tyres last or suffering if they went too hard too soon, and had their tyres' performance "drop off a cliff". However, for their second year as Formula One's sole tyre supplier, Pirelli will be looking to enhance the battle for pole position by introducing special qualifying tyres and the spectacle of drivers being able to really attack for these key laps on Saturday afternoon looks set to provide exhilarating drama.

Regarding the mix of teams and drivers for the 20-race campaign, there is little change among the top teams, although a driver merry-go-round is promised to break out as several top players will be out of contract at the end of the season. So, for this year at least, Red Bull Racing will continue to field Sebastian Vettel and Mark Webber; McLaren has Jenson Button and Lewis Hamilton, while Ferrari is represented by Fernando Alonso and Felipe Massa. Although there is no change to the status quo, it will be extremely interesting to see whether Lewis Hamilton can get his mojo back, eliminate the mistakes that peppered his 2011 season and so attempt to establish himself once again as the team's leading driver after Button made himself the "go to" figure with some mature, intelligent drives to victory. The team itself will also be looking to ensure some of the mistakes that it made last year do not happen again. Expect Alonso to dominate Massa once more in what will most likely be their last season together and, on last year's form, for the same to happen with

Vettel lording it over Webber at Red Bull – unless the Australian can take the battle to Vettel again, as he did in 2010.

Behind the top three teams, Mercedes GP will also have driver continuity, with Michael Schumacher and Nico Rosberg partners for a third year. Their hopes of catching the big guns have been boosted by a major influx of design and engineering talent.

There are no new teams, but the battle to carry the Lotus name that was fought out last year between Lotus Renault GP and Team Lotus has been settled, with the latter changing its name to Caterham.

If you want to keep an eye out for what might be the biggest surge, look to Williams for this once-dominant team has hooked up again with Renault, as it was in its title-winning days of the 1990s, when this partnership resulted in five constructors' titles in six years. Despite a few lean years, it still has a sizeable workforce and so has the staff to mount the fightback. The midfield looks set to be made up of Force India, Sauber and Toro Rosso. At the tail, Virgin Racing has scrapped its concept of having a car designed only by CFD and might well advance because of this, while HRT can only hope that it's a case of third time lucky.

With Vettel talking, incredibly, of raising his game for 2012, his rivals know that they have a challenge of extraordinary magnitude ahead of them. Most of all, they will be praying their teams' designers can give them machines with which they will be able to take the fight to the German.

RED BULL RACING

This is the team all others must aspire to beat, for Adrian Newey's cars are the ones "pushing the envelope" the most in their quest for speed. With no changes known for 2012, expect more of the same for Sebastian Vettel and Mark Webber.

Red Bull Racing provided the car to have last year and Sebastian Vettel did the rest. Paired together again, can anyone topple them?

Consider the bald facts of Red Bull Racing's 2011 World Championship campaign and it's a swathe of wins, fastest laps, points galore and victory in both the drivers' and constructors' championships. Perhaps the most telling feat of all, however, was the fact that Sebastian Vettel put one of its RB7s on pole for the opening round in Melbourne and either he or team-mate Mark Webber then took pole at each of the next 14 grands prix.

The RB7s' performance advantage was not as great in the races, when the McLarens and occasionally the Ferraris were able to match them. Yet, even with KERS and DRS to assist in overtaking, pole is still the best place to be and Vettel made it work for him time and again by driving as if his life depended on it for the first two laps to ensure that he was out of range of his pursuers when their DRS was enabled from lap 3 onward.

For 2012, perhaps Newey will have allowed enough space within the RB8 to accommodate the KERS, unlike last year's sleek body. In fact, if the team had an Achilles' heel in 2011, it was in the way in which those additional, power-boosting technologies worked. Or, more to the point, *did not* work, with Webber seeming to suffer more failures that left him unable to defend from any

KEY MOMENTS AND KEY PEOPLE

TEAM HISTORY

Few sports have as many teams to have reinvented themselves as F1. Red Bull Racing started as Stewart GP in 1997. It looked smart, but achieved little until Johnny Herbert produced a surprise win at the Nürburgring in a wet/dry race of 1999. Ford bought the team for 2000 and renamed it Jaguar Racing, with Mark Webber its star driver. Then, in 2005, Dietrich Mateschitz's Red Bull money turned it into Red Bull Racing and the key to its subsequent success was the signing of design genius Adrian Newey from McLaren in 2006.

CHRISTIAN HORNER

Horner rose from karts to F3000 as a driver but then realized that he was not quite quick enough to go any further so instead turned to team management. His team, Arden, remains at the front in F1 feeder formula GP2, but he handed over the reins long ago in joining Red Bull Racing for 2005. He must have done a good job as he took over as team principal from 2006 and the team has risen to the top of the pile.

Driver	Nationality	Races	Wins	Pts	Pos
Sebastian Vettel	German	19	11	392	1st
Mark Webber	Australian	19	1	258	3rd

McLaren driver closing in and pressing their KERS button.

These KERS failures became fewer as the season progressed, but what did not was the way in which the RB7s consumed their tyres on high-speed circuits, which explains why team principal Christian Horner, Newey and co seldom looked more relieved than when Vettel held it together to win at Spa-Francorchamps.

One massive advantage of Vettel and Red Bull Racing wrapping up both titles early last year was that they could afford to swing their attention toward developing this year's car earlier than their rivals. And in a sport where success is achieved by fractions, every week of design and development counts.

Although F1 is a cyclical sport, with teams coming and going at the head of the pack, Red Bull Racing looks set for a run of dominance at least until the end of next year because that is when the next major set of rule changes are to be implemented. This is when the current engines will be consigned to the scrapheap and a new range of 1.6-litre V6s introduced. At this point Red Bull Racing will have to hope engine partner Renault gets it more right than rival manufacturers. Yet, even in this, Red Bull's increasing predominance has landed it an advantage as it will

now be given a say in the design of the new-generation engine and this could help it to fit in with Newey's notoriously parsimonious space allocations as he continues to seek the most aerodynamic way of packaging.

Vettel and Webber will remain the driving line-up, perhaps for the final time, but the dynamics of this pairing have changed irrevocably as the Australian can no longer even pretend he is the equal of the German as Vettel has put his stamp on proceedings with two drivers' titles in the past two years. In 2010 there was some parity and chopping and changing of order whether or not Vettel happened to be favoured by the management, but with Vettel racking up six wins in the first eight races and Webber scoring none, the debate was over. With the car better suited to his driving style, Vettel was undoubtedly the team's number one and he produced an all-but-flawless set of races.

FOR THE RECORD

Country of origin:	England
Team base:	Milton Keynes, England
Telephone:	(44) 01908 279700
Website:	www.redbullracing.com
Active in Formula One:	From 1997 (as Stewart until 2000, then as Jaguar Racing until 2004)
Grands Prix contested:	261
Wins:	28
Pole positions:	39
Fastest laps:	22

THE TEAM

Chairman:	Dietrich Mateschitz
Team principal:	Christian Horner
Chief technical officer:	Adrian Newey
Head of race engineering:	Ian Morgan
Head of car engineering:	Paul Monaghan
Chief designer:	Rob Marshall
Head of vehicle performance:	Mark Ellis
Head of aerodynamics:	Peter Prodromou
Team manager:	Jonathan Wheatley
Test driver:	Jean-Eric Vergne
Chassis:	Red Bull RB8
Engine:	Renault V8
Tyres:	Pirelli

> "The loss of exhaust-related downforce for 2012 is a big change because we've developed our car around that for the past two years, so it will have a knock-on effect in all sorts of areas."
>
> **Adrian Newey**

There was plenty to cheer about for Christian Horner, Dietrich Mateschitz and Adrian Newey.

To become the youngest Formula One champion in history in 2010 was one thing, but to follow it up with another triumph in 2011 proved that Sebastian Vettel is the right driver in the right place on the right form at the right time.

Vettel almost did not put a foot wrong last year. If any criticism might have had the 24-year-old thinking through the close season, it would be that he is not the best at overtaking. Yet, he did not have to do much passing as he put his RB7 on pole 15 times in last year's 19 rounds, usually being clear by the first corner.

Indeed, aware that the performance advantage he possessed when the RB7 was in qualifying trim was greater proportionally than in race trim over the best of the pursuers, usually McLaren and Ferrari, Vettel displayed a priceless ability to blast far enough clear on the opening two laps to be too far in front for his closest rival to be allowed to engage their DRS to try and pass him as they had to be within 1s to be allowed to open the slot in their rear wing and thus be quicker in a straight line to attempt a passing move. His performances at the Circuit de Catalunya and Monaco's street circuit bore all the hallmarks of a world champion as his RB7 was certainly not the fastest in race trim, yet he stayed ahead all the way to the finish.

Vettel has a contract that keeps him at Red Bull Racing until the end of 2014 and

Sebastian does not often look this introspective as victory follows victory.

provided that Adrian Newey continues to produce F1's pace-setting car for him, there is no reason why he would want to go anywhere else. Indeed, with the total support he receives from team owner Dietrich Mateschitz, Red Bull motorsport

advisor Helmut Marko and team principal Christian Horner, why would he want to join any other team, other than curiosity as to what it would be like to race for Ferrari or McLaren?

It's easy to smile when the wins keep rolling in, but Vettel appears to have a bulletproof buoyancy and his sense of humour is appreciated by all around him.

TRACK NOTES

Nationality:	GERMAN
Born:	3 JULY 1987, HEPPENHEIM, GERMANY
Website:	www.sebastianvettel.de
Teams:	BMW SAUBER 2007, TORO ROSSO 2007-08, RED BULL RACING 2009-12

CAREER RECORD

First Grand Prix:	2007 UNITED STATES GP
Grand Prix starts:	81
Grand Prix wins:	21
	2008 Italian GP, 2009 Chinese GP, British GP, Japanese GP, Abu Dhabi GP, 2010 Malaysian GP, European GP, Japanese GP, Brazilian GP, Abu Dhabi GP, 2011 Australian GP, Malaysian GP, Turkish GP, Spanish GP, Monaco GP, European GP, Belgian GP, Italian GP, Singapore GP, Korean GP, Indian GP
Poles:	30
Fastest laps:	9
Points:	773
Honours:	2010 & 2011 F1 WORLD CHAMPION, 2006 EUROPEAN FORMULA 3 RUNNER-UP, 2004 GERMAN FORMULA BMW CHAMPION, 2003 GERMAN FORMULA BMW RUNNER-UP, 2001 EUROPEAN & GERMAN JUNIOR KART CHAMPION

MAKING THE MOST OF LUCKY BREAKS

Some drivers win championships by a point, but Sebastian Vettel signalled his intent in 2004 when he dominated the German Formula BMW ADAC series, winning 18 of the 20 rounds. Red Bull was backing him by this point and he used the energy drinks company's support to step up to the F3 Euroseries. Fifth overall behind champion Lewis Hamilton in 2005, he was runner-up behind another British driver, Paul di Resta, in 2006. After starting 2007 in World Series by Renault, however, he was given his F1 break when Robert Kubica promoted him from its test line-up to a race seat when Kubica himself became injured. Later in the year he was given a full-time ride when he replaced Scott Speed at Scuderia Toro Rosso. A year later, he had given the Italian team its first win, fittingly at Monza. Promoted to the senior Red Bull team for 2009, Sebastian won four grands prix before adding five more in 2010 to become the youngest-ever World Champion.

MARK WEBBER

Having really pushed his Red Bull Racing team-mate Sebastian Vettel in 2010, last year was less kind to this competitive Australian as the young German dominated across the season and left him in his wake on a regular basis.

The big question for Mark Webber as he prepares for the 2012 season is just what he can do to put himself on an equal footing with team-mate Sebastian Vettel, having lost out in their confrontations last year. Look at the record book: with Webber winning just one race to Vettel's 11 across the 19 rounds, the balance had certainly swung away from him.

The problem in 2011, it seems, was that Webber was simply harder on his tyres and suffered the performance drop-off that went with it, which was particularly marked on the rubber that new supplier Pirelli provided. So, he is going to have to hope this year's car, the RB8, enables him to drive as hard as he desires without using up the rubber so much, or else he will have to change his driving style.

When that is under control, Webber will also have to hope the performance-enhancing KERS works better for him than it did in 2011, when a lack of space under the sculpted bodywork caused it to often overheat and so stop working, thus hampering his ability to overtake cars ahead and hold off those pressing from behind.

Mark is back for another crack in 2012, anxious to re-establish his in-house rivalry.

After last year, there can be no doubt that Webber is the team's number two driver, but he appears to have become accustomed to this and has stopped lashing out against it, as he did in 2010.

At the age of 35, Webber knows that his time left in Formula One may be short and that the contract extension signed last summer takes him through only until the end this year. However, his name has been mentioned in dispatches as a possible Ferrari driver for 2013 when the driver market opens up, but with Red Bull's junior drivers Jaime Alguersuari, Sebastien Buemi, Daniel Ricciardo and Jean-Eric Vergne not yet pressing their case strongly enough for promotion to Red Bull's senior team, Webber may still be with the team next year.

TRACK NOTES

Nationality:	AUSTRALIAN
Born:	27 AUGUST 1976, QUEANBEYAN, AUSTRALIA
Website:	www.markwebber.com
Teams:	MINARDI 2002, JAGUAR 2003-04, WILLIAMS 2005-06, RED BULL RACING 2007-12

CAREER RECORD

First Grand Prix:	2002 AUSTRALIAN GP
Grand Prix starts:	177
Grand Prix wins:	7
	2009 German GP, Brazilian GP, 2010 Spanish GP, Monaco GP, British GP, Hungarian GP, 2011 Brazilian GP
Poles:	9
Fastest laps:	13
Points:	669.5
Honours:	2001 FORMULA 3000 RUNNER-UP, 1998 FIA GT RUNNER-UP, 1996 BRITISH FORMULA FORD RUNNER-UP & FORMULA FORD FESTIVAL WINNER

WORKING HIS WAY TOWARD THE TOP

The Australian racing scene does not have much strength or depth and so Mark Webber had to head for Britain to complete his Formula Ford education. Success in the Formula Ford Festival at Brands Hatch marked him out as one to watch and investment from Australian rugby legend David Campese, a friend of his father's, helped him into F3 for 1997. Then, despite winning races, a lack of cash meant no promotion to F3000, as planned. Instead, Mercedes snapped him up for its GT racing programme. This went well, but two years later he was back in single-seaters and ended the 2001 season as runner-up to Justin Wilson in F3000. This was good enough to land him an F1 seat for 2002. He scored on his debut with tail-end Minardi, but progressive moves to Jaguar Racing, then Williams moved him toward the front of the grid. Wins only started to look likely after he moved to Red Bull Racing, with the first coming his way at the 2009 German GP.

McLAREN

McLaren ended last year with six race wins but no titles and it will be seen as a failure if it cannot land either the constructors' title or the drivers' title for its first rate line-up of Jenson Button and Lewis Hamilton.

Expect more strident battles between McLaren team-mates Jenson Button and Lewis Hamilton in the season ahead.

McLaren is the ultimate model for how to build a centre of automotive excellence, for not only does it have the capability to become the dominant team again, but Ron Dennis has masterminded an expansion programme that he hopes will reduce the F1 team's proportion of McLaren's takings to just 10% of its total. To do so, he is expanding the automotive and applied technologies side of the company, which will focus on hybrid technologies as well as the production of road-going and racing versions of its MP4-12C.

Financing this expansion will involve the construction of a further factory alongside the McLaren headquarters outside Woking - a significant stake in McLaren Automotive was sold last August to Singapore business tycoon Peter Lim. The McLaren Applied Technology Centre will be built on the other side of the road from the McLaren Technology Centre and the newly-completed McLaren Production Centre, where the MP4-12C is built, and will employ as many as

400 new people, as well as being a centre for education to bring in the next generation of engineers and designers.

So, these are more bold steps from this most innovative and ambitious of teams, but what of the core element that Bruce

KEY MOMENTS AND KEY PEOPLE

TEAM HISTORY
Founder Bruce McLaren was that rare thing: a driver/engineer. Already a grand prix winner, he began building racing cars in 1964 and expanded to include Can-Am and Indycars, F5000 and F2 before being killed while testing in 1970. When taken over by Teddy Mayer, the team won drivers' titles with Emerson Fittipaldi (1974) and James Hunt (1976) before Ron Dennis took control to turn McLaren into the dominant force, with a championship for Niki Lauda in 1982, then multiple successes for Alain Prost, Ayrton Senna and Mika Hakkinen. Lewis Hamilton's is the most recent title: from 2008.

MARTIN WHITMARSH
Always on the lookout for those with the skills to propel it ahead of the opposition, McLaren recruited Whitmarsh from British Aerospace in 1989. As a mechanical engineer, he was made head of operations and fitted in so well that he was promoted to managing director of McLaren's racing division in 1997. Thereafter, he took on more and more of a role in the team's management and eventually took over completely when Dennis stepped back in 2009.

2011 DRIVERS & RESULTS

Driver	Nationality	Races	Wins	Pts	Pos
Jenson Button	British	19	3	270	2nd
Lewis Hamilton	British	19	3	227	5th

McLaren established in 1966 - the F1 team? Well, it failed to match Red Bull Racing last year but came a clear second, a long way clear of Ferrari, in the constructors' cup rankings. There were several cases of the team fumbling pit stops and not getting their tactics right in qualifying, but these were not the difference between success and failure. So, for 2012, the Paddy Lowe-led technical squad will have to produce a superior car if McLaren are to stand a chance of claiming its first constructors' title since 1998.

To do so, the team's long-standing practice of making one year's car the responsibility of one design crew and then alternating with another the following year has been dropped. Whether this will lead to the team not taking a major gamble - for example, with a part such as the complex exhaust system that was tried and then dropped last year - remains to be seen, but Lowe and co know you do not beat Red Bull's ex-McLaren design genius Adrian Newey by playing it safe.

One major change is that former Williams' technical director Sam Michael has moved across to become sporting director. In this role he'll be responsible for the organizational side of the team rather than the engineering and will call the strategic shots from the pit wall during the races. In doing so, he'll be the first person to hold this post since early 2009, when Dave Ryan was fired for his role in Lewis Hamilton not telling the truth to the stewards at the Australian GP.

There are no changes on the driving front, though, with Hamilton and Jenson Button staying on for a third season together, and this is a significant positive as they get on and work well as a pair. However, Hamilton, who is generally quicker over a flying lap, will have spent the winter trying to work out how to prevent himself from tripping up. Staying clear of the race stewards would be a step in the right direction, as would keeping his frustrations in check, as it was Button who delivered more often when the chips were down, largely through applying a more intelligent and considered approach to tyre and fuel conservation. The pair will be bolstered by long-term McLaren test driver Pedro de la Rosa opting to stay on rather than seek a race drive.

FOR THE RECORD

Country of origin:	England
Team base:	Woking, England
Telephone:	(44) 01483 728211
Website:	www.mclaren.com
Active in Formula One:	From 1966
Grands Prix contested:	704
Wins:	175
Pole positions:	148
Fastest laps:	148

THE TEAM

Team principal:	Martin Whitmarsh
Managing director:	Jonathan Neale
Engineering director:	Paddy Lowe
Design & development director:	Neil Oatley
Sporting director:	Sam Michael
Chief aerodynamicist:	Doug McKiernan
Head of vehicle design:	Andrew Bailey
Head of race operations:	Simon Roberts
Head of vehicle engineering:	Mark Williams
Team manager:	David Redding
Chief race engineer:	Philip Prew
Test drivers:	Pedro de la Rosa, Gary Paffett
Chassis:	McLaren MP4-27
Engine:	Mercedes V8
Tyres:	Pirelli

"We are often fighting at the end of a year, and I cannot recall a year when we've said halfway through that we should back off. We have a very good fighting spirit."
Martin Whitmarsh

Engineering director Paddy Lowe is drenched by Jenson Button after victory in Canada.

JENSON BUTTON

With last season adding to Jenson Button's reputation as a racer when he displayed considerable class and application in outscoring McLaren team-mate Lewis Hamilton, he will be hoping for a car that will be able to beat the Red Bulls in the season ahead.

Having answered his critics in 2010, in leaving Brawn GP as World Champion to take on Lewis Hamilton at McLaren only to emerge with honours pretty much even, Jenson Button went one better in 2011 when he responded to further criticism that he stood little chance against Hamilton by proving himself the more polished performer of the duo. This has made him that rare beast: an F1 driver who appears to be raising his game even after more than a decade at the sport's top level.

Watch any interview with Button or study his behaviour after a race with his rivals and you can see that he is a thoroughly decent and well-liked individual, and it's this, as well as his driving that has meant he fits in so well at McLaren and has helped him enter what was seen as Hamilton's camp and in short, made him an integral part of the team. Add to this his uncanny ability to perform when the chips are down – and especially when track conditions are mixed, as he did to supreme effect in working his way from the back of the field to the front in the Canadian GP – and you can see why he has made himself so popular down Woking way.

Jenson laid down a marker in 2011 when he outraced Hamilton, and will want more.

The quality and precision of his driving and particularly his overtaking in the second half of last season was a joy to behold and the comparison with the more crash-prone Hamilton showed a driver already exceptionally popular with the team in an even better light.

The second half of last season was marked by Button and McLaren continuing their negotiations about a combined future; it was always assumed the deal would be done, but talk of Button looking to Ferrari for 2013 kept surfacing, so he and his management team proved that they too know how to play a good hand of poker before signing a long-term deal with McLaren.

TRACK NOTES

Nationality:	BRITISH
Born:	19 JANUARY 1980, FROME, ENGLAND
Website:	www.jensonbutton.com
Teams:	WILLIAMS 2000, BENETTON/ RENAULT 2001-02, BAR/HONDA 2003-08, BRAWN 2009, McLAREN 2010-12

CAREER RECORD

First Grand Prix:	2000 AUSTRALIAN GP
Grand Prix starts:	209
Grand Prix wins:	12
	2006 Hungarian GP, 2009 Australian GP, Malaysian GP, Bahrain GP, Spanish GP, Monaco GP, Turkish GP, 2010 Australian GP, Chinese GP, 2011 Canadian GP, Hungarian GP, Japanese GP
Poles:	7
Fastest laps:	6
Points:	811
Honours:	2009 FORMULA ONE WORLD CHAMPION, 1999 MACAU FORMULA THREE RUNNER-UP, 1998 FORMULA FORD FESTIVAL WINNER, BRITISH FORMULA FORD CHAMPION & McLAREN AUTOSPORT BRDC YOUNG DRIVER, 1997 EUROPEAN SUPER A KART CHAMPION, 1991 BRITISH CADET KART CHAMPION

A TALENT THAT FINALLY DELIVERED

After the past three seasons of being at the head of the field, it's hard to remember before that Jenson Button had spent nine years getting nowhere fast in Formula One. This had come as a surprise to those who watched him collect title after title in karting and then replicate that form in junior single-seaters. Jenson started in cadet karts at the age of eight. After starring on the British and European scene, he moved to cars and was an immediate hit in Formula Ford, winning the British title. He looked set to achieve a similar result in F3 in 1999, but ended up third. However, a strong test for the Prost F1 team changed his plans to return for the title as Williams took notice and he won a shoot-out for its second seat for 2000. He progressed through the year, but a move to Benetton was not a hit as the team languished and it was not until his fourth year with BAR/Honda that he eventually won, at Hungary in 2006.

LEWIS HAMILTON

Last season was not Lewis Hamilton's greatest F1 campaign as it was littered with incident and he was accused by the British media of being a losing focus. However, no one can deny he is one of the quickest out there.

Lewis Hamilton has been part of the McLaren machine since a teenage kart racer when he went on to achieve a world title and considerable success with the men from Woking. However, there were signs last year that his behaviour was troubling them, his visits to the stewards' office becoming a bore and some of his comments not showing him - and thus the team - in a good light.

Yes, there were supreme displays, such as when he won the Chinese GP and even more so after he triumphed in Germany, but there were also collisions at Monaco, Spa and Singapore. This led to questions over Hamilton's state of mind, with even long-term supporter Sir Jackie Stewart worrying that perhaps he needed someone to manage him better.

Last year's change to Pirelli tyres made the racing more interesting as the teams struggled to understand the rubber and thus get the best out of them, but Hamilton soon got to grips with them in qualifying. In race conditions, though, it was his McLaren team-mate Jenson Button who displayed a more refined touch to be stronger in the closing stages. That said, the differences only added to the intrigue.

Lewis is determined to put a troubled 2011 behind him and is sure to win more races.

What Hamilton's legions of fans are eager to see in 2012 is a driver who still takes a look at overtaking manoeuvres others would never consider. They want him to avoid ruining races with pit stops for new nose wings or drive-through penalties

and so ditch his feeling of persecution. Most of all, they would be thrilled to see his attack rewarded with another world title to add to the one already landed at his second attempt in 2008.

TRACK NOTES

Nationality:	BRITISH
Born:	7 JANUARY 1985, STEVENAGE, ENGLAND
Website:	www.lewishamilton.com
Teams:	McLAREN 2007-12

CAREER RECORD

First Grand Prix:	2007 AUSTRALIAN GP
Grand Prix starts:	90
Grand Prix wins:	17
	2007 Canadian GP, United States GP, Hungarian GP, Japanese GP, 2008 Australian GP, Monaco GP, British GP, German GP, Chinese GP, 2009 Hungarian GP, Singapore GP, 2009 Hungarian GP, Singapore GP, 2010 Turkish GP, Canadian GP, Belgian GP, 2011 Chinese GP, German GP, Abu Dhabi GP
Poles:	19
Fastest laps:	11
Points:	723
Honours:	2008 FORMULA ONE WORLD CHAMPION, 2006 GP2 CHAMPION, 2005 EUROPEAN FORMULA THREE CHAMPION, 2003 BRITISH FORMULA RENAULT CHAMPION, 2000 WORLD KART CUP CHAMPION & EUROPEAN FORMULA A KARTING CHAMPION, 1999 ITALIAN INTERCONTINENTAL A KARTING CHAMPION, 1996 McLAREN MERCEDES CHAMPION OF THE FUTURE, 1995 BRITISH CADET KARTING CHAMPION

A STAR FROM HIS VERY FIRST RACE

So smooth was his progress that Lewis Hamilton seemed to fly through from junior karting to F1 without breaking into a sweat. British Cadet Kart Champion at the age of 10 in 1995, he collected not just titles galore in the years that followed (including the World Kart title), but far more importantly, the patronage of McLaren principal Ron Dennis. This really made itself worthwhile when Hamilton moved through Formula Renault to F3 with McLaren's financial assistance. European F3 champion at his second attempt in 2005, he made great strides to achieve the rare feat of winning the GP2 crown at his first attempt in 2006 and an F1 ride at McLaren opened up for him in 2007. After scoring his first win mid-season in Canada, he added three more and only lost the drivers' title at the final round. In 2008, he put this right, with fifth place gained on the last lap at the final round enough to help him pip Ferrari's Felipe Massa.

FERRARI

The pressure began to be exerted last year when it became clear that, although quick on some tracks, Ferrari's best was not enough. This season, Stefano Domenicali's squad must deliver on a regular basis to keep Luca di Montezemolo happy – and Fernando Alonso, too.

Alonso will continue to be Ferrari's driving force and will win races if given a car capable of matching the Red Bulls and McLarens.

There is a view that Ferrari is Formula One. This certainly is not healthy as no sport should revolve around one team, but it's undeniably the team most fans look to. So long as it's in the mix for winning, the fans are happy. However, even though Fernando Alonso won once last year and led other races, Ferrari president Luca di Montezemolo expects more. In short, he wants Ferrari's lead driver to become World Champion and, perhaps even more so, he is keen for Ferrari to win the constructors' title for the first time since 2008.

Although there has been no change in the driver line-up, with Alonso once again supported by Felipe Massa, one key to Ferrari's possible improvement is that it has a new face in charge of producing a pace-setting chassis: long-time McLaren engineer, Pat Fry. He arrived at Ferrari last year as deputy technical director, but was soon put in charge of chassis development following the departure of technical director Aldo Costa after the team's poor start to the season,

which produced just one podium finish – third place for Alonso at Istanbul – in the first five rounds. Luca Marmorini continued to be in charge of engines and electronics, while Corrado Lanzone was promoted to run the production department.

KEY MOMENTS AND KEY PEOPLE

TEAM HISTORY
The first racing car to bear Enzo Ferrari's name appeared in 1946 and Ferrari is the only team whose involvement with the World Championship stretches back to the inaugural year, 1950. Its list of champions starts in 1952 with Alberto Ascari. Looking at the list of other Ferrari champions – Juan Manuel Fangio (1956), Mike Hawthorn (1958), Phil Hill (1961), John Surtees (1964), Niki Lauda (1975 and 1977), Jody Scheckter (1979), Michael Schumacher (2000 to 2004) and Kimi Raïkkönen (2007) – shows success has not been continuous, though.

PAT FRY
Pat's move to Ferrari for 2011 as assistant technical director came as a shock for he was seen as a McLaren man through and through. He began his career working on missiles at Thorn EMI, but became involved in active suspension for Benetton from 1987, going on to become a race engineer. In 1993, he moved to McLaren to head up its test team, but from 1995 was a race engineer before becoming chief engineer in 2002, then taking engineering responsibility of each new car from 2005.

2011 DRIVERS & RESULTS

Driver	Nationality	Races	Wins	Pts	Pos
Fernando Alonso	Spanish	19	1	257	4th
Felipe Massa	Brazilian	19	0	118	6th

After the closing race of the 2010 World Championship in Abu Dhabi, in which poor race strategy hampered Alonso's slim chances of landing the drivers' title, there was something of a witchhunt and one of the resultant changes was the arrival of strategist Neil Martin from Red Bull Racing. He took the place on the pit wall of former shot-caller Chris Dyer, who was transferred to factory-based duties following the fiasco at Yas Marina.

From Ferrari's lofty perspective there were few high points last year, but at the head of these must be the team's sudden improvement in form at the British GP on the 60th anniversary of its first F1 win, fittingly at the same venue. This came after the change to the blown diffuser rules seemed to suit Ferrari in particular and Alonso chased after the leading Red Bulls, then gained second place when Mark Webber had a wheelnut stick at his second pit stop and Sebastian Vettel's rear jack was broken. So, yes, there was some fortune but Alonso was in the right place to benefit from it.

From the Canadian GP onward, the trend last year was upward for Ferrari, with Alonso the driver to produce the goods when required, Massa less so. And, with Alonso contracted until 2016, this explains the fevered speculation as to who will fill the second seat from 2013. Massa may stay on, but Domenicali is keen to field Robert Kubica, if the Pole manages to recover from arm injuries suffered in a rallying accident. Also in the reckoning are Jenson Button, Mark Webber, Nico Rosberg, Sergio Pérez and GP2 pacesetter Jules Bianchi, which will act as a stick to beat Massa into delivery in the season ahead. How he responds, especially if the car proves less than out-and-out competitive, remains to be seen.

What is definite, though, is that team principal Domenicali has brought Ferrari new respect in the paddock as he is prepared to talk to the other teams and has put the reign of predecessor Jean Todt firmly in the shade. Now, when the teams want to be united, they can do so whereas Todt used to ally the team with the FIA, which in turn would side with Ferrari, usually to the detriment of solidarity.

FOR THE RECORD

Country of origin:	Italy
Team base:	Maranello, Italy
Telephone:	(39) 536 949111
Website:	www.ferrari.com
Active in Formula One:	From 1950
Grands Prix contested:	831
Wins:	216
Pole positions:	205
Fastest laps:	225

THE TEAM

President:	Luca di Montezemolo
Chief executive officer:	Amedeo Felisa
Team principal:	Stefano Domenicali
Chassis director:	Pat Fry
Engine & electronic director:	Luca Marmorini
Production director:	Corrado Lanzone
Sporting director:	Massimo Rivola
Chief designer:	Nikolas Tombazis
Chief aerodynamicist:	Marco de Luca
Chief engineer:	Mattia Binotto
Test drivers:	Jules Bianchi, Giancarlo Fisichella, Marc Gene
Chassis:	Ferrari F12
Engine:	Ferrari V8
Tyres:	Pirelli

"It is crucial to understand the tyre performance to make sure that we really use that as a performance factor because I think there is a lot to learn after last season on that."

Stefano Domenicali

Pat Fry brought experience from McLaren and will be looking to make even more of a mark.

Sebastian Vettel was a worthy champion last year, but few feel Fernando Alonso might not have managed the same in the same car. This year, the ever-competitive Alonso will be praying Ferrari gives him the tools to do the job.

There's no driver in Formula One with an image of win-at-all-costs competitiveness so intense as Fernando Alonso. He is the very image of the dead-eyed gunslinger made all the more powerful as he has a history of hitting his targets. This has not always made him popular with the British media for many of his scalps have been claimed from British drivers and he can appear dour. But to Alonso, that matters not – he simply gets the job done, seldom making mistakes and proving a threat everywhere. His drive to victory at last year's British GP, when the blown-diffuser rules came Ferrari's way, was a classic example of maximizing every opportunity.

There were races last year in which Alonso knew his car would not have the pace of the Red Bulls or McLarens across the race distance but he went for it anyway, seizing the glory of leading in the Spanish GP. He then did the same at the Italian GP later in the year to give the Tifosi a treat. Then, when his rival powered past, all he could do was press on and hope for better in 2012.

This ambition will have Alonso giving team principal Stefano Domenicali as much grief about the need to build a pace-

Fernando is a driver who will never ever give up if there's a hint of a win to be had.

setting car for 2012 as Ferrari president Luca di Montezemolo will undoubtedly be applying. After all, although he has two world titles to his name (won with Renault in 2005 and 2006), Fernando wants at least one more before he hangs up his helmet

and there is no time like the present. After all, no one knows what lies around the corner and no champion likes to languish in an uncompetitive car. So, Ferrari's little Prince is primed for action.

TRACK NOTES

Nationality:	SPANISH
Born:	29 JULY 1981, OVIEDO, SPAIN
Website:	www.fernandoalonso.com
Teams:	MINARDI 2001, RENAULT 2003-06, McLAREN 2007, RENAULT 2008-09, FERRARI 2010-12

CAREER RECORD

First Grand Prix:	2001 AUSTRALIAN GP
Grand Prix starts:	178
Grand Prix wins:	27
	2003 Hungarian GP, 2005 Malaysian GP, Bahrain GP, San Marino GP, European GP, French GP, German GP, Chinese GP, 2006 Bahrain GP, Australian GP, Spanish GP, Monaco GP, British GP, Canadian GP, Japanese GP, 2007 Malaysian GP, Monaco GP, European GP, Italian GP, 2008 Singapore GP, Japanese GP, 2010 Australian GP, German GP, Italian GP, Singapore GP, Korean GP, 2011 British GP
Poles:	20
Fastest laps:	19
Points:	1086
Honours:	2010 FORMULA ONE RUNNER-UP, 2005 & 2006 FORMULA ONE WORLD CHAMPION, 1999 FORMULA NISSAN CHAMPION, 1997 ITALIAN & SPANISH KART CHAMPION, 1996 WORLD & SPANISH KART CHAMPION, 1995 & 1994 SPANISH JUNIOR KART CHAMPION

A DRIVER IN A HUGE HURRY

Fernando Alonso was such a superstar in karts that he was forced to bide his time after claiming the world title in 1996 when he was 15 and therefore too young to move up to car racing. He finally started in cars in 1999 and promptly won the Formula Nissan series, having already bypassed Formula Renault and Formula Three. Vaulting on in 2000 to F3000 (the last step before F1), Fernando showed immense class, scoring a runaway win at Spa-Francorchamps. Snapped up by Flavio Briatore, he found himself gaining F1 experience with Minardi in 2001, where he did well. Briatorte then used Alonso as a test driver for Renault in 2002 before letting him lead the team's driving challenge of 2003. Before moving on to McLaren, his efforts were rewarded with two titles (2005 and 2006). This was not a match made in heaven, though, and while he won races and was only pipped to the 2007 title, Fernando returned to Renault before transferring to a more profitable relationship with Ferrari for 2010.

FELIPE MASSA

This will be Massa's seventh season with Ferrari and it's likely to be his last after he failed to add to his tally of 11 wins or indeed to get anywhere near the podium last year but instead languished in Fernando Alonso's shadow.

Formula One is a harsh environment but then so it should be, being the pinnacle of the sport. Naturally, Felipe Massa will know as well as anyone that his form of 2011 was not good enough to keep him at Ferrari after his contract expires at the end of this year. Sure, Ferrari's 150 Italia was only occasionally superior to the McLaren MP4-26 and only once, at the British GP, to the Red Bull RB7. However, Massa was consistently slower than team-mate Fernando Alonso and in the cold light of analysis, that is not enough if Ferrari ever wants to win the constructors' title again.

Check the records and Massa has not secured a grand prix since the 2008 season, in which he came within a whisker of beating Lewis Hamilton to the drivers' title. Indeed, he failed to win a grand prix in the first nine races of the 2009 season, only once being called to the podium before suffering potentially life-threatening head injuries in Hungary. And since his comeback in 2010, Massa's best results were second-place finishes on his race return in Bahrain and later in the German GP, albeit when he was instructed to hand victory to Alonso. In

Felipe knows that a second year without a win will certainly end his Ferrari career.

2011, his best was a quartet of fifth places. The frustration was clear for all to see when he lost a decent result in Singapore after Lewis Hamilton clipped him and gave him a puncture. Frankly, you could not blame him for his outburst.

With all this hovering over him, aware that his team's future lead choice would be Robert Kubica (if he recovers fully from his rallying accident), Massa spent much of 2011 feeling unloved, and increasingly so as even podium visits proved beyond him. That said, the Brazilian's acceptance of always playing the supporting role to Alonso might yet keep him in Ferrari's second seat, while some soon-to-be-out-of-contract top guns may find themselves out of a job.

TRACK NOTES

Nationality:	BRAZILIAN
Born:	25 APRIL 1981, SAO PAULO, BRAZIL
Website:	www.felipemassa.com
Teams:	SAUBER 2002 & 2004-05, FERRARI 2006-12

CAREER RECORD

First Grand Prix:	2002 AUSTRALIAN GP
Grand Prix starts:	153
Grand Prix wins:	11
2006 Turkish GP, Brazilian GP, 2007 Bahrain GP, Spanish GP, Turkish GP, 2008 Bahrain GP, Turkish GP, French GP, European GP, Belgian GP, Brazilian GP, 2011 GP	
Poles:	15
Fastest laps:	14
Points:	582
Honours:	2008 FORMULA ONE RUNNER-UP, 2001 EUROPEAN FORMULA 3000 CHAMPION, 2000 EUROPEAN & ITALIAN FORMULA RENAULT CHAMPION, 1999 BRAZILIAN FORMULA CHEVROLET CHAMPION

FOLLOWING A PRECEDENT

Brazilian racing drivers have been coming to Europe to finish off their junior single-seater education since the Fittipaldi brothers led the way in the late 1960s and so Felipe Massa was following in a long tradition when he won the 1999 Brazilian Formula Chevrolet title, then took the plane to Europe. In fact, he secured not only the Italian Formula Renault title, but the European one too. Without a budget to advance to F3 in 2001, he tried the cheaper but more powerful cars of the second-rank F3000 Euro series and won the title. Indeed, Massa's form on testing a Sauber F1 car shocked many. Having given Kimi Räikkönen his F1 break in 2001, Peter Sauber gambled again with Felipe. The speed was there, but he was wild and benefited from spending 2003 as a Ferrari test driver. After two more years with Sauber, he moved to a race seat at Ferrari in 2006, only to be pipped to the 2008 title by Lewis Hamilton. Then, in 2009, he was lucky to survive a head injury.

MERCEDES GP PETRONAS

Ross Brawn achieved miracles in 2009 when he revived Honda Racing, renamed it and won both titles. The big question is whether he can reclaim some of that chassis magic to take Mercedes GP to the top as it takes on its third campaign.

Michael Schumacher will be anxious to continue the stronger form he displayed through last year into the season ahead.

There was an element of good fortune in Brawn GP having the right technology – a double-decked diffuser – to set the pace in 2009, as it had guessed how to maximize the rulebook. However, Jenson Button and team principal Ross Brawn delivered to take both titles. So, with precious little new for 2012, the question is whether the team will be able to come up with something novel that will give drivers Nico Rosberg and Michael Schumacher a chance to leave their rivals behind them and win races.

So, what will it take for Mercedes GP to earn its place in the limelight? Brawn believed that a stronger technical and design side was needed and so he busied himself last summer in achieving just that, signing a host of established talent to enable the team to build a car the equal of any of its rivals. Indeed, Brawn talked of adding 100 more staff.

Former Renault mastermind Bob Bell had already joined as technical director when, at the end of last September, both

Aldo Costa and Geoff Willis followed him to Mercedes GP. Costa, previously Ferrari's technical director, goes back a long way

with team principal Brawn as they worked together when Schumacher scored his run of five consecutive drivers' titles

KEY MOMENTS AND KEY PEOPLE

TEAM HISTORY

Mercedes is one of several manufacturers to return to F1 after previous involvement. In this case, it proved the dominant force in 1954 and 1955, even exceeding its own form when fighting Auto Union in the 1930s. However, after pulling out following the Le Mans disaster of 1955, Mercedes' subsequent involvement was as an engine supplier only until it took over Brawn GP and rebadged it for 2010, with Ross Brawn staying at the helm with assistance from Mercedes' Norbert Haug. Brawn GP had been formed from Honda Racing (previously BAR) when it quit at the end of 2008.

ROSS BRAWN

In 1979, Brawn was senior aerodynamicist at Williams, then at Force in 1984 and later, chief designer at Arrows (1986). His first posting as a technical director was with TWR Racing in 1989, taking him away to sports cars, but he returned to hold the post at Benetton, then Ferrari (working in tandem with Michael Schumacher) before taking over Honda Racing in late 2007 and then running it under his own name in 2009 to land the constructors' title.

2011 DRIVERS & RESULTS

Driver	Nationality	Races	Wins	Pts	Pos
Nico Rosberg	German	19	0	89	7th
Michael Schumacher	German	19	0	76	8th

for Ferrari, from 2000-04. He will be engineering director. Willis, on the other hand, arrives from a spell attempting to sort out HRT and is to be in charge of technology. He knows the team well, having worked with many of the staff back in the pre-Brawn GP days when it was BAR, then Honda Racing. The design team has been bolstered by the arrival of John Owen as chief designer, working with Loïc Bigois (aerodynamics) and Craig Wilson (vehicle dynamics).

One of the keys to Mercedes GP going forward is entering the season ahead with a car with more grip, so it won't suffer tyre degradation as much as 2011's W02 did and then perhaps the McLarens won't be the only silver-grey cars at the sharp end of the field. To that end Brawn stated last summer that the design of the W03 would include a longer wheelbase as well as some more radical ideas in its search for speed and consistency. In many ways, as the W02 clearly was not able to challenge for wins, even when gains were found in the second half of the season from its exhaust-blown diffuser, this made it easier for Brawn to decide to concentrate on the W03's design earlier than the team otherwise might have done. Do not forget, though, that exhaust-blown diffusers are being banned, so Mercedes ought to be able to claw back their performance deficit in this area.

One beneficial carry-over to 2012 is the driver line-up, with Rosberg and Schumacher seemingly working well together, which had not been something that looked likely when Schumacher was a late signing for 2010. If Schumacher manages to take the drivers' title this year, it would be his eighth title won in conjunction with Ross Brawn, following their earlier success at Benetton and then Ferrari.

When there was talk last summer of Schumacher not staying on for a third year with Mercedes GP, Paul di Resta and Nico Hulkenberg were the names discussed as replacements. Both will be in the frame again this time around for 2013, but the likelihood of them getting a race seat depends largely on how well Schumacher goes, whether the seven-time World Champion is still enjoying himself as Mercedes maximizes his promotional value and whether Rosberg decides that his best chance of winning races and titles lies with another team. Either driver is talented enough to prove a more-than-capable replacement.

"Our technical organization has been strengthened by the arrival of Bob Bell and, working closely with Ross [Brawn], he has identified areas in which we can improve still further."
Norbert Haug

FOR THE RECORD

Country of origin:	England
Team base:	Brackley, England
Telephone:	(44) 01280 844000
Website:	www.mercedes-gp.com
Active in Formula One:	From 1999
(as BAR until 2005, as Honda Racing until 2008 and then Brawn GP in 2009)	
Grands Prix contested:	226
Wins:	9
Pole positions:	8
Fastest laps:	4

THE TEAM

Team principal:	Ross Brawn
Chief executive officer:	Nick Fry
Vice-President, Mercedes-Benz Motorsport:	Norbert Haug
Technical director:	Bob Bell
Engineering director:	Aldo Costa
Technology director:	Geoff Willis
Chief designer:	John Owen
Head of aerodynamics:	Loïc Bigois
Head of vehicle engineering:	Craig Wilson
Sporting director:	Ron Meadows
Chief designer:	John Owen
Test driver:	tba
Chassis:	Mercedes MGP W03
Engine:	Mercedes V8
Tyres:	Pirelli

Ross Brawn has really beefed up the team's technical side and its operating structure.

MICHAEL SCHUMACHER

It took two seasons for Michael Schumacher to rediscover his form after three years away, but he will only add to his record tally of seven titles and 91 wins if Mercedes GP can supply him with a car relatively more competitive than last year's W02.

On days when things are not going right for Schumacher or he has just crashed, one wonders why he has come back from an extremely comfortable retirement. Yet, when the seven-times World Champion is embroiled in a wheel-to-wheel battle, working off his instincts, it makes sense.

Last year, after a troubled F1 return in 2010, when he was outperformed by team-mate Nico Rosberg, he started showing flashes of his old self. His qualifying form was still inferior to Rosberg's and these flashes were interspersed with collisions that made him look past his best, but the spark was there. It first showed itself with fourth place in the Canadian GP, Schumacher demonstrating his wet-weather driving skills, then was repeated with fifth places in Belgium and Italy. The gain came, it seemed, from him learning how to extract the most from the Pirelli tyres in race conditions.

This return to form was a relief to Mercedes GP big guns Ross Brawn and Norbert Haug as it justified their faith in him and so warded off paddock talk of how Schumacher ought to stand down and not take up the third year of his contract. There is one factor of the early

Michael showed last year that he still has the pace to win if he has the right car.

Schumacher that remains, though, and this is his use of robust tactics, such as the defence of his position when pressed by Hamilton at the Italian GP. Some might not like it, but it shows that Schumacher has not backed off.

TRACK NOTES

Nationality:	GERMAN
Born:	3 JANUARY 1969, KERPEN, GERMANY
Website:	www.michael-schumacher.de
Teams:	1991 JORDAN, 1991-95 BENETTON, 1996-06 FERRARI, 2010-12 MERCEDES

CAREER RECORD

First Grand Prix:	1991 BELGIAN GP
Grand Prix starts:	288
Grand Prix wins:	91

1992 Belgian GP, 1993 Portuguese GP, 1994 Brazilian GP, Pacific GP, San Marino GP, Monaco GP, Canadian GP, French GP, Hungarian GP, European GP, 1995 Brazilian GP, Spanish GP, Monaco GP, French GP, German GP, Belgian GP, European GP, Pacific GP, Japanese GP, 1996 Spanish GP, Belgian GP, Italian GP, 1997 Monaco GP, Canadian GP, French GP, Belgian GP, Japanese GP, 1998 Argentinian GP, Canadian GP, French GP, British GP, Hungarian GP, Italian GP, 1999 San Marino GP, Monaco GP, 2000 Australian GP, Brazilian GP, San Marino GP, European GP, Canadian GP, Italian GP, US GP, Japanese GP, Malaysian GP, 2001 Australian GP, Malaysian GP, Spanish GP, Monaco GP, European GP, French GP, Hungarian GP, Belgian GP, Japanese GP, 2002 Australian GP, Brazilian GP, San Marino GP, Spanish GP, Austrian GP, Canadian GP, British GP, French GP, German GP, Belgian GP, Japanese GP, 2003 San Marino GP, Spanish GP, Austrian GP, Canadian GP, Italian GP, US GP, 2004 Australian GP, Malaysian GP, Bahrain GP, San Marino GP, Spanish GP, European GP, Canadian GP, French GP, British GP, German GP, Hungarian GP, Japanese GP, 2005 US GP

Poles:	68
Fastest laps:	75
Points:	1517
Honours:	2004, 2003, 2002, 2001, 2000, 1995 & 1994 F1 WORLD CHAMPION, 1990 GERMAN F3 CHAMPION, 1988 GERMAN FORMULA KÖNIG CHAMPION

BECOMING F1'S GREATEST DRIVER

Michael Schumacher was brought up on a kart track run by his father Rolf and his natural balance and killer instinct led to good results in karts. On graduating to Formula König in 1988, he did so well that he wrapped up the title with rounds to spare, so advanced to Formula Ford, where he also won. It took two goes to land the German F3 title, but it was what happened next that made his career. Without the money to advance to F3000 in Europe, he bought a ride in the Japanese series and won. Then, when Jordan's Bertrand Gachot was jailed during 1991, Schumacher took his ride. He impressed and Benetton signed him. Titles followed in 1994 and 1995, but what put him into a class of his own was turning Ferrari into a winning machine and claiming five titles in a row from 2000. Then, at the end of 2006, Ferrari forced him into retirement. However, dabbling in motorbike racing did not bring titles, so he was ready when Mercedes returned to F1.

NICO ROSBERG

Rosberg's target this year, however realistic, must be to become a grand prix winner for, after six years in the sport's top category, he has to take the next step up. And it can be done – just ask Jenson Button who became a winner in his seventh season.

A F1 driver's currency only lasts for so long, and the big step from promising rookie to grand prix winner is one that a driver has to take if he wants to be in a position to take a tilt at winning the World Championship. However, key to this vital step is landing a ride with a team who will give him the equipment with which to do the job, to become a regular podium visitor and occasional grand prix winner at the very least.

Nico Rosberg, six-year veteran of Williams and Mercedes GP, and a driver good enough to set the fastest lap on his Formula One debut, knows all the above only too well, with the message reinforced by his father Keke, World Champion for Williams in 1982. So, Rosberg will have spent the close-season praying Ross Brawn and the design team led by Loïc Bigois at Mercedes GP Petronas can produce a car that will fight closer to the front of the field, a car that outperforms at least the Ferraris and the McLarens, if not the Red Bulls.

The team rates Rosberg, though, appreciating his stark intelligence and consistent approach, and Brawn said at

Nico really needs to win now that he is starting his seventh season of Formula One.

the start of last year that he thought him good enough to become World Champion. So, it's largely down to the machinery, then.

However, one of the more interesting comparisons over the past two seasons has been how Rosberg has put team-mate Michael Schumacher in the shade, adding to his reputation. Yet, as 2011 progressed, the gap between them first came down and was then overturned as Schumacher began to work out how to handle the Mercedes MGP W02's problems with tyre degradation and so allowed his race-craft of old to re-emerge.

If this year's Mercedes MGP W03 continues to hold him back, Rosberg will have to hope that his reputation remains sufficiently strong so that he can team up with Ferrari, a team known to be interested in him as a potential replacement for Felipe Massa to race alongside Fernando Alonso for 2013. Wins are what drivers want, and the rest will follow.

TRACK NOTES

Nationality:	GERMAN
Born:	27 JUNE 1985, WIESBADEN, GERMANY
Website:	www.nicorosberg.com
Teams:	WILLIAMS 2006-09,
	MERCEDES 2010-12

CAREER RECORD

First Grand Prix:	2006 BAHRAIN GP
Grand Prix starts:	108
Grand Prix wins:	0
(best result: second, 2008 Singapore GP)	
Poles:	0
Fastest laps:	2
Points:	306.5
Honours:	2005 GP2 CHAMPION,
	2002 FORMULA BMW CHAMPION, 2000
	EUROPEAN FORMULA A KART RUNNER-UP

COMING OUT OF THE SHADOWS

With 1982 World Champion Keke Rosberg his father, it was always likely that Nico would at the very least try his hand at karting. This he did, but he was put in the shade by his team-mate Lewis Hamilton on several occasions, including the time when he finished runner-up in the 2000 European Formula A series. However, when Nico went it alone in cars, he immediately shone, winning the German Formula BMW title in 2002. His second campaign in the F3 Euroseries left him fourth overall in 2004, but it all came right in 2005, when he became the GP2 champion ahead of Heikki Kovalainen. Naturally, F1 followed and he raced for Williams in 2006, setting fastest lap on his debut. However, a four-year spell with the team fell short of victory, with second in Singapore (2008) his best result. Then, contrary to critics' expectations, he stood up well to the arrival of Michael Schumacher to newly renamed Mercedes GP in 2010, outscoring him 142 points to 72.

LOTUS RENAULT GP

Last year's Renault team has a new name, Lotus, for 2012 and it will be looking to put itself back on the rails after a season of patchy form that started with a surprise podium finish but was soon heading downhill from there.

The arrival of Kimi Raïkkönen as team leader and Romain Grosjean as number two left no place for Vitaly Petrov in the 2012 season.

The big news for 2012 is the return of 2007 World Champion Kimi Raïkkönen to Formula One after a two-year spell in the World Rally Championship. Whether this will be enough to propel the Lotus team forward remains to be seen, but it needs to rediscover its momentum.

So patchy was this team's form last year that it dropped from the mix near the front of the field and its name hit the news principally due to clashes with Team Lotus over which of them should bear the Lotus name. Eventually, Team Lotus backed down and will race as Caterham.

Ranked a distant fifth overall in 2010, when it was known as Renault, the team had reason to believe that they might achieve more in 2011 when the season started with a third-place finish for Vitaly Petrov in the Australian GP and another for Nick Heidfeld next time out at Sepang. However, it ended up with less than half of the previous year's tally. So, team principal Eric Boullier's job for the close season was

to build up the team's structure again to return to a level of competitiveness with which it could once more chase podium finishes and, after a year of inconsistent form, achieve this on a regular basis.

The season went off the rails before

KEY MOMENTS AND KEY PEOPLE

TEAM HISTORY
This is a team with a confused identity. It started life as Toleman, became Benetton, then Renault and is now Lotus, but not the same team that was Lotus last year or the original Lotus that shone under Colin Chapman. Its greatest success came in the 1990s as Benetton, when it helped Michael Schumacher to two titles and again, a decade later when it did the same as Renault for Fernando Alonso under the management of Flavio Briatore. The team was dubbed Lotus Renault for 2011 out of deference to Group Lotus.

JAMES ALLISON
Versed in speed from being the son of the head of the Royal Air Force, who also enjoyed a passion for vintage cars, James studied mechanical engineering at Cambridge, using his specialization in aerodynamics to land a job at Benetton in 1991. After studying under Willem Toet, he moved to Larrousse, where he stayed until the team folded. Following this, he went back to Benetton in 1995. A spell at Ferrari followed, but he once more returned to Benetton (now renamed Renault), rising to become technical director in 2005.

2011 DRIVERS & RESULTS

Driver	Nationality	Races	Wins	Pts	Pos
Vitaly Petrov	Russian	19	0	37	10th
Nick Heidfeld	German	11	0	34	11th
Bruno Senna	Brazilian	19	0	2	18th

it had even started when Robert Kubica suffered a terrible accident while competing in a rally in the close season. At a stroke, Lotus Renault GP (as it was then known) lost its primary asset. In came Heidfeld as a replacement, but it was not the same for he soon became swamped and there was none of the spark or driven attitude that the Pole would have provided, week in, week out. With almost all other drivers already signed up for 2012, Boullier understandably chose to wait for Kubica.

Therefore, it came as little surprise last autumn that the team's plans hinged on whether Kubica would be physically ready to race again in F1. If he proved that he could, Boullier and his colleagues would have re-signed him in an instant. Indeed, while a true racer, he comes with the added benefit of not chasing the accoutrements of fame and fortune, focusing all his time on making both himself and the car go faster. So, the driver decision was in limbo.

With strong backing from Russia, Petrov was always likely to stay, but the decision to replace Heidfeld after the first 11 races for underperforming, thus paving the way for Bruno Senna to step up from the test ride, was revealing. Senna's surname obviously retains resonance the world over because of his uncle Ayrton. However, when Senna was immediately quicker, Petrov's reputation took a battering and it was discussed that he too might be replaced,

with Rubens Barrichello mentioned in dispatches for his technical knowledge and general input. However, Romain Grosjean, long-time Renault development driver and a Renault racer in 2009, also waited in the wings after winning the GP2 title and landed the second seat.

Expect this year's Renault chassis to be one of the more standard ones as technical director James Allison reckoned the R31's innovative forward-facing exhausts hindered rather than helped the team last year, believing not only were they hard to develop but they also proved difficult to operate on low-speed circuits. The problems around this exhaust system came to the fore when the team's relative competitiveness declined as the season went on.

Organisationally, Paul Seaby has been promoted to the team manager's role when John Wickham declined to stay on after fleetingly returning to F1 to replace the outgoing Steve Nielsen after overtaking an efficiency study first.

"Last year we produced a car at the start of the season that could fight for podiums. Now we understand why we couldn't catch up, but I'm confident that we'll again be delivering a good car."
Eric Boullier

FOR THE RECORD

Country of origin:	France
Team base:	Enstone, England
Telephone:	(44) 01608 678000
Website:	www.lotusrenaultgp.com
Active in Formula One:	From 1977-85, then from 2002
Grands Prix contested:	301*
Wins:	35
Pole positions:	50
Fastest laps:	31

* Note these stats do not include the 238 races that the team ran as Toleman, then Benetton

THE TEAM

Chairman:	Gerard Lopez
Team principal & managing director:	Eric Boullier
Technical director:	James Allison
Deputy technical director:	Naoki Tokunaga
Chief designer:	Tim Densham
Head of aerodynamics:	Dirk de Beer
Operations director:	John Mardle
Track operations director:	Alan Permane
Team manager:	Paul Seaby
Race engineers:	Simon Rennie & Mark Slade
Test driver:	tba
Chassis:	Lotus
Engine:	Renault V8
Tyres:	Pirelli

Eric Boullier lost his number one before last year and will welcome a steadier ride into 2012.

KIMI RAIKKONEN

Kimi really is back from the cold as he spent the two years since quitting Ferrari contesting the World Rally Championship on snow, ice and gravel. The big question is whether he has rediscovered the drive to compete in F1, along with its PR demands.

Kimi Raïkkönen, World Champion for Ferrari in 2007, is a rare thing: a driver who has left Formula One of his own volition, then returned. He had grown tired of the demands. Instead, he loved the freedom of the World Rally Championship, the challenge of competing on ice, gravel and snow. However, the signs were there that this still was not what he sought as he considered stock car racing in the USA and also endurance racing.

Then came the news that he was looking at F1 again. This seemed unlikely to many, who felt that he did not have the desire to get back into this pressured world but he entered into negotiations with Williams. Lofty financial demands were a likely stumbling block and talks faltered. Then, as last season ended, the news broke that he had signed a two-year F1 deal: to return with Lotus Renault GP as team leader.

No one should ever doubt Raïkkönen's speed for he remains one of the most talented drivers to race on this stage, as demonstrated by his propensity to win at the more difficult circuits such as Spa-Francorchamps. However, insiders are

Kimi wanted to try different things but says he has never lost his love for Formula One.

asking whether he will be able to maintain his apparent enthusiasm driving a car likely to be in the midfield rather than at the front, as the McLarens and Ferraris he raced before used to be.

If the team has its car ready in good

time and he can get some useful testing in pre-season, then Kimi might revel in doing what he likes best - driving a racing car very fast - perhaps enough to help him bear carrying out the obligatory PR duties that he loathes so much.

TRACK NOTES

Nationality:	FINNISH
Born:	17 OCTOBER 1979, ESPOO, FINLAND
Website:	www.kimiraikkonen.com
Teams:	SAUBER 2001, McLAREN 2002-06, FERRARI 2007-09, LOTUS 2012

CAREER RECORD

First Grand Prix:	2001 AUSTRALIAN GP
Grand Prix starts:	157
Grand Prix wins:	18

2003 Malaysian GP, 2004 Belgian GP, 2005 Spanish GP, Monaco GP, Canadian GP, Hungarian GP, Turkish GP, Belgian GP, Japanese GP, 2007 Australian GP, French GP, British GP, Belgian GP, Chinese GP, Brazilian GP, 2008 Malaysian GP, Spanish GP, 2009 Belgian GP

Poles:	16
Fastest laps:	35
Points:	569
Honours:	

2007 FORMULA ONE WORLD CHAMPION, 2003 & 2005 FORMULA ONE RUNNER-UP & 2000 BRITISH FORMULA RENAULT CHAMPION, 1999 BRITISH FORMULA RENAULT WINTER SERIES CHAMPION, 1998 EUROPEAN SUPER A KART RUNNER-UP & FINNISH KART CHAMPION & NORDIC KART CHAMPION

FROM KARTS TO F1, TO RALLYING

From the moment that he started kart racing, Kimi Raïkkönen had talent to spare. National and international titles followed, then someone mentioned him to Steve Robertson. As the former racer was eager to move into driver management, he took a look and subsequently snapped him up to race in Formula Renault in Britain. After landing the British title, Robertson arranged for Kimi not to move to F3 but to have an F1 test. Amazingly, he impressed Peter Sauber enough for the team boss to give him his F1 break in 2001 after 23 car races. He scored on his debut in Melbourne and that was enough for McLaren to sign him for 2002. Runner-up to Michael Schumacher in 2003, Raïkkönen was second again in 2005, behind Fernando Alonso. As a Ferrari driver in 2007, he took the title at the final round. He then spent 2010 and 2011 in the World Rally Championship with Citroen, both times ranking tenth, with a best finish of fifth in Turkey in his first year.

It was a long wait and Romain had said that he would give up on Formula One forever if he did not land a ride for 2012, but the Frenchman held his nerve and now has a fulltime ride with Lotus Renault GP and a target to aim for in team-mate Kimi Raïkkönen.

The selection of drivers for the Lotus Renault GP team's attack for the 2012 World Championship was a complicated process. Firstly, the team was waiting for a prognosis on Robert Kubica's recovery from the dreadful injuries that he suffered in a rallying accident at the start of last year. Then it sought a lead driver to replace him, landing 2007 World Champion Kimi Raïkkönen. And following this, it had to decide who would fill its second seat.

Vitaly Petrov was the favourite, but an outburst against the team wrecked his chances. Romain was tipped to get the ride, but he had to convince the team to take him ahead of Bruno Senna and even Rubens Barrichello. In the end his French nationality helped swing it as this keeps the Total group on board as sponsor.

Romain is a driver with a prodigious record in the junior single-seater formulae and so had truly earned his chance. However, it appeared that he had blown his shot at Formula One when he was given a ride by the Renault team in 2009 after Nelson Piquet Jr was moved aside and yet still did not deliver.

For whatever reason this did not work,

Romain failed to shine in F1 at the end of 2009, but is better prepared this time.

Romain had to step down a level, rebuild his career and get himself ready for a second crack at the big time. No mean task in a sport where drivers soon get forgotten once they've left the F1 stage, but he kept the backing of Gravity driver management and was helped hugely when Gravity's Eric Boullier became the Renault F1 team principal for 2010.

All that Romain could do was to rediscover his winning touch and this he succeeded in doing in no uncertain manner (see box below). More importantly, he discovered a new approach to his racing and feels that he's arriving back in F1 with the same team, albeit now racing as Lotus, with a new maturity. His career setbacks have made him stronger and more focused, and he will grab this opportunity with both hands.

TRACK NOTES

Nationality:	FRENCH
Born:	17 APRIL 1986, GENEVA, SWITZERLAND
Website:	www.romaingrosjean.com
Teams:	RENAULT 2009, LOTUS 2012

CAREER RECORD	
First Grand Prix:	2009 EUROPEAN GP
Grand Prix starts:	7
Grand Prix wins:	0 (best result: 13th, 2009 Brazilian GP)
Poles:	0
Fastest laps:	0
Points:	0
Honours:	2011 GP2 CHAMPION & GP2 ASIA CHAMPION, 2010 AUTO GP CHAMPION, 2008 GP2 ASIA CHAMPION, 2007 FORMULA THREE EUROSERIES CHAMPION, 2005 FRENCH FORMULA RENAULT CHAMPION, 2003 SWISS FORMULA RENAULT 1600 CHAMPION

CHAMPIONSHIP TITLES GALORE

Romain is a driver who delivers and has done so consistently ever since he started car racing by winning the Swiss Formula Renault 1600 title in 2003. At two-yearly intervals, he added the French Formula Renault and then European Formula Three titles. Then came race-winning form in GP2 in 2008, when he ranked fourth and then even stronger form in the early races of 2009 before he was given his Formula One break by Renault from the European GP onward, replacing Nelson Piquet Jr. At the end of the season, having achieved a best result of 13th at Interlagos and having lost his F1 ride with Renault, Romain considered quitting, but he had a change of heart and in 2010 stepped back and raced in the FIA GT1 Championship, winning two rounds in a Matech Competition Ford GT before winning the Auto GP series for old A1GP cars. Then it was back to GP2 again for 2011, starting off by winning the four-race GP2 Asia series, then landing the main title.

SAHARA FORCE INDIA

Improving form toward the end of last year gave a hint of what might lie ahead in 2012 as Force India is clearly a team on the up, with much of the credit going to its engine and transmission deals with Mercedes and McLaren.

Adrian Sutil (above) and rookie Paul di Resta collected points at an ever-greater rate through 2011 and the team should expect more in 2012.

Force India started to deliver last year and its high points include rookie Paul di Resta qualifying sixth for the British GP, then finishing sixth in Singapore and Adrian Sutil achieving the same finish at the Nürburgring, one place ahead of di Resta. This reflected the progress that the team made through the season, which is not normally the way teams with smaller budgets.

Much of the credit for this improvement for Vijay Mallya's white cars, with the green and orange stripes of India bedecking their livery, is due to the technical partnership with McLaren, who supplies Force India with Mercedes engines and McLaren transmissions. These are indeed strong building blocks on which technical director Andrew Green can base the package.

Indeed, so good was the progress last year as a radical aerodynamic package was introduced at the Spanish GP, effectively to upgrade what had been a revised version of the 2010 car with which they had started the season and this

began the team's advance up the order. As di Resta and Sutil racked up points in the latter half of the year, they overhauled Sauber and it then became clear that they

might stand a chance of toppling Renault to end the year as fifth best team in the constructors' championship, especially as Renault's point-gathering seemed to

KEY MOMENTS AND KEY PEOPLE

TEAM HISTORY
This team started life in F1 in 1991, when it was entered by Eddie Jordan, who had run a successful F3000 team. Its first win came in Belgium (1998) and the team won sporadically until it was sold to Russian Alex Shnaider in 2005. This was the start of a changing of identity, as it was known as Midland F1, then two years later as Spyker after the Dutch sports car builder bought the controlling share. Then, in 2008, Vijay Mallya took over as owner and the team name was changed to Force India.

ANDREW GREEN
The British designer arrived at Force India from Virgin Racing for 2011 in the wake of the departures of James Key, then Mark Smith. His career in racing design has been a long one, dating back to working on Reynard's F3000 cars from 1987, before becoming a designer at Jordan in 1991, followed by a spell as a race engineer from 1995. After moving to BAR as chief designer in 1998, Green moved on to Red Bull Racing.

2011 DRIVERS & RESULTS

Driver	Nationality	Races	Wins	Pts	Pos
Adrian Sutil	German	19	0	42	9th
Paul di Resta	British	19	0	27	13th

FOR THE RECORD

Country of origin:	England
Team base:	Silverstone, England
Telephone:	(44) 01327 850800
Website:	www.forceindiaf1.com
Active in Formula One:	From 1991
	(as Jordan, then Midland in 2005
	and Spyker in 2007)
Grands Prix contested:	358
Wins:	4
Pole positions:	3
Fastest laps:	3

THE TEAM

Chairman & team principal:	Vijay Mallya
Co-owner:	Michiel Mol
Team director:	Bob Fernley
Chief operating officer:	Otmar Szafnauer
Technical director:	Andrew Green
Design project leader:	Akio Haga
Team manager:	Andy Stevenson
Project leader:	Ian Hall
Head of aerodynamics:	Simon Phillips
Chief race engineer:	Dominic Harlow
Test driver:	tba
Chassis:	Force India VJM05
Engine:	Mercedes V8
Tyres:	Pirelli

have dried up. What was impressive is that Force India got to the point where it expected to score on every outing rather than just hoping. Many onlookers were impressed not just by the speed but the consistency, too. After all, almost all of the team's 2009 points came in just two races – in the Belgian and Italian GPs – and many were confused by how a team that could claim pole position and race to second place at Spa-Francorchamps in Giancarlo Fisichella's hands and race to fourth at Monza with Sutil driving might then drop back into the pack a month later.

Green can feel pleased with the progress that he has made since being appointed technical director in June 2010 to replace James Key after he left to join Sauber and his initial replacement Mark Smith headed off for Lotus. Apart from seven years with other teams, Green has been with Jordan, from which this team evolved, since 1991.

Last year the drivers generally acquitted themselves well and while Mallya heaped considerable praise on first-year F1 racer di Resta, he kept the Scot and team-mate Sutil on tenterhooks regarding 2012 in announcing last September that he was not planning to name his drivers for this year until last year's World Championship was over. Di Resta might be confident of staying as he had performed with such maturity and no little speed, as well as

conducting himself in a model manner out of the cockpit. Sutil, on the other hand, may be quicker, but has lost all novelty in being around in F1 for five years. Keeping both on their toes was the presence of Nico Hulkenberg as Force India's third driver. Already he'd proved himself more than capable, spending his rookie F1 season racing for Williams and like di Resta, he is viewed by many as a possible Mercedes GP driver for the future, or a future Force India driver of course, which is why both di Resta and Sutil were aware that there was no guarantee of their seats for 2012. In the end, Sutil lost out to Hulkenberg.

At some stage in the future Force India would love to run an Indian driver and it instigated a F1 academy last year, starting with a karting competition to identify the best of the sub-continent's young stars.

The team is called Sahara Force India this year as computer magnate Saharasri Subrata Roy Sahara has invested in them, buying some of Mallya's shares.

"If we want to be anywhere in the constructors' championship, then we need to build a car that is capable of racing and being competitive everywhere, not just on high-speed circuits like Spa and Monza."

Vijay Mallya

Mallya's decision to use McLaren technology and Mercedes power has helped the team advance.

PAUL DI RESTA

Here is a rare thing: a driver who disappointed no one in his rookie Formula One season. Perhaps this was down to having greater maturity, being 24 when he hit F1, but the results were enough to earn him his second season with Force India.

Motor racing runs in Paul di Resta's family genes. His father, Louis, used to race in Formula Ford, his uncle George was a racer too, as are George's sons, Dario and Marino Franchitti, with the former a multiple Indycar champion. So, it comes as no surprise given this grounding that Paul was immersed in motorsport from an early age as he grew up in Scotland.

While his family background might explain his love of racing, and the honing of his skills on the track, what makes Paul such a find for F1 is that he has clearly watched and learned from Dario as his cousin landed DTM and Indycar titles, and as a result his off-track demeanour is first-class, making him even more of an asset for any team that runs him.

Having friends in high places helps too, and Mercedes-Benz motorsport boss Norbert Haug snapped up this former winner of the McLaren Autosport BRDC Young Driver award when he ran out of cash to continue his single-seater career after winning the European Formula Three title in 2006 and so was unable to advance to GP2. Instead, Mercedes placed him in touring cars as part of its

Paul impressed everyone not only with his pace but also his maturity in his rookie year.

DTM attack. Then, after he won that title too, Haug found him his place in F1, with Mercedes-equipped Force India. A second season with the team could have him perfectly prepared to step across and race for Mercedes GP next year if Michael

Schumacher decides to retire again when his latest contract expires.

Scoring points in his first two grands prix was impressive, with Paul taking 10th place finishes in both Australia and Malaysia. Then, as the car became more competitive after a mid-season slump in form relative to its rivals, he started getting among the points on a regular basis, showing considerable aplomb in the manner in which he raced unruffled to finish sixth on the streets of Singapore.

This is a driver with a definite future. It's just a question of which team he will advance to next.

TRACK NOTES

Nationality:	BRITISH
Born:	16 APRIL 1986, UPHALL, SCOTLAND
Website:	www.pauldiresta.com
Teams:	FORCE INDIA 2011-12

CAREER RECORD	
First Grand Prix:	2011 AUSTRALIAN GP
Grand Prix starts:	19
Grand Prix wins:	0 (best result: sixth, 2011 Singapore GP)
Poles:	0
Fastest laps:	0
Points:	27
Honours:	2010 GERMAN TOURING CAR CHAMPION. 2006 EUROPEAN FORMULA THREE CHAMPION & FORMULA THREE MASTERS WINNER, 2001 BRITISH JICA KART CHAMPION, 1998 SCOTTISH OPEN KART CHAMPION, 1997 BRITISH CADET KART CHAMPION, 1995 SCOTTISH CADET KART CHAMPION

GROOMED BY MERCEDES-BENZ

Paul followed in the wheeltracks of his cousins Dario and Marino Franchitti in racing karts, stepping up to car racing after collecting a cluster of national titles. His first step was into Formula Renault and he had the distinction of marking his maiden season by beating Lewis Hamilton in the final round of the series at Oulton Park. Then, after another strong season in which he ranked third, Paul advanced to Formula Three for 2005. At the second time of asking, he won the F3 Euroseries ahead of a German driver by the name of Sebastian Vettel. Yet this is where his career took a different course as he could not afford to graduate to GP2 for 2007 and so accepted Mercedes' offer to race in the DTM. He took to touring cars straightaway and was series runner-up behind Timo Scheider in 2008. After doing some F1 tests for Force India, Paul landed the DTM title in 2010 before Mercedes eased his passage to F1 with Force India for 2011.

NICO HULKENBERG

Nico is a driver with a remarkable pedigree and he is back for a second season in a Formula One race seat after a year in which he only went out in Friday practice. It will be intriguing to see how the German fares against his team-mate Paul di Resta.

Stepping back from a race seat with Williams in 2010 to the reserve driver position with Force India for the 2011 season was a definite move backward, but this promising German went through last year confident that he had a contract in place for a race ride in 2012.

So, when Force India kept delaying its driver announcement until deep into December, people started to worry that he would not be racing in the year ahead. Then it all fell into place when it was announced that Nico and Paul di Resta would be the team's drivers.

This will be an intriguing pairing as di Resta built some impressive momentum in his rookie year, earning plaudits as he went, yet Nico ended his maiden season of F1 in 2011 with pole position in the penultimate event, the Brazilian GP, when he struck as weather conditions changed on a wet/dry day.

Both drivers are European Formula Three Champions, albeit with di Resta reaching F1 only via a detour through the German Touring Car Championship.

Nico, on the other hand, arrived after a powerful surge up the ladder of

Nico had a contract but had to sweat on the sidelines before his 2012 seat was settled.

single-seater formulae was capped with his domination of the GP2 series in 2009, achieving greater control of this tricky series than any GP2 rookie before him and outracing his far more experienced team-mate Pastor Maldonado, who was

ironically the driver who took his place at Williams last year.

So, just how good is Nico? We will find out in the year ahead, but his form in Friday practice sessions last year suggests that he is more than up to the task, with his technical feedback much appreciated by the team. Indeed, Force India's chief engineer Dominic Harlow credited Nico with helping with much of the progress the team achieved through the year, thanks to his mileage on its simulator. Furthermore, few drivers who have been so rapid in the junior formulae ever fail to impress given, the right F1 break.

TRACK NOTES

Nationality:	GERMAN
Born:	19 AUGUST 1987, EMMERICH, GERMANY
Website:	www.nico-hulkenberg.net
Teams:	WILLIAMS 2010, FORCE INDIA 2012

CAREER RECORD

First Grand Prix:	2010
Grand Prix starts:	19
Grand Prix wins:	0 (best result: sixth, 2010 Hungarian GP)
Poles:	1
Fastest laps:	0
Points:	22
Honours:	2009 GP2 CHAMPION, 2008 EUROPEAN FORMULA THREE CHAMPION, 2007 MASTERS FORMULA THREE WINNER, 2006/07 A1GP CHAMPION, 2005 GERMAN FORMULA BMW CHAMPION, 2003 GERMAN KART CHAMPION, 2002 GERMAN JUNIOR KART CHAMPION

A DRIVER WHO COLLECTS TITLES

Sitting on the sidelines as Force India's third driver in 2011 was the first real hiccough in Nico's meteoric racing career. He was a double national champion on the German karting scene, then made an instant impact on German Formula BMW as soon as he was old enough to graduate, winning the title in 2005. Although driving an unfancied Ligier chassis in F3, he did well against the predominant Dallaras and enhanced his reputation over the winter in winning the A1GP World Cup for Germany. Looked after by the Schumacher brothers' manager Willi Weber, he was placed in the F3 Euroseries for 2007, but had the unusual experience of placing third overall. Avenging himself in 2008, Nico was crowned champion. Then came GP2 in 2009 and Nico was that rare thing, a rookie GP2 champion. So it was that his five wins from 20 starts landed him not just the title but his F1 breakthrough with Williams. The highlight of this was qualifying on pole in changeable conditions in Brazil.

SAUBER

Low-profile yet efficient, Sauber's Formula One involvement often slips beneath the radar, but this is a team that is starting to make progress in its eternal battle under Peter Sauber's guidance to advance from the front of the midfield pack.

Both Kamui Kobayashi and Sauber seemed to go off the boil last year and the Swiss team's drivers must qualify better in the season ahead.

Progress can often come from change, whether that is a change in the rules, the driver line-up or even the team personnel. In Sauber's case, with a settled technical team, the change is most likely to come as the result of serious investment. Cash has not always been in abundance for the Swiss-based team but a considerable wave of money flowing in from Mexico since the start of 2011 after Sauber signed rookie Mexican racer Sergio Pérez should start to make a difference in the season ahead.

Technical director James Key has produced some good cars before, when at Jordan, and his designs since joining Sauber have been quick out of the box. Yet this is Sauber's eternal conundrum since their relative pace atrophies as the season progresses. Larger and better-funded teams then pull ahead and so points-scoring drives previously attainable on a regular basis in the first half of the season become all but out of reach, dropping the team down the rankings in the constructors' championship and so costing it the prize money that helps put funds back into the pot for the development of the following year's car.

Now, with the financial involvement of Carlos Slim, the world's richest man,

KEY MOMENTS AND KEY PEOPLE

TEAM HISTORY
Founded by racer Peter Sauber, the Swiss constructor started off making sports cars in the 1970s, later building cars for F3. However, Sauber truly made its name when it ran Mercedes' sports car attack the 1980s, winning the 1989 Le Mans 24 Hours. They discussed trying F1 together, but Sauber went it alone in 1993 and has been there ever since. BMW bought a stake in the team in 2006, but after Robert Kubica won in Canada (2008), the deal came to an end in 2009 and Sauber is now back at the helm – and intends to stay there.

PETER SAUBER
A hill-climb competitor in his native Switzerland, Sauber turned to racing sports cars in the 1970s, but increasingly focused on building cars for others to race instead, both sports cars and F3. One of his F3 drivers, Max Welti, became involved with Sauber's sports car team and convinced Mercedes to fit its engines to the cars. A fruitful partnership followed and the money the German manufacturer paid Sauber helped convince him that he could afford to try F1.

2011 DRIVERS & RESULTS

Driver	Nationality	Races	Wins	Pts	Pos
Pedro de la Rosa	Spanish	1	0	0	20th
Kamui Kobayashi	Japanese	19	0	30	12th
Sergio Pérez	Mexican	18	0	14	16th

adding to the coffers and in turn attracting backing from other Mexican companies with global aspirations, the regular loss of competitiveness should be a thing of the past, provided Key and his designers continue to come up with in-season tweaks and developments to keep the Ferrari-powered Sauber C31 in the hunt.

The clearest goal for the C31 is to raise its game to be able to work its tyres more effectively and so get more heat into them to enable the drivers to slot in more quick runs in qualifying. Conversely, the C30s were light on their tyres in race trim, but the drivers had been hampered in starting from further back on the grid than desired, often having to fight their way past those who qualified ahead of them but whose cars had inferior race pace. Obviously, on circuits where overtaking is difficult, this proved ruinous to their chances and caused Sergio Pérez in particular to take risks that did not always pay off. This qualifying performance shortfall also explained why both drivers - and Pérez in particular due to his ability to be easy on his tyres - led to them heading out into races with a strategy planned for making fewer pit stops than their rivals around them in an attempt to get ahead.

One massive plus for the team in all of this is that Peter Sauber is a racer through and through, and he has clearly enjoyed

the past two seasons since he has put his team back on the map as his own in essence and deed after four years of being known as BMW Sauber after the German manufacturer took control and left him largely on the sidelines. Indeed, Sauber has said that he will never again sell the team, as he did before the 2006 season when BMW came flexing its chequebook.

Another advantage is that both Kamui Kobayashi and Pérez are settled at the team and have the pace to compete with anyone they find near them on the grid. With Kobayashi now entering his third full season, mistakes ought to be reduced - important since every point will count in the battle to climb the constructors' championship. Whether either can improve on Kobayashi's fifth place in last year's Monaco GP remains to be seen, however.

FOR THE RECORD

Country of origin:	Switzerland
Team base:	Hinwil, Switzerland
Telephone:	(41) 44 937 9000
Website:	www.sauberf1team.com
Active in Formula One:	From 1993
(but from 2006 to 2010 as BMW Sauber)	
Grands Prix contested:	325
Wins:	1
Pole positions:	1
Fastest laps:	2

THE TEAM

Team principal & owner:	Peter Sauber
Managing director:	Monisha Kaltenborn
Technical director:	James Key
Chief designer:	Christoph Zimmermann
Head of aerodynamics:	Willem Toet
Head of track engineering:	Giampaolo Dall'Ara
Team manager:	Beat Zehnder
Test driver:	Esteban Gutierrez
Chassis:	Sauber C31
Engine:	Ferrari V8
Tyres:	Pirelli

"Although it was only his second full F1 season, Kamui has grown into his role extremely well and he's already taking responsibilities that naturally fall to the more experienced driver in the team."
Peter Sauber

James Key is hoping that his drivers will mature in their second season together at Sauber.

Although not so spectacular in 2011 as in 2010, Kamui Kobayashi remains extremely important in Formula One circles for keeping Japan's attention on the grands prix. Yet it will take a move to a top-ranked team if he wants to win races.

After two full seasons with Sauber, now is the time for Kobayashi to be seen as part of the Formula One establishment rather than just an impressive newcomer, so the Japanese driver needs to get serious, eliminate all mistakes and deliver results, race in, race out, whatever the state of competitiveness of his car.

For so many drivers, the challenge of making it up the greasy pole to the sport's pinnacle – Formula One – is all encompassing. However, their ascent is forgotten once they've reached the F1 paddock and only their results in grands prix count thereafter. So, after Kobayashi made a considerable impact in his two outings for Toyota at the end of 2009, then delighted with bold overtaking moves for Sauber in 2010, his 2011 season made less of a positive impression. The reason for this downswing in reputation was that rookie team-mate Sergio Pérez got straight onto Kobayashi's pace and if ever there was a case of a driver realizing his rookie days were over, this was it.

Fifth place in Monaco was a huge fillip for Kamui and the team, but as ever with Sauber, their relative level of

Kamui needs to hit the form he showed in 2010 to keep his reputation as a charger.

competitiveness dwindled as the year progressed. Because of this, championship points became increasingly hard to come by, causing Kamui to consider his run to points-scoring results – in six consecutive rounds from Sepang to Montreal – with

increasing nostalgia as summer turned to autumn. Still, by the start of August, Peter Sauber had Kamui's signature on the dotted line for another campaign this year. Knowing the increased investment in the team that arrived from Mexico along with Pérez ought to bear more fruit in 2012, perhaps Kamui and his legion of fans in Japan will have a little more to cheer about in the months ahead. Certainly, the sight of this driver on the attack in a more competitive car will excite fans and TV directors alike as he probes to pass and then goes for moves that others might not think possible.

TRACK NOTES

Nationality:	JAPANESE
Born:	13 SEPTEMBER 1986, HYOGO, JAPAN
Website:	www.kamui-kobayashi.com
Teams:	TOYOTA 2009, BMW SAUBER/SAUBER 2010-12

CAREER RECORD

First Grand Prix:	2009 BRAZILIAN GP
Grand Prix starts:	40
Grand Prix wins:	0
	(best result: fifth, 2011 Monaco GP)
Poles:	0
Fastest laps:	0
Points:	65
Honours:	2008 GP2 ASIA CHAMPION, 2005 EUROPEAN & ITALIAN FORMULA RENAULT CHAMPION, 2003 JAPANESE FORMULA TOYOTA RUNNER-UP, 2001 ALL-JAPAN ICA KART CHAMPION, 2000 SUZUKA KART CHAMPION

SACRIFICES ALONG THE WAY

Kamui Kobayashi's route to the top was one of sacrifices. Since leaving Japan's junior formulae after a successful career in karts and then single-seaters, Kamui took at the age of just 17 a voyage into the unknown by venturing Europe to further his racing career. Yet Kamui blossomed in this alien environment and at his second attempt in 2005, won the European and Italian Formula Renault titles, achieving a level of success that Japanese drivers had not achieved before. When he followed this up by ranking fourth overall in the 2007 European F3 series, he confirmed his talents and stepped up to GP2. A winner second time out, at the Circuit de Catalunya, he went on to win the winter series before returning for a second full season of GP2. However, before it was over, he was drafted in to Toyota's F1 team for the final two races and impressed enormously. Then, in 2010, Kamui proved to be one of the great entertainers and added a second sixth-place finish.

SERGIO PÉREZ

After a hugely impressive debut F1 season in which he proved the master of tyre preservation, this young Mexican is already making the top teams sit up and take notice. What he needs now is a season of consolidation at Sauber.

Raw speed and the ability to put on a charge through the field marked Sergio Pérez out as he rose through the junior categories, most especially in GP2, so it came as a major surprise last year that what stood out was his ability to make a set of tyres last longer than almost anyone else. In short, the young Mexican's image was transformed and he quickly gained a host of admirers within the paddock for the way that he drove like a F1 driver of considerable experience rather than a 21-year-old rookie.

From the very first race, too, he proved the equal of highly-rated Sauber team-mate Kamui Kobayashi. The way that Pérez made a single-stop strategy work for him at Melbourne, driving in unflustered style from start to finish, caused everyone to sit up and take notice. It was a great shame, then, that his seventh place finish – one position ahead of Kobayashi – was subsequently deleted as the Saubers were disqualified for having an illegal curvature of the top element of their rear wing.

As one would expect in a rookie campaign, there were mistakes through 2011, especially in the heat of the midfield

Sergio enjoyed a good rookie season and displayed a surprising degree of maturity.

battle, including contact in China and Hungary, but these did not detract from his smooth and effective style. That said, he was fortunate to miss only one race after crashing during qualifying at Monaco's chicane and being knocked

unconscious. He missed the following race in Canada, then reckons that it took him a further three races to get back to full fitness.

Leading the queue of admirers of the Mexican's talents is Scuderia Ferrari and they might even want Pérez as Fernando Alonso's number two from 2013, but his form in the year ahead will dictate whether or not this proves to be the case.

Another considerable attraction is that Sergio is Mexican and the world's richest man, Carlos Slim, looks increasingly like making a major investment in this most high-profile of sporting stages, so cash will probably be bestowed on any team for which Pérez drives. In these financially straitened times, that is a major plus and certainly enriches his prospects.

TRACK NOTES

Nationality:	MEXICAN
Born:	26 JANUARY 1990, GUADALAJARA, MEXICO
Website:	www.sergioperez.mx
Teams:	SAUBER 2011-12

CAREER RECORD

First Grand Prix:	2011 BAHRAIN GP
Grand Prix starts:	17
Grand Prix wins:	0
Poles:	0
Fastest laps:	0
Points:	14
Honours:	2010 GP2 RUNNER-UP, 2007 BRITISH F3 NATIONAL CLASS CHAMPION

ALWAYS CHASING THE RACING

Like so many of his contemporaries from outside Europe, Sergio Pérez had to leave home at a young age to further his racing career. Having shown well in karting in his native Mexico, he headed for the USA at 14. Then, aged 15 in 2005, Sergio travelled to Europe to race in German Formula BMW. After being given a taste of more power representing Mexico in A1GP, he contested the National class in the 2007 British F3 Championship and won that. He then raced in the main class of 2008, but was beaten to the title by Jaime Alguersuari and had to settle for ranking fourth overall. His next taste of power came in that year's GP2 Asia series, in which he won two races. The main GP2 series was his next target, but the then 19-year-old did not match his speed with results and so it took until Sergio's second GP2 campaign – in 2010 – for him to shine. Despite winning four races, he was to be disappointed as he ended the year as runner-up to Pastor Maldonado.

SCUDERIA TORO ROSSO

There has been a changing of the guard at Scuderia Toro Rosso, with both Jaime Alguersuari and Sebastien Buemi discovering that Red Bull does not offer the chance to be groomed for stardom forever, replacing them with two new drivers.

Neither Sebastien Buemi (above) nor Jaime Alguersuari did enough to hold onto their drives this year, meaning a clean start for the team.

Back in 2006, when Red Bull magnate Dietrich Mateschitz bought Minardi and renamed the Italian team as Scuderia Toro Rosso, the plan was to use it to develop the next generation of drivers, with the pick of these being selected to fill any vacancy at Red Bull Racing.

It was cost-effective too, as the team used an updated version of the previous year's Red Bull chassis built by Red Bull Technologies. However, that all changed when a rule was passed outlawing this practice for 2010 onward and Toro Rosso had to face up to the cost of designing and building its own cars, which was not easy with a staff of just 225.

While Mateschitz and his motorsport advisor Helmut Marko still want to bring on the best of the rising stars on their books and give them F1 experience to find out whether or not they have the full set of talents required to be in a position to fill any vacancy at Red Bull Racing should one arise, there were murmurs last year that

they would rather do so more cheaply. The way to do this is to place them with other teams rather than run one of their own to meet this function. However, with

Abu Dhabi's sovereign wealth fund Aabar Holdings buying a large stake in the team to add to its 40% stake in Mercedes GP, perhaps the team will be able to expand

KEY MOMENTS AND KEY PEOPLE

TEAM HISTORY
From 1985 to 2005, Scuderia Toro Rosso was Minardi, a team that was big on heart, though small of budget. It helped young drivers to get a foot on the F1 ladder, but little more. Then, after Paul Stoddart gave up his battle to keep the team afloat, it was sold to Red Bull drinks magnate Dietrich Mateschitz as a junior team to his main Red Bull Racing attack. And so it became Scuderia Toro Rosso and upset the plans after beating its senior partner to score a first win through Sebastian Vettel at Monza in 2008.

FRANZ TOST
Cutting a slightly less high profile than Red Bull Racing boss Christian Horner, Tost is another driver-turned-team-manager. Having reached F3, he took control of the Walter Lechner racing school in his native Austria in the mid-1980s. After moving on to work for Willi Weber's management company from 1995, he joined Williams to run its track operations from 2000. Then, when Scuderia Toro Rosso was created, Mateschitz brought him in as team principal.

2011 DRIVERS & RESULTS

Driver	Nationality	Races	Wins	Pts	Pos
Jaime Alguersuari	Spanish	19	0	26	14th
Sebastien Buemi	Swiss	19	0	15	15th

FOR THE RECORD

Country of origin:	Italy
Team base:	Faenza, Italy
Telephone:	(39) 546 696111
Website:	www.scuderiatororosso.com
Active in Formula One:	From 1985
	(as Minardi until 2005)
Grands Prix contested:	449
Wins:	1
Pole positions:	1
Fastest laps:	0

THE TEAM

Team owner:	Dietrich Mateschitz
Team principal:	Franz Tost
Technical director:	Giorgio Ascanelli
Team manager:	Gianfranco Fantuzzi
Chief designer:	Luca Furbatto
Chief aerodynamicist:	Nicolo Petrucci
Deputy head of aerodynamics:	J Tomlinson
Chief engineer:	Laurent Mekies
Technical co-ordinator:	Sandro Parrini
Logistics manager:	Domenico Sangiorgi
Chassis:	Toro Rosso STR7
Engine:	Ferrari V8
Tyres:	Pirelli

rather than wither, especially if the holding company then increases its share, as has been predicted.

As a sign of how Aabar Holdings might use the team, Spanish oil company Cepsa, one of many organizations owned by Aabar, had its logos appear on the Toro Rossos toward the end of last season and it was seen by many that Spanish driver Jaime Alguersuari had become the favoured one ahead of team-mate Sebastien Buemi.

However, this proved misleading as both Alguersuari and Buemi were dropped by the team last December and replaced by two other Red Bull junior programme drivers: Daniel Ricciardo and F1 rookie Jean-Eric Vergne.

A new stream of income will also help the team to become more aggressive in its chassis development through the season, which is an area where it has fallen down in the past when technical director Giorgio Ascanelli's aspirations have been kept in check. He has been joined by Luca Furbatto from McLaren to take Ben Butler's place, with Jon Tomlinson brought in to run the team's wind tunnel in Bicester.

Last year produced point-scoring drives on 10 occasions, with Alguersuari achieving the team's best finish with seventh in the Italian GP. However, snapping around for the minor points was all the team could hope for, and that an accident or two would take out the frontrunners and so promote their drivers.

In the 2012 season, however, there will be increasing pressure from the teams that ranked behind them last year, with Williams in particular expected to raise its game in the season ahead now that its cars will be powered by Renault engines. In light of this, Toro Rosso may have to face up to another financial problem in that it cannot be sure its end-of-year ranking will be as high as last year's eighth, thus reducing the travel money it will receive from FOM for 2013. So, in short, more expenditure is needed even for the team to remain where it is in the rankings, but at least Aabar Holdings can afford that, if it needs to do so. If not, Scuderia Toro Rosso will revert to its position of old when it went racing as Minardi and a top 10 finish was a target seldom achieved.

"One has to remember that when Toro Rosso was established in 2005, it was done so with the intention of providing a first step into Formula One for the youngsters in the Red Bull junior driver programme."

Franz Tost

Franz Tost continues to lead Red Bull's second team, principally to develop its future drivers.

Just when it looked as though Scuderia Toro Rosso had no ride for him in 2012, and a seat at HRT or Caterham beckoned, the Italian team snapped him up in December as it changed its guard. This is Daniel's big break as it moves him into the midfield.

Daniel had been happy enough getting Formula One experience on Fridays at grands prix with Scuderia Toro Rosso when, midway through last year, his Red Bull backing propelled him into a far better way to learn about F1. He was put in a fulltime F1 ride. This was not with Toro Rosso, as had been predicted for both of its regular drivers - Jaime Alguersuari and Sebastien Buemi - were under probation as there were no vacancies. The ride was with HRT instead, coming when Narain Karthikeyan was dropped after the European GP.

Certainly, this was a retrograde step in terms of lap time as the Spanish-financed team very much brought up the rear of the grid, but it gave Daniel the opportunity to experience race starts, managing pit stops and racing wheel-to-wheel.

Not surprisingly, no points were accrued and Daniel's best result was 18th place, which he achieved at the Hungaroring and Buddh International. However, no more than that could be expected in this tail-end car. For racing with a chance of winning, Daniel at least

Daniel will want to show what he can do in a car far more competitive than his HRT.

had his Formula Renault 3.5 programme to fall back on, but even with a win at each of Monza and Monaco, missing races so that he could attend grands prix meant that he'd never be likely to

challenge for the title and eventually ended up fifth.

However, what was important was how promising Red Bull thought he was and he energy drinks company proved that it sees him as having good potential by slotting him in to the Toro Rosso line-up for 2012, elevating both he and new team-mate Jean-Eric Vergne above Alguersuari and Buemi in Red Bull's cutthroat staircase of talent. Do well and you might be promoted to the Red Bull Racing squad. Pull up just short, though, and your ride is over and your ride towards the stars terminated. It's intense, but a chance all the same.

TRACK NOTES

Nationality:	AUSTRALIAN
Born:	1 JULY 1989, PERTH, AUSTRALIA
Website:	www.danielricciardo.com
Teams:	HRT 2011, TORO ROSSO 2012

CAREER RECORD	
First Grand Prix:	2011 BRITISH GP
Grand Prix starts:	11
Grand Prix wins:	0 (best result: 18th, 2011 Hungarian GP, Indian GP)
Poles:	0
Fastest laps:	0
Points:	0
Honours:	

2010 FORMULA RENAULT 3.5 RUNNER-UP, 2009 BRITISH FORMULA THREE CHAMPION, 2008 EUROPEAN FORMULA RENAULT RUNNER-UP & WESTERN EUROPE CHAMPION

CHASING A DREAM ACROSS THE GLOBE

Daniel started karting at the age of 10, but competing in pan-Australian series was expensive as he was based in Perth on the country's western flank. Instead, once he had turned 16, Daniel tried three races in Australian Formula Ford before entering the Formula BMW Asia series. He ranked third in that and had a couple of races in the British series. Moving to Europe fulltime in 2007, he raced in the Italian and European Formula Renault series before shining in his second year in the category, winning the Western Europe zone title and finishing runner-up to Valterri Bottas in the main European series. What really impressed his backers, Red Bull, though, was when he won the British F3 title at his first attempt in 2009. Stepping up to Formula Renault 3.5 in 2010, he won four times for Tech 1 Racing and placed second overall behind Mikhail Aleshin. He raced on in the category in 2011, but landed the second HRT F1 drive mid-season and never looked back.

JEAN-ERIC VERGNE

Jean-Eric could be just the driver that French Formula One fans have been waiting for. Not only is he a proven winner but he has the backing of Red Bull and this might yet land him a ride with a top team for 2013 if he matches his promise.

The greatest break in Jean-Eric's career has to be the moment when he was signed up by Red Bull's young driver programme. Identified as a driver of considerable potential, he was thus financed to have a shot at racing's junior single-seater formulae. In winning continuously, he was kept on board by the energy drink giant as others were jettisoned. Winning the British Formula Three title in 2010 added his name to that most prestigious series' list of famous winners. With former World Champions Emerson Fittipaldi, Nelson Piquet, Ayrton Senna and Mika Hakkinen all landing the crown on their ascent to Formula One, and the likes of Rubens Barrichello and Johnny Herbert also becoming champion, its pedigree is clear for all to see.

However, Jean-Eric's biggest break came when he was racing in the Formula Renault 3.5 series last year, vying over race wins with Robert Wickens. For it was as that season drew to a close that the 21-year-old Frenchman got the nod to step up and attend the final couple of grands prix of the season with Scuderia Toro Rosso. He grabbed the chance with both hands and

Jean-Eric impressed in his late-season F1 runs and could be the surprise of 2012.

by all but matching Alguersuari's pace in practice first time out at Yas Marina. Yet, it was what followed; when he was fastest of all in the younger driver test there after the Abu Dhabi GP, lapping less than half a second off Sebastian Vettel's pole time

in the same pace-setting Red Bull. This convinced the company that Jean-Eric needed an F1 race seat, finding space for both himself and fellow Red Bull protégé Daniel Ricciardo for 2012 by kicking out both Alguersuari and Toro Rosso teammate Sebastien Buemi.

Knocking on the door of F1 is one thing, but Jean-Eric has rapped just once and walked straight in. His Toro Rosso will not be able to match the Red Bulls, but this is one driver who has found his way straight to the midfield and could easily use it as a springboard to the big time.

TRACK NOTES

Nationality:	FRENCH
Born:	25 APRIL 1990, PONTOISE, FRANCE
Website:	www.jeanericvergne.com
Teams:	TORO ROSSO 2012

CAREER RECORD

First Grand Prix:	2012 AUSTRALIAN GP
Grand Prix starts:	0
Grand Prix wins:	0
Poles:	0
Fastest laps:	0
Points:	0

Honours:
2011 FORMULA RENAULT 3.5 RUNNER-UP, 2010 BRITISH FORMULA THREE CHAMPION, 2009 EUROPEAN FORMULA RENAULT RUNNER-UP & WESTERN EUROPE RUNNER-UP, 2008 FRENCH FORMULA RENAULT CHAMPION, 2007 FRENCH FORMULA CAMPUS CHAMPION, 2001 FRENCH CADET KART CHAMPION

SUCCESS ALL THE WAY

Jean-Eric was an early starter in karts, beginning his racing career at the age of 10 in 2000. He went on to be crowned French cadet kart champion in 2001 and then worked his way up through the age groups and categories to become runner-up in the European ICA series in 2005 and runner-up again in 2006 in the French Elite Championship. Jean-Eric graduated to car racing in 2007 and immediately landed the Formula Campus title with six wins. What really marked him out, though, was winning the French Formula Renault title in 2008, which he followed up by finishing as runner-up in the European series of 2009. He then followed Daniel Ricciardo's example in landing the British F3 title as a rookie in 2010, thanks to 13 wins in 30 starts, and had his first taste of F1 testing with Scuderia Toro Rosso. With further test outings promised for 2011, Jean-Eric raced in Formula Renault 3.5, winning five times en route to being runner-up, edged out by Robert Wickens.

WILLIAMS

A new engine deal with Renault might just mark the start of a comeback for the once pace-setting team to work its way forward again after a slide to the rear of the midfield pack. Pastor Maldonado will lead their renewed attack.

Pastor Maldonado remains for a second season with Williams and is hoping that Renault engines and Qatari investment will improve the cars.

Watching Williams attempt to compete last year was extremely depressing for the team's many fans for its descent into mediocrity was at best sad, bearing in mind how it once ruled the roost in its days of pomp in the 1980s and 1990s. The fact that it took the Williams drivers until the sixth round last year to as much as register their first points of the campaign, and for ninth place at that, illustrates just how much trouble they were in.

All is not lost, though, as Williams has extra incentive to make advances this year when the new tie-up with Renault could lead to it becoming one of the Regie's two works teams as the French manufacturer refines its focus. Bearing in mind how successful Williams and Renault have been in the past, with five constructors' titles in six years for the two between 1992 and 1997, during which time Nigel Mansell, Alain Prost, Damon Hill and Jacques Villeneuve landed the drivers' titles of 1992, 1993, 1996 and

1997 respectively, this has to be seen as a promising development.

While Sir Frank Williams remains as team principal, founding partner Patrick Head has

stood down as director of engineering to stay at base and focus instead on developing Williams' hybrid technology division. As a result, there has been wholesale change in

KEY MOMENTS AND KEY PEOPLE

TEAM HISTORY
Sir Frank Williams' passage through F1 has been one of highs and lows. He started by running cars for others from 1969-76 before deciding to run his own team. Williams started out with engineer Patrick Head in 1977 and after Alan Jones became their first World Champion in 1980, the pair added drivers' titles for Keke Rosberg (1982), Nelson Piquet (1987), Nigel Mansell (1992), Alain Prost (1993), Damon Hill (1996) and Jacques Villeneuve (1997), there have been precious few more wins and no more titles.

MIKE COUGHLAN
Hooked by motorsport as a child, Mike studied mechanical engineering then went in 1981 to work for Tiga. He made it to F1 with Lotus in 1984. After a spell with Benetton in 1990, Mike joined Tyrrell then moved to Ferrari in 1993, then to Arrows in 1997. After becoming technical director in 1999, he joined McLaren in 2002 and was chief designer until 2007, but spent two years on the sidelines for alleged espionage before returning in 2011 to re-establish his name with Williams.

2011 DRIVERS & RESULTS

Driver	Nationality	Races	Wins	Pts	Pos
Rubens Barrichello	Brazilian	19	0	4	17th
Pastor Maldonado	Venezuelan	19	0	1	19th

the technical department. Out have gone long-serving technical director Sam Michael, off to become sporting director at McLaren, and chief aerodynamicist Jon Tomlinson, too. In their place are Mike Coughlan and Jason Somerville – designer Coughlan's first appointment in F1 since leaving McLaren under a cloud following an industrial espionage charge. Even this transfer seemed tricky, though, as the NASCAR team for which he had been working, Michael Waltrip Racing, contested his contract. Somerville, meanwhile, returns to the team as chief aerodynamicist after spells at Toyota and Renault.

Since its great days and subsequent partnership with BMW from 2000 until 2005, cash has been a problem for Williams and last year the global economic slump made it hard for the team to replace long-standing sponsors whose contracts had come to an end. So, with this in mind, chairman Adam Parr led a move to float the team on the stockmarket and duly attracted some welcome finance to go with the millions arriving from Venezuela once GP2 champion Pastor Maldonado arrived to fill the second seat and so race alongside Rubens Barrichello. Since then, considerable investment has flowed in from Qatar, with a technology centre being built in the Middle Eastern country as part of this relationhip.

On the driving front, Barrichello and Maldonado performed reasonably last year, but when it became clear that the team was not entirely happy with the Brazilian veteran's input, other drivers began visiting the Williams' headquarters at Grove to discuss the possibility of taking the lead seat. Most fêted of all was Kimi Raïkkönen, but in the interim the 2007 World Champion has been away from F1 – competing in the World Rally Championship and also trying his hand at NASCAR stock cars – and his motivation has proved unreliable in the past. Force India's Adrian Sutil talked to the team but Bruno Senna became a late favourite There was talk, fleetingly, of Nico Hulkenberg returning after his year as Force India's reserve driver but again that came to naught. So, Pastor Maldonado and most likely Bruno Senna will be at the wheel of this year's FW34 and will be hoping the car/engine package is competitive enough for them to gather points on a regular basis.

FOR THE RECORD

Country of origin:	England
Team base:	Grove, England
Telephone:	(44) 01235 777700
Website:	www.attwilliams.com
Active in Formula One:	From 1972
Grands Prix contested:	623
Wins:	113
Pole positions:	126
Fastest laps:	130

THE TEAM

Team principal:	Sir Frank Williams
Co-owner:	Toto Wolff
Chairman:	Adam Parr
Chief executive officer:	Alex Burns
Technical director:	Mike Coughlan
Chief operations engineer:	Mark Gillan
Chief designer:	Ed Wood
Chief of aerodynamics:	Jason Somerville
Senior systems engineer:	tba
Team manager:	Dickie Stanford
Test driver:	Valtteri Bottas
Chassis:	Williams FW34
Engine:	Renault V8
Tyres:	Pirelli

"As a team, we have a massive task ahead of us, but everyone is absolutely resolute that we don't have another season like 2011 and we all look forward to better times ahead."
Mark Gillan

Frank Williams has lost Patrick Head's support at the races but has a new team behind him.

Bruno Senna's career has not run seamlessly, having been forced to take a year out in 2009 before landing his Formula One break, then starting last year without a drive. However, the second Williams' seat just might be the break he has been waiting for.

The name Senna resonates throughout the sport as Bruno's uncle Ayrton was one of the all-time greats until tragedy struck when he was killed racing Formula One at Imola in 1994 after claiming three world titles. So, even before Bruno turned a wheel to begin his racing career, the expectation was there - along with the pressure that goes with it.

After two brief spells in F1, with tail-end HRT in 2010 and then half a season with Renault last year at the very point when it lost form, it's still hard to judge what Bruno can offer from behind the wheel. All those who work with the young driver like and respect him; indeed many ceded his supporters had been right all along when he returned to Formula One for last year's Belgian GP at Spa-Francorchamps after Renault dropped Nick Heidfeld, promptly qualifying an impressive seventh. Sadly, after a poor start Bruno had to wait until a second outing at Monza before scoring his first F1 points - coming home ninth, one lap down on Sebastian Vettel's winning Red Bull, but right on the tail

Bruno's family name carries heavy expectation but few doubt his talent.

of Paul di Resta's Force India. Yet the remaining races were not so kind and many were unsure when he came into the final reckoning for the second Williams' drive of 2012.

Having a healthy package of sponsorship from his native Brazil to accompany the obvious driving talent he displayed in winning GP2 races in 2008 made Bruno very attractive to the team from Grove. However, just 26 grands prix to his name, all with teams in the midfield at best, leave him a long way short of the record-breaking 325 grand prix starts offered by compatriot Rubens Barrichello, to say nothing of Rubens' experience in having spent the past two years with the team. To many, a fresh face as Williams re-establishes itself is just what the team needs - and the polite and personable Bruno brings just that, as well as more speed than he has been able to demonstrate so far in F1.

TRACK NOTES

Nationality:	BRAZILIAN
Born:	15 APRIL 1982, SAO PAULO, BRAZIL
Website:	www.brunosenna.com.br
Teams:	HRT 2010, RENAULT 2011, WILLIAMS 2012

CAREER RECORD	
First Grand Prix:	2010 BRAZILIAN GP
Grand Prix starts:	26
Grand Prix wins:	0
	(best result: 9th, 2011 Italian GP)
Poles:	0
Fastest laps:	0
Points:	2
Honours:	2008 GP2 RUNNER-UP

WITH HIS FAMILY'S PERMISSION

Ayrton Senna always considered his nephew Bruno to be quick in karts when they larked about together on breaks from F1. However, his untimely death in 1994 when Bruno was 12 resulted in family opposition to the young man racing. When he was 22, his mother finally agreed to let him try, starting with the British Formula BMW series. Returning to Britain in 2005, he raced in F3 and seized two second-place finishes. After a strong start in 2006, winning the first three races, Bruno ranked third overall. However, it was on moving up to the more powerful GP2 category that his catch-up programme came good as he won on only his third outing. Returning with iSport in 2008, Bruno grabbed himself two more wins and finished the year as runner-up to Giorgio Pantano. Yet despite his famous surname he failed to step up to F1 in 2009, instead racing in sports cars. Then in 2010, he made it - albeit only with tail-end HRT - achieving a best finish of 14th place.

Pastor Maldonado certainly brings the cash with him to clinch his Williams' ride, but he also brings speed and application to the cockpit and will be hoping that, in 2012, Williams can offer him the car with which to start scoring points on a regular basis.

When a driver has spent four years trying to break into Formula One from GP2, you might forgive him for being disappointed if he does so armed with a car that has scarcely an outside chance of victory. Indeed, he would not be a true racing driver if he did not feel upset at not having a shot at the top step of the podium. However, Venezuelan rookie Pastor Maldonado simply knuckled down to his driving, accepted his Williams FW33 would only help him to points if others fell off ahead of them and concentrated on learning his craft.

In so doing, Pastor did something difficult last year in that he managed, as a rookie driver, to impress Williams' director of engineering Patrick Head, a man not normally given to offer praise freely. It was not just his raw speed, something he'd displayed for years in GP2, which earned this accolade but also his ability to learn. Indeed, with the most experienced tutor of all in team-mate Rubens Barrichello, a veteran of more than 300 grand prix starts, he had plenty of knowledge to take on board and Head is convinced that he will be better still in

Pastor had a steep learning curve in 2011, which will put him in good stead for 2012.

2012, when he visits circuits for a second time around.

One problem last year was that Pastor started the season with just 500 miles of testing under his belt and he then covered only 17 laps in the first two grands prix, making him feel somewhat short of much needed mileage. Another problem was that the FW33 was not particularly driveable during the first half of the year because it lacked the balance that the drivers needed to be confident. Then, in the second half of the season, the car started to consume its rear tyres at too great a rate.

For his second season of F1, with the cash from Venezuela still a much-needed part of the deal as far as Williams are concerned, Pastor must continue to mature in his driving and so eliminate the occasional bouts when over-enthusiasm clouds his judgement. Most of all, he must refrain from crashing, as Williams is no great fan of that.

PASTOR'S PERSEVERANCE PAYS OFF

After winning kart championships at home in Venezuela, Pastor Maldonado headed for Europe in 2002 to experience the challenge of tougher single-seater series. Starting with Formula Renault in Italy and winning the winter series in 2003, he was Italian champion of 2004, winning an F1 test with Minardi as a prize. He was then signed up as a member of the Renault Driver Development programme and advanced to World Series by Renault for 2005, ranking third in the series of 2006. Moving up to GP2, he had high hopes of a quick transition to F1 so that he could become the first Venezuelan since Johnny Cecotto in 1984. However, after interrupting his season by breaking his collarbone, the F1 feeder formula was to be his home for four years. He was a winner in each of these, but left empty-handed until 2010 when he became champion, having reduced the number of accidents that had previously peppered his career to produce wins at six different circuits through the year.

TRACK NOTES

Nationality:	VENEZUELAN
Born:	9 MARCH 1985, MARACAY, VENEZUELA
Website:	www.pastormldonado.com
Teams:	WILLIAMS 2011-12

CAREER RECORD

First Grand Prix:	2011 AUSTRALIAN GP
Grand Prix starts:	19
Grand Prix wins:	0
	(best result: 10th, 2011 Belgian GP)
Poles:	0
Fastest laps:	0
Points:	1
Honours:	2010 GP2 CHAMPION, 2004 ITALIAN FORMULA RENAULT CHAMPION, 2003 ITALIAN FORMULA RENAULT WINTER CHAMPION

CATERHAM F1 TEAM

After a year of wrangling with Lotus the car manufacturer over its use of the Lotus name, this year the team is coming out fighting as Caterham F1, while the ambitious owner demands a move up the order from his experienced drivers.

Heikki Kovalainen will continue to lead the charge, this time driving a Caterham, as the team gives its all in a bid to move up into the midfield.

Even keen followers of Formula One will be slightly confused at the opening round of this year's World Championship as what was formerly Team Lotus in 2011 has now been renamed Caterham F1 Team and the team that fielded Renaults last year as Lotus Renault GP will now be running F1 cars called Lotus.

Last year, these naming right issues were time consuming for both teams. Malaysian automotive manufacturer Proton (owners of Group Lotus) backed what had been the Renault team, while Tony Fernandes' outfit, which started racing in 2010, was known as Team Lotus after seeking permission from 1976 World Champion James Hunt's brother David, who had bought the rights to the name after Lotus's racing team closed in 1994. With Fernandes buying Caterham Cars, ironically a company formed to continue the production of Lotus 7 road-going sports cars, this gave him the chance to pin another name on his cars' flanks for 2012.

Fernandes has a personal face in a corporate world but no entrepreneur builds up businesses as he does without a backbone of steel. Rest assured no stone will be left unturned as he pushes chief technical officer Mike Gascoyne and his design team to build a more competitive car for 2012. Finishing the best of the three

KEY MOMENTS AND KEY PEOPLE

TEAM HISTORY
The team started life in 2009, preparing for 2010, but linked itself to Team Lotus, which closed its doors in 1994 when the name was bought by David Hunt and the team was given permission to use it. The original Team Lotus was a remarkable outfit, with founder Colin Chapman not only building exciting road cars but coming up with revolutionary ideas to make his F1 cars go faster. Jim Clark won titles in 1963 and 1965, Graham Hill in 1968, Jochen Rindt (1970), Emerson Fittipaldi (1972) and Mario Andretti in 1978, but then the money ran out.

MIKE GASCOYNE
The man charged with making the team successful has been in F1 since joining McLaren as an aerodynamicist in 1989. Spells at Tyrrell, Sauber and then Tyrrell again followed before Gascoyne moved to Jordan, helping it to its most successful season in 1999. After moving on to Benetton in 2001, he became Toyota's technical director in 2004, then returned to Jordan (as Spyker, then Force India) before returning to his native Norfolk when Team Lotus re-emerged.

2011 DRIVERS & RESULTS

Driver	Nationality	Races	Wins	Pts	Pos
Jarno Trulli	Italian	18	0	0	21st
Heikki Kovalainen	Finnish	19	0	0	22nd
Karun Chandhok	Indian	1	0	0	28th

teams who joined the World Championship for 2010, that is to say ahead of Virgin Racing and HRT, is not enough.

Helping Gascoyne in this task is Mark Smith, who arrived from Force India last summer. Both are extremely aware that the higher a team places in the constructors' championship, the more money they receive from the prize fund to help with travel costs in this increasingly far-flung circus. Their forces were recently bolstered by the arrival of McLaren's head of aerodynamics John Iley.

Perhaps the most important factor in the cars qualifying and racing nearer the front was the extension of its deal with Renault for engine supply through to the end of 2013. In conjunction with this, Red Bull Technology will continue to supply gearboxes. And to the drivers' delight, the team will use KERS for the first time, which will help in both attack and defence. Finally, they will also have use of Williams' wind tunnel, ensuring these gains can be maximized.

Gascoyne believes one of the reasons why the team ought to advance is that this will be the first year when he and the design team will not be fitting a new engine and gearbox into the car. Combine this with a larger design team plus the benefits of double the wind tunnel time and the ingredients are in place for a more competitive package.

One factor that the team is facing up to is that its HQ would be better situated in England's "Motorsport Valley", which runs around London from Northampton in the East via Banbury to Woking rather than remaining at its base at Hingham, Norfolk. Indeed, with its cars no longer entered as Lotuses, the symbolic connection with the original Team Lotus's home county no longer has the same importance. To this end, the ex-Arrows site in Leafield has been bought.

Fernandes opted to keep Heikki Kovalainen and Jarno Trulli, although last year there was concern that Trulli had lost his pace. As it turned out, the power steering was not offering sufficient feel to give him the confidence to attack and Fernandes had long discussions with the Italian before re-signing him. Give Trulli a more competitive car with steering feel, though, and he may yet get into the lower reaches of the top 10 on good days.

"We've always been a proper racing team, but we were constrained by the limitations of being a new team. Now it's time to move on and get on with beating the opposition."
Mike Gascoyne

FOR THE RECORD

Country of origin:	England
Team base:	Hingham, England
Telephone:	(44) 01953 851411
Website:	www.caterhamracing.my
Active in Formula One:	From 2010*
Grands Prix contested:	38
Wins:	0
Pole positions:	0
Fastest laps:	0

* This team has nothing to do with the Lotus team that ran in F1 from 1958-94.

THE TEAM

Team owner & team principal:	Tony Fernandes
Chief executive officer:	Riad Asmat
Chief technical officer:	Mike Gascoyne
Head of operations (Asia):	Mia Sharizman
Sporting director:	Steve Nielsen
Technical director:	Mark Smith
Performance director:	John Iley
Sporting director:	Steve Nielsen
Team manager:	Graham Watson
Chief engineer:	Jody Egginton
Test driver:	tba
Chassis:	Caterham CT-12
Engine:	Renault V8
Tyres:	Pirelli

Tony Fernandes is piling pressure on Mike Gascoyne (right) to propel the team up the order.

HEIKKI KOVALAINEN

As the more impressive of Lotus's drivers last year, Heikki Kovalainen was first to be signed to lead what team owner Tony Fernandes hopes will be a more competitive assault as Caterham F1 aims to work its way up the grid in 2012.

All a driver can do is race with what they've got and Heikki Kovalainen demonstrated the merits of doing just that last year, impressing those who chose to look at how the Team Lotus duo were getting on toward the bottom of the order rather than simply following the battle for the lead of the grand prix.

Although Heikki and team-mate Jarno Trulli always expected to beat the best from Virgin and HRT, any race in which he finished ahead of a driver from any of the midfield teams was considered a triumph by Team Lotus, such was the team's relative lack of experience and budget.

Life in F1 has certainly been varied for the sparky Finn as he rose from his maiden season with long-time supporters Renault to join McLaren, became a grand prix winner at the Hungarian GP in 2008, discovered what it's like to be in the shadow of another driver - Lewis Hamilton at McLaren - and now how it feels to head out racing with a tail-end team with next to no chance of scoring a single point.

One thing that emerged in 2011 was that Kovalainen held the upper hand over

Heikki performed miracles that went unnoticed save by those who looked hard.

Trulli, even in qualifying, which has long been the Italian driver's forte. Much of this was down to Trulli struggling to get feeling from the Lotus T128's steering, but it cemented Kovalainen's position as team

owner Tony Fernandes' chosen driver and perhaps chased away some of the dark clouds gathering over him after he was sidelined by Hamilton at McLaren.

Yet with better times promised, Kovalainen is back for a third year with the team, now renamed Caterham F1 Team. Heikki is pumped up with the confidence built from doing a really good job last year and he deserves a swathe of better results, but one can only feel the years are passing by and so any future openings with top teams will not be taken by this driver, now in his 30s but one of the latest crop of young guns.

TRACK NOTES

Nationality:	FINNISH
Born:	19 OCTOBER 1981, SUOMUSSALMI, FINLAND
Website:	www.heikkikovalainen.net
Teams:	RENAULT 2007, McLAREN 2008-09, LOTUS/CATERHAM 2010-12

CAREER RECORD

First Grand Prix:	2007 AUSTRALIAN GP
Grand Prix starts:	90
Grand Prix wins:	1
	2008 Hungarian GP
Poles:	1
Fastest laps:	2
Points:	105
Honours:	2005 GP2 RUNNER-UP, 2004 FORMULA NISSAN WORLD SERIES CHAMPION & CHAMPION OF CHAMPIONS AT THE RACE OF CHAMPIONS, 2000 NORDIC KARTING CHAMPION

CHOOSING HIS OWN CAREER PATH

Unlike his contemporaries in rural Finland, Heikki Kovalainen was more into racing than rallying and subsequently rose to become Nordic kart champion by the age of 18. This success was followed by a season in the British Formula Renault Championship the next year and his speed was sufficient for promotion to British Formula Three in 2002. After ranking third overall, and finishing second in the Macau F3 race, Kovalainen advanced to World Series by Nissan, winning the title in his second year, in 2004. He then put his name up in lights in beating Michael Schumacher at the multi-discipline indoor Race of Champions tournament before moving on to GP2 with Arden International in 2005 and ending the year as runner-up to Nico Rosberg. Kovalainen then became Renault's F1 test driver for 2006 before stepping up to a race seat in 2007. After moving to McLaren in 2008, he won the Hungarian GP but was wholly overshadowed by team-mate Lewis Hamilton and so after two seasons moved to Lotus for 2010.

JARNO TRULLI

It has been eight years since Jarno Trulli scored his only grand prix win (for Renault). He now faces his 16th season in Formula One with a team – Caterham F1 – that offers him next to no chance of adding to the tally.

Staying on in Formula One year after year, hoping either to attain glory or perhaps to regain it, is perhaps a game of diminishing returns. Rubens Barrichello is much the arch exponent of this, with 19 seasons under his belt, but Jarno Trulli (38 this summer) is in pretty much the same category with 15 F1 campaigns now behind him.

The Italian's lengthy career has been peppered by stunning flashes of speed, near-misses and that one win, for Renault at Monaco in 2004, but more recently it has been one of disappointment after any promise showed by Toyota faded.

Jarno then stepped back to join Team Lotus in 2010 only to find himself at the back of the pack. Keeping one's commitment in such circumstances might not be easy, especially for an individual like Trulli, who has strong interests away from the circuits, most notably cycling and running.

Jarno is and always has been an exceptionally intense and thoughtful individual, so he must have spent much of last year beating himself up when he could not get to grips with the Lotus

Jarno struggled to get a feel for his car last year and needs to race hard or quit.

T128. Hard as he tried, he simply failed to get the feel he wanted from his car's steering and so he struggled to commit on qualifying laps and thus lost out to team-mate Heikki Kovalainen.

Fortunately, Jarno's form in races was fine. However, by mid-season, as the team's technical experts scrambled to upgrade the power steering to suit him, the situation became so bad in qualifying that he agreed to stand down to make way for reserve driver Karun Chandhok to race in his place in the German GP.

Around this time, Jarno entered into talks with team owner Tony Fernandes about their future together and this was later concluded so he has to hope in the season ahead that 2012 is more competitive and proves to be a case of third time lucky for him.

TRACK NOTES

Nationality:	ITALIAN
Born:	13 JULY 1974, PESCARA, ITALY
Website:	www.jarnotrulli.com
Teams:	MINARDI 1997, PROST 1997-99, JORDAN 2000-01, RENAULT 2002-04, TOYOTA 2005-09, LOTUS/CATERHAM 2010-12

CAREER RECORD	
First Grand Prix:	1997 AUSTRALIAN GP
Grand Prix starts:	256
Grand Prix wins:	1
	2004 Monaco GP
Poles:	4
Fastest laps:	1
Points:	246.5
Honours:	1996 GERMAN FORMULA 3 CHAMPION, 1995 ITALIAN KARTING CHAMPION, 1994 EUROPEAN & NORTH AMERICAN KARTING CHAMPION, 1991 WORLD KARTING CHAMPION

A LOT OF SPEED, BUT JUST ONE WIN

From the high starting point of being World Kart Champion at 17, Jarno Trulli was simply not prepared to hang about when he moved to car racing. For him, there was no Formula Ford or Formula Renault, merely graduation direct to F3. That was midway through 1995 and he then beat Nick Heidfeld to the German F3 title in 1996. Following this, his intention was to skip F3000 and move directly to F1, which he did – with a late deal to race for Minardi. By mid-season, however, he'd moved on to Prost, to replace French driver Olivier Panis, who'd broken his legs. There, Trulli shocked everyone in leading much of the Austrian GP. Through his subsequent career with Jordan and Renault, he became acknowledged as a qualifying expert when his car was seldom the most competitive but at least he was able to win at Monaco in 2004. Moving on to Toyota in 2005, there were more flashes of speed when the car allowed, but joining Lotus for 2010 suggested he was in F1's last chance saloon.

HRT

This is a team that has yet to find form and the main news surrounding it concerns its change of ownership. So, the arrival of Thesan Capital last year might help HRT to find the financial footing on which to build in its third year of F1.

HRT's cars were the slowest of all through 2011 and the indicators do not suggest that matters will change a great deal for the season ahead.

HRT is a team still to hit its stride. Having started life as Campos Meta F1, the name was changed to Hispania Racing Team even before its first race of 2010, after founder and ex-F1 driver Adrian Campos backed out and the helm was taken up by businessman José Ramón Carabante. The team has struggled through its first two seasons, so the real key to the season ahead is whether the injection of cash from Thesan Capital can point it in the right direction.

Barwa Addax GP2 team owner Alejandro Agag, son-in-law of former Spanish Prime Minister José María Aznar, was also seen mixing with HRT last summer and his political connections might help open more doors for further finance that is essential if HRT is to afford the personnel to build more competitive cars.

It's not just money that makes a team work, though, and HRT was wise to allow former Force India boss Colin Kolles to run the team from his base at Greding in Germany rather than follow Campos'

dream of being based in Madrid. There were more people with racing team experience available to Kolles in Germany, especially

after the closure of the Toyota F1 team at the end of the 2009 season, so it's with some concern that paddock insiders heard

KEY MOMENTS AND KEY PEOPLE

TEAM HISTORY
Created as one of three new teams for 2010, HRT had a chequered history even before the first race as ex-racer Adrian Campos found he did not have the cash to start his own team so handed over control to businessman José Ramón Carabante. He has since taken a reduced role as venture capitalists Thesan Capital bought a controlling share in 2011, leaving Colin Kolles to run proceedings from his German base rather than the planned Spanish headquarters. The best result across HRT's first two campaigns has been Vitantonio Liuzzi's 13th place at Montreal in 2011.

JACKY EECKELAERT
HRT's sporting director started out as a driver in Formula Ford. However, the Belgian turned to the technical side in the 1980s and ran KTR's F3 team before stepping up to F3000 with DAMS in 1990. After a spell in touring cars with Peugeot, Eeckelaert broke into F1 when Jordan ran Peugeot engines in 1996. From being a senior engineer with the Prost team, he joined Sauber in 2000, then Honda Racing in 2006 before joining HRT.

2011 DRIVERS & RESULTS

Driver	Nationality	Races	Wins	Pts	Pos
Vitantonio Liuzzi	Italian	19	0	0	23rd
Narain Karthikeyan	Indian	9	0	0	26th
Daniel Ricciardo	Australian	10	0	0	27th

FOR THE RECORD

Country of origin:	Spain
Team base:	Madrid, Spain
Telephone:	tba
Website:	www.hispaniaf1team.com
Active in Formula One:	From 2010
Grands Prix contested:	38
Wins:	0
Pole positions:	0
Fastest laps:	0

THE TEAM

Team owners:	Thesan Capital
Team principal:	Luis Perez-Sala
Chief executive officer:	Saul Ruiz de Marcos
Head of design:	Jacky Eeckelaert
Team manager:	Boris Bernes
Chief aerodynamicist:	Stephane Schosse
Chief engineer:	Antonio Cuquerella
Chief mechanic:	Sören Morgenstern
Test driver:	tba
Chassis:	HRT F112
Engine:	Cosworth V8
Tyres:	Pirelli

Thesan Capital's mooted plans of relocating the team to Valencia to turn it into an all-Spanish team, using either the buildings left by the Americas Cup yachting teams now competition has quit for a fresh home base in San Francisco or a new facility in Madrid. This concern is based on the fact that no successful F1 team has ever been located in Spain, meaning a lack of designers, engineers and fabricators as well as the hobbled state of the Spanish economy.

At least in an attempt to help it understand F1, Thesan Capital appointed Spanish ex-Minardi racer Luis Pérez-Sala as an advisor last July. At that point, though, it was thought most likely the team would stay operating from Kolles' established base in Germany rather than start from scratch in Spain. But last December Kolles quit and Sala became the new team principal.

With a UK-based design facility being mooted, there are clearly changes on the technical side, with last year's technical director Geoff Willis returning to Williams. Former Brawn GP technical director Jorg Zander was expected to fill the gap after a spell on the sidelines but then decided against the move. Stephane Schosse, formerly of Toyota, Sauber and Ligier, did make the move, joining as chief aerodynamicist and reporting to Jacky Eeckelaert, who has been promoted to head of design.

Wherever the team settles, the build of this year's cars must come first as there were concerns last autumn that they might not be ready for the start of the 2012 season.

Last year's highest-place finish for an HRT was when Vitantonio Liuzzi finished 13th in the crash-strewn Canadian GP, but the team's average finish was 19th, the lowest of all 12 teams, so focusing on this season early made good sense.

On the driving front HRT has pursued a Spanish theme in employing the services of Pedro de la Rosa as lead driver. At 41 years of age, he is no rising star but Pedro brings highly-rated chassis developing skills from all his years as a McLaren test driver. The team will gain greater benefit from this rather than out and out racing skill.

The team's second seat can only be seen as a way into Formula One.

"We must be aware that assuming responsibilities such as designing the car or moving the headquarters to Spain are huge tasks and we still have a lot of work ahead."

Luis Perez-Sala

Former F1 racer Luis Perez-Sala has taken over from Jose Ramon Carabante (above).

PEDRO DE LA ROSA

Michael Schumacher has proved that drivers aged over 40 can still compete in F1, and that is good news for 41-year-old Pedro as he looks forward to what might be his first full season of F1 since 2002, having joined HRT from McLaren's test squad.

Pedro de la Rosa will turn 41 just before this year's opening race in Melbourne's Albert Park. That is quite an age in Formula One circles, even though Michael Schumacher is still in the mix at 43. However, Pedro is back in a race seat once again not as a multiple World Champion but because he is Spanish (like his team HRT), has knowledge of the Pirelli tyres from being the Italian manufacturer's test driver last year and possesses some of the most finely-honed car development skills after many years as a test driver for McLaren.

HRT had considered running Pedro in 2010, when it planned to enter F1 as Campos Meta F1, but he was edged aside as the quest for finance became increasingly more important than experience, with Karun Chandhok, Sakon Yamamoto and Christian Klien all joining Bruno Senna in the team's line-up at some stage in its inaugural season. Pedro landed a ride with Sauber instead, but was replaced by Nick Heidfeld with five races to go and thus returned to the role most helpful to him in making his F1 return, in once again becoming a McLaren test driver.

Pedro is delighted to have a race ride again, but life will be very different from McLaren.

For 2012, with investment in place from Thesan Capital, he will get his chance with the Spanish team after all. Indeed, with a contract for both this year and next in his pocket, Pedro has been given the most

unlikely of opportunities. His last full-time ride, with Jaguar Racing in 2002, seems a long time ago but he stands the chance of really helping his team to develop for the pace of HRT's drivers has not yet been of prime concern for the team. Indeed, many feel that a driver of Pedro's calibre and technical excellence is far more likely to find those chunks of lap time than someone younger and perhaps faster. Trouble is, it's not just a few seconds that HRT needs to make up but more like a handful! Yet in these trying times for the team, Pedro's ambassadorial skills will also undoubtedly be called into play.

TRACK NOTES

Nationality:	SPANISH
Born:	24 FEBRUARY 1971, BARCELONA, SPAIN
Website:	www.pedrodelarosa.com
Teams:	ARROWS 1999-2000, JAGUAR 2001-02, McLAREN 2005-06, SAUBER 2010-11, HRT 2012

CAREER RECORD	
First Grand Prix:	1999 AUSTRALIAN GP
Grand Prix starts:	85
Grand Prix wins:	0
(best result 2nd, 2006 Hungarian GP)	
Poles:	0
Fastest laps:	1
Points:	35
Honours:	1997 FORMULA NIPPON CHAMPION & JAPANESE GT CHAMPION, 1995 JAPANESE F3 CHAMPION, 1992 BRITISH & EUROPEAN FORMULA RENAULT CHAMPION, 1990 SPANISH FORMULA FORD CHAMPION, 1989 SPANISH FORMULA FIAT UNO CHAMPION

A DRIVER WHO TRAVELS TO RACE

With the Spanish government tipped to help HRT in F1, this completes the circle as Pedro de la Rosa's early career was given a boost when he was sponsored to travel to England in 1991 after becoming Formula Ford champion. In 1992, he became British and European Formula Renault champion. Formula 3 proved harder, but he bounced back in winning the Japanese title in 1995 and rose still further after securing the Formula Nippon and Japanese GT titles of 1997. He then became a test driver for Jordan, doing well enough to be signed to race for Arrows in 1999. Two years there and two years with Jaguar Racing proved little as points were hard to come by for these mid-ranking teams, but he then became a test driver for McLaren in 2003, where he learned a lot – with the bonus of standing in when Juan Pablo Montoya was injured in 2005, and after he quit midway through 2006, taking second in Hungary (2006). Following this, Pedro raced for Sauber in 2010 and in Canada last year.

JAIME ALGUERSUARI*

A sudden decision last December ended Jaime's stint at Scuderia Toro Rosso and so he found himself on the driver market with just two seats on offer for 2012, leaving him as favourite to make up an all-Spanish HRT line-up.

A snap decision to revert to being the team with which Red Bull introduces the up-and-coming stars of its driver development programme to Formula One was the reason why the Red Bull motorsport board decided to dump Jaime and team-mate Sebastien Buemi. They had been in the team since 2009 and several questioned whether they were ultimately better than the next two drivers on their list: Daniel Ricciardo and Jean-Eric Vergne. So, in an instant, out they went.

Jaime's response was dignified in the extreme, saying that he appreciated the support that Red Bull had given him since he was a 15-year-old racing in karts, even highlighting that with five million unemployed in Spain he should not feel too hard done by. Interestingly, though, Jaime said that he had thought it crazy when Red Bull elevated him to F1 midway through 2009 when he was 19 and had not driven even a kilometre in a F1 car.

Looking at his form last year, when the Toro Rosso STR6 was good, Jaime would

Jaime's sudden presence in the HRT line-up completes an all-Spanish set-up.

fly. He was not as sharp in qualifying as Buemi, being outqualified 13 times in 19 grands prix, but in races Jaime would perform better, working his way up the order into points-scoring finishes on

seven occasions, which was no mean performance considering the team ranked only eight overall. His top result was seventh place, which he recorded both at Monza and Yeongam.

For the year ahead, with extremely limited options thanks to having been led to believe that his ride was safe for 2012, Jaime's best chance of staying in an F1 race seat is to step back to tail-end HRT – a team that would love him as he is Spanish as well as quick, thus helping with its marketing.

* Not confirmed at time of going to press.

TRACK NOTES

Nationality:	SPANISH
Born:	23 MARCH 1990, BARCELONA, SPAIN
Website:	www.jalguersuari.com
Teams:	TORO ROSSO 2009-11, HRT 2012

CAREER RECORD

First Grand Prix:	2009 HUNGARIAN GP
Grand Prix starts:	46
Grand Prix wins:	0 (best result: seventh, 2011 Italian & Korean GPs)
Poles:	0
Fastest laps:	0
Points:	31
Honours:	2008 BRITISH F3 CHAMPION, 2007 ITALIAN FORMULA RENAULT RUNNER-UP, 2006 ITALIAN FORMULA RENAULT WINTER SERIES CHAMPION

FROM TWO TO FOUR WHEELS

Jaime's father "Tortajada" raced motorbikes, but Jaime moved from karts to cars as his father became involved in race promotion after his career came to an end and was involved in the organization of World Series by Renault. This would have been too advanced a starting point, so Jaime Jr headed to race in Italian Formula Junior in 2005 when only 15. The next two years were spent contesting the Formula Renault Euroseries and Jaime ranked fifth in that in 2007. What followed surprised everyone as he graduated to the competitive British F3 series and not only did he go on to win races as a rookie but he also won the title aged just 18. And so he reached World Series by Renault in 2009 and was going strongly with Carlin Motorsport when he was called up mid-season by Scuderia Toro Rosso, thanks to being a Red Bull development driver, to replace Sebastien Bourdais. He remained with the team through 2010, peaking with ninth place at both Sepang and Yas Marina.

MARUSSIA VIRGIN RACING

It was all-change for Virgin Racing last year when it ditched Nick Wirth and his all-CFD approach and signed a technical partnership deal with McLaren instead, signalling the intent to move away from the rear of the grid in 2012.

Timo Glock is remaining for another season with Marussia Virgin Racing, kept happy by a determined push to make the cars more competitive.

Formula One is far too complicated for it to be a case of third time lucky for Virgin Racing, and also the gap from the back of the grid to the front is too great to close in one leap, but hopefully it will be a case of third time better and progress will be made away from the last two rows of the grid.

The big change for this year's MVR03 is that it will not, like its predecessors, have been designed entirely by Computational Fluid Dynamics, which has clearly not worked on the team's first two designs. It may well be proven in years to come that Nick Wirth had the right idea but he is no longer involved as technical director and we may have to wait a few years longer until CFD-only designs are the way to go. Instead, veteran Toleman, Benetton and Renault technical chief Pat Symonds are now on board to oversee the design and production of this year's car, which gained an extra boost when the focus swung toward and thus away from the MVR02 with several races still to run last year.

Key to the team's progress is its deal with McLaren. This differs from the one held by Force India as it is based around

the provision of aerodynamic input and the use of McLaren's wind tunnel rather than the provision of an engine and

KEY MOMENTS AND KEY PEOPLE

TEAM HISTORY
One of the new wave of teams to hit F1 in 2010, Virgin Racing is based - as Jordan once was, 20 years earlier - on an established racing team. This was Manor Motorsport, an outfit successfully led in international single-seater categories by John Booth, with the likes of Kimi Raïkkönen and Lewis Hamilton, having previously been run by Manor in Formula Renault. A technical partnership with Wirth Research led to the first two cars being designed wholly in CFD and produced without using a wind tunnel. Investment from Russian supercar manufacturer Marussia swelled the coffers for 2011.

JOHN BOOTH
One of the stars of the British Formula Ford scene into the 1980s, John Booth hoped to become a top racing driver but he was too large to fit Formula Three cars easily and was also short on budget. Instead, he set up Manor Motorsport and ran cars for others instead. The outfit grew from the national formulae to running teams on the international stage. Then, from the end of 2009, he handed over the reins to concentrate on the then all-new Virgin F1 outfit.

2011 DRIVERS & RESULTS

Driver	Nationality	Races	Wins	Pts	Pos
Jérôme d'Ambrosio	Belgian	19	0	0	24th
Timo Glock	German	19	0	0	25th

FOR THE RECORD

Country of origin:	England
Team base:	Banbury, England
Telephone:	(44) 01909 517250
Website:	www.marussiavirginracing.com
Active in Formula One:	From 2010
Grands Prix contested:	38
Wins:	0
Pole positions:	0
Fastest laps:	0

THE TEAM

Team principal:	John Booth
Technical director:	Pat Symonds
Engineering director:	Nickolay Fomenko
Chief designer:	John McQuilliam
Deputy design chief:	Rob Taylor
Chief aerodynamicist:	Richard Taylor
Head of race engineering:	Mark Herd
Sporting director:	Graeme Lowdon
Team manager:	Dave O'Neill
Test driver:	tba
Chassis:	Marussia MVR03
Engine:	Cosworth V8
Tyres:	Pirelli

gearbox. It should certainly help Virgin Racing to produce an effective chassis that can support development through the course of the season, especially with McLaren design personnel stationed at Virgin's new headquarters in Banbury, Oxfordshire. With this move, Virgin Racing will finally have the whole of its operation under one roof as opposed to having the team based in South Yorkshire and its design wing, then Wirth Research, in Bicester. Even in these days of easy communication, being located in one building must help to avoid those critical gaps in communication that can occur and can make a small mistake into a large one in this business in which the time-scale for everything is infinitesimal.

Another advantage of the move away from Dinnington, near Sheffield to the heart of England's motorsport crescent is that this will only entice more leading designers, engineers and craftsmen to the team in the years ahead. That said, the former Ascari Cars' facility is expected to be home to the team for only three or four years before it plans to move to a purpose-built facility at Silverstone. In addition to this assistance, the drivers are able to use McLaren's ultra-advanced driver simulator at Woking to help develop the car and work on potential set-ups for each circuit visited, offering a level of input and experience that has become so diminished for drivers in recent seasons, in which in-season testing has been banned.

John Booth continues as team principal and the former racer's level-headed approach is likely to gel well with Symonds and the crew as they chip away at reducing their lap time deficit to the fastest cars.

On the driving front, Timo Glock has been retained for a third year as the team's lead player. The German will be looking to improve on last year's best result, 15th place at both the Canadian GP at Montreal and the Italian GP at Monza, or even on the pair of 14th place finishes recorded by 2011 team-mate Jérôme d'Ambrosio in the season-opener in Melbourne and the Canadian GP.

This year, F1 novice Charles Pic will occupy the team's second seat.

"We've got a lot more scope for developing and designing the 2012 car, especially with the facilities at Woking that have become available to use, such as the wind tunnel and technical rigs."
John Booth

As a former racer, John Booth brings a level-headed approach to being team principal.

Back for a third straight season with Virgin Racing, the industrious German will be hoping a wholesale change of design technique and personnel can move the team away from the back two rows of the grid.

It's been a long and often undulating journey from when Timo made his Formula One debut with Jordan back in 2004 to preparing for another campaign with Marussia Virgin Racing for 2012. However, the often intense German driver is back for more, now accustomed to contesting grands prix for a tail-end team rather than in the more rarefied heights of the starting grid occupied when he raced for Toyota in 2008 and 2009.

Last year, midway through his second season with Virgin and still starting most races from the penultimate row of the gird, with only the pair of HRTs behind himself and team-mate Jérôme d'Ambrosio, Timo was not sure whether he wanted to stay on. The reason was because he no longer believed in technical director Nick Wirth's approach of designing the car by computer alone, through CFD. This did away with the need to put models in wind tunnels, but the result – the Virgin MVR02 – was not competitive against its rivals bar HRT.

However, Wirth and the team parted company, causing Timo to think again, and he soon agreed to sign up for 2012. Actually, for 2013 and 2014 as well. This

Timo has signed until 2014, but may want to move on if no progress can be made.

will put money in his bank account but the big question is whether it will put any championship points in Timo's pot.

The biggest plus is that Marussia Virgin Racing has signed a technical partnership deal with McLaren and this will entail not only the assistance of McLaren aerodynamicists in the MVR03's design but the use of McLaren's state-of-the-art wind tunnel, too. One can only feel that progress will come, as after the team was built from scratch the crew spent 2010 learning the ropes and 2011 realizing CFD-only design might not yet be the solution. So, provided that lessons have been learnt, Timo and his rookie team-mate Charles Pic may yet get closer to points in the season ahead, although Timo is more aware than most that for every fraction of a second the bottom teams cut from their lap times, the top teams can cut two.

Expect more honest application and dogged drivers that go unnoticed.

TRACK NOTES

Nationality:	GERMAN
Born:	18 MARCH 1982, LINDENFELS, GERMANY
Website:	www.timo-glock.de
Teams:	JORDAN 2004, TOYOTA 2008-09, VIRGIN RACING 2010-12

CAREER RECORD	
First Grand Prix:	2004 CANADIAN GP
Grand Prix starts:	72
Grand Prix wins:	0
(best result: second, 2008 Hungarian GP, 2009 Singapore GP)	
Poles:	0
Fastest laps:	1
Points:	51
Honours:	2007 GP2 CHAMPION, 2001 GERMAN FORMULA BMW CHAMPION, 2000 GERMAN FORMULA BMW JUNIOR CHAMPION

A CAREER THAT NEEDED REBUILDING

Timo Glock really stood out in his early racing career, the reason being he had the much-admired knack of winning championships. The first came in 2000, when he was crowned German Formula BMW Junior champion. After winning the senior German Formula BMW title in 2002, he stepped up to German F3. However, there was no title as he ranked third. Fifth overall was his position at the end of the 2003 F3 Euroseries, but Timo's backers eased his way into Jordan's F1 line-up midway through 2004, when the team dropped Giorgio Pantano. Better still, he scored on his debut. Yet there was no ride for 2005, so he went to Champ Car and raced well. F1 was still his aim, though, so he risked stepping back to GP2. He did not win the title but did so in 2007 and was subsequently signed by Toyota for its 2008 F1 attack, collecting two second places before the team closed. Since 2010, Timo has driven for Virgin Racing.

CHARLES PIC

This French Formula One novice is undoubtedly talented, being a race winner in GP2, but he is also well funded. This has propelled him to the head of the list of F1 hopefuls and landed him the second seat at Marussia Virgin Racing, alongside Timo Glock.

Coming from a family made exceptionally rich through transporting Total's fuels around France certainly helped when young Charles decided that he wanted to start racing karts. Later, he would ascend through the junior single-seater ranks. And it's helping him even now as Marussia Virgin Racing still needs extra finance to assist in its aim of dragging itself from the back few rows of the grid and developing its new facility at Banbury into one that is truly cutting-edge.

Pic undoubtedly knows how to win races because he has been doing just that in powerful single-seater categories since 2008 and this can never be underestimated as young drivers approach the door to Formula One. In truth, though, what made him extra-attractive to Marussia Virgin Racing in an unusually crowded driver market is the fact that his family can help to pay the bills.

For French F1 fans, it's good news indeed as the country that started motor racing with city-to-city races at the end of the nineteenth century has had a lean time in its highest category for the

Marussia Virgin Racing ought to offer Charles a good place to learn his F1 craft.

past decade or so and still looks back fondly to the 1980s and the success of Jacques Laffite, Didier Pironi, Patrick Depailler and Alain Prost. Since then, largely due to the withdrawal of previously

extremely generous government assistance to young drivers, the nation's involvement has dwindled, made all the more apparent as their involvement with teams all but ended and they have since lost their grand prix.

Pic might be the first of a new wave of drivers to get the French interested again as he is young – he turns 22 a month before the opening round in Australia – and looks fashionable. However, Marussia Virgin Racing certainly would not be expected to provide him with a car capable of scoring points so he should be able to learn his craft in relative anonymity, which is no bad thing. His real worth will be realized if he can develop the technical touch to match his speed. That said, Charles has enough cash behind him to remain an attractive prospect for 2013, even if he does not quite hit the top notes.

A WINNER AT EVERY LEVEL

Charles Pic was French Junior Kart Champion at the age of 14 in 2004 and showed competitive form again in 2005, but championship titles simply eluded him. As soon as he was old enough to race cars (2006), he moved up. Starting Formula Campus, he ranked third. Formula Renault followed, and Charles ranked third in the European Championship and fourth in the French Series. Stepping up quickly, he advanced for the Formula Renault World Series of 2008 and grabbed two wins. Back for more in 2009, he was once again a winner and rose to third overall while Bertrand Baguette dominated. A win in the Asian GP2 series set him up for a full GP2 campaign in 2010, when he was once more a winner but ranked only tenth before improving to fourth, collecting wins at Catalunya and Monaco plus a pair of second places for the Barwa Addax team as Romain Grosjean became champion. His younger brother Arthur is also a racer, competing in the Renault World Series last year.

TRACK NOTES

Nationality:	FRENCH
Born:	15 FEBRUARY 1990, MONTELIMAR, FRANCE
Website:	www.charles-pic.com
Teams:	MARUSSIA VIRGIN 2012

CAREER RECORD	
First Grand Prix:	2012 AUSTRALIAN GP
Grand Prix starts:	0
Grand Prix wins:	0
Poles:	0
Fastest laps:	0
Points:	0
Honours:	2005 ITALIAN JUNIOR KART CHAMPIONSHIP RUNNER-UP

Monza's first chicane is often the scene of much activity on the opening lap, as shown last year when Vitantonio Liuzzi got on the grass and speared into the pack.

TALKING POINT: BRITANNIA RULES THE WAVES

France hosted the first Grand Prix, Germany set the pace and Italy has the greatest passion for grand prix racing but Britain leads the way and through ingenuity has made itself the home of the sport.

Anyone watching the opening race of the inaugural World Championship at Silverstone in 1950 would have been left in no doubt that Italy was grand prix racing's pre-eminent nation as Alfa Romeo dominated, filling the first three places. French Lago-Talbots came fourth and fifth, with the best-placed British cars – ERAs – three laps adrift in sixth and seventh. By the mid-1950s, when Mercedes-Benz had arrived and conquered all before it and no British manufacturer appeared capable of stepping up to the challenge, things looked bleak as far as the nation's interest in motor racing's ultimate class was concerned. Yet something clicked as eight of today's 12 F1 teams are based in England, British drivers have won 214 of the 847 grands prix and 14 drivers' titles, while British teams fill nine of the top 10 places in the table for the teams with the most grand prix wins – kept off the top only by Ferrari.

That something was ingenuity and design genius, which achieved what money was unable to do. Through the efforts of Surbiton-based Cooper in mounting the engine behind the driver and then Norfolk-based Lotus in turning out the first F1 cars built around a monocoque and later introducing ground effects, small British teams transformed the sport and displayed a speed of thought and an ability to almost instantly embrace new ideas. None of the industry giants, such as Alfa Romeo or Mercedes, could match that speed of thought, though. Without a chain of command above them, neither Charles and John Cooper nor Lotus chief Colin Chapman had anyone stopping them

from getting on immediately to try their latest design notion.

It soon became clear that British designers led the way when it came to moving ahead in F1. In time, the specialist small industries sprung up to supply them and none more successfully than Northampton-based Cosworth Engineering, which took Ford's investment and built F1's most successful engine: the Ford Cosworth DFV. As a result of the availability of this engine, a vanguard of teams appeared that would most likely not otherwise have been able to afford to try F1. Williams is a prime example of this and the step on the ladder offered by the DFV helped the motor racing team and constructor on its way toward nine constructors' championship titles.

The gathering of tailor-made suppliers, wind tunnels, carbon fibre specialists and highly-trained personnel drove the industry on and now there is an arc of companies around London: from Woking (home of McLaren) curving to the west of the capital through Brackley (Mercedes GP) and Milton Keynes (Red Bull Racing) to Brixworth (Mercedes-Benz High Performance Engines) that covers or produces every aspect, part and skill required to produce cutting-edge F1 cars. Conversely, being based in Switzerland, like Sauber, guarantees fresh mountain air but makes other elements in producing an F1 car all the more difficult, with attracting the most qualified personnel being a prime example because they don't wish to uproot their families from English homes and schools.

Such excellence of industry and chain of supply is one thing, but there is

little reason why British drivers rose to the top, especially as there has never been a government-backed manufacturer helping them into the sport. Yet after Mike Hawthorn became the first British World Champion when racing for Ferrari in 1958, leaving fellow British racers Stirling Moss, Tony Brooks, Roy Salvadori and Peter Collins filling second to fifth places overall, nine other British drivers have shared 13 more drivers' titles between them: Graham Hill (1962 and 1968), Jim Clark (1963 and 1965), John Surtees (1964), Jackie Stewart (1969, 1971 and 1973), James Hunt (1976), Nigel Mansell (1992), Damon Hill (1996), Lewis Hamilton (2008) and Jenson Button (2009).

Much of the reason for this comes from Britain's national racing scene, being the most competitive in the world. Britain's Formula Ford and Formula Three championships continue to be where many of the world's up-and-coming drivers head to see if they've got what it takes to make it to the top, with Emerson Fittipaldi, Jody Scheckter, Ayrton Senna and Mika Hakkinen among those to prove themselves there. In racing against the finest, rising British stars have the best incentive to improve and it's perhaps the merit of this that has helped the aforementioned World Champions to hone their skills.

Left: The British GP has a rich history at Silverstone and it can also guarantee a knowledgable capacity crowd every summer.

Below: Jim Clark and Colin Chapman combined at Lotus in the early 1960s to drive British teams to the forefront.

Below: The McLaren Technology Centre is proof of how British teams are powered by technology and inspiration, helping them to expand into the general automotive market.

TALKING POINT: THE RACE TO JOIN THE GRAND PRIX CIRCUS

As the World Championship calendar changes by the year and more and more countries vie to host a grand prix, which ones will make way for them?

Countries host rounds of the World Championship either through historical continuity or burning ambition backed by the financial clout to afford one, and meanwhile a constant battle rages between those in the former category trying to resist the government-backed push of the latter.

After decades of little change to the calendar, with the majority of grands prix held in Europe, the World Championship has changed out of all recognition over the past 10 years and as the calendar is now extended to 20 races, the European element has been reduced to less than half of the races. In have come races for China, India, Korea, Abu Dhabi and Bahrain, while out have gone the Austrian, French and San Marino grands prix. The racers of even the 1990s wouldn't have believed the change, although there are of course further changes either underway or in the pipeline, with the United States GP about to be restored for the first time since the last of its races on the Indianapolis infield course in 2007 on an all-new circuit near Austin, Texas, with a further race planned for New Jersey in 2013. Russia will be breaking new ground, though, with plans to host its first-ever F1 event in 2014 at another all-new circuit being built at the Black Sea coastal resort of Sochi, base of the 2014 Winter Olympics.

A number of countries around Southeast Asia are also keen to land a grand prix and South Africa would relish a return to the calendar, with Argentina and Mexico also keen to rejoin the show. However, with the teams stating that they don't wish to contest any more than 20 grands prix a year to avoid burnout among personnel, some of the more established races will have to lose their spot to accommodate newcomers.

The first candidate was Turkey since the event has simply not excited the population sufficiently to encourage them to attend since its debut of 2005. Of the more long-standing events, the Belgian GP appears to be in the weakest position, being in financial difficulty with its contract set to expire this year. There have been suggestions that it might share a date with a French GP, thus hosting a race in alternate years only. For fans who revere the great circuits, the potential loss of Spa-Francorchamps is of real concern. It would be very good news for France, though - desperate to get back on board, having last held a grand prix in 2008.

Germany, a country with an equally considerable history of motorsport, is also facing financial problems and was recently forced to scale back to host races alternately between the Nürburgring and Hockenheim. This was bad enough for the fans, but the pattern of alternation has also left both circuits out of pocket. This contract for alternation is in place through until 2018.

Much as Germany held two grands prix each year when Michael Schumacher was in his heyday, so Spain has enjoyed two since Fernando Alonso's success made F1 popular there. In future, Barcelona and Valencia are likely to alternate to free up another date for a grand prix further afield.

Fortunately, a few of the longstanding events are safe, at least for now. For many years, F1 ringmaster Bernie Ecclestone took digs at Silverstone, saying it was substandard and required investment to keep its place on the calendar. Despite no investment from the government, the British GP is safe until 2027, thanks to considerable rebuilding work. Another classic track, Monza, appears equally safe - so long as pressure from environmental groups can be quelled. Only Monaco, the jewel in F1's crown, seems eternally sure of hosting a grand prix.

While financial difficulties abound the world over, political unrest can also affect the calendar, as Bahrain discovered in 2011 when it lost its Grand Prix. A return depends on the promise of no repeats. So, while everyone welcomes global expansion and F1 being taken to new markets, there is a genuine concern that F1, in turning its back on historic venues for the World Championship, is chopping off its nose to spite its face.

62

Right: Abu Dhabi showed what can be done with an unlimited budget, but few other hosts will be able to match Yas Marina.

Left: Singapoore has been a big hit with its night race, but already there is talk of moving the event out of the city centre to avoid the disruption that it causes.

Below: Bernie Ecclestone and President Vladimir Putin have done a deal for Russia to have a grand prix at Sochi, home of the next Olympic winter games, from 2014.

This aerial view of the approach to Albert Park's Turn 13 shows just how life can go on as normal for much of the populace even when the Grand Prix comes to Melbourne.

KNOW THE TRACKS 2012

The World Championship calendar is in a constant state of flux and the early twenty-first century years will be seen as a period of considerable expansion for Formula One. After South Korea joined the championship calendar in 2010 and India last year, the teams are all set for the USA's return to the fray in 2012.

When one looks back at the seemingly ceaseless expansion of the World Championship since its inaugural season in 1950, what once seemed totally surprising rapidly becomes something that fails to raise even an eyebrow or two. Take the Hungarian GP, for example, a race that appeared to break all the accepted norms when it popped up behind the Iron Curtain in 1986, bringing perhaps the most capitalist sport to what was then the communist heartland. Now this race is very much part of the furniture, although the World Championship keeps on changing its identity. Indeed, if you had said a decade ago that not only would India have a grand prix but it would be contested by an Indian driver, few would have believed you.

As part of the great plans for global expansion, grands prix were later granted by supremo Bernie Ecclestone to nations not only outside Formula One's European heartland but off the motorsport radar, too - countries like Malaysia, followed by Middle Eastern nations such as Bahrain and Abu Dhabi. The booming economies of China and later Korea, then India joined the party while Singapore built a temporary street circuit and made it all the more enticing by holding its grand prix after dark. Not only did this look even more exciting on the television screen but it also fitted in with daytime viewing hours for the key European market. Taking matters still further, Abu Dhabi used its oil wealth to fund the construction of F1's glitziest and most extravagant circuit at Yas Marina.

So, in the space of a decade or more, the traditional World Championship calendar became a thing of the past, with the number of European races becoming proportionally fewer as the

flyaway races became more numerous. Indeed, last year the total number of races grew from the traditional 16 to what should have been 20 before the Bahrain GP was lost to continuing political unrest in the run-up to its planned season-opening date.

Now, with the French GP sidelined until a deal to alternate with the financially-beleaguered Belgian GP at Spa-Francorchamps can be settled, and with the German GP teetering in no-man's land because both Hockenheim and the Nürburgring are in financial difficulties, this means that three of the World Championship's traditional grands prix, their histories going way back in the record books, are either in peril or on the brink of being lost altogether. One has to hope these races can be secured for the future for it never helps to lose such links with the past. Indeed, should they fall, it would mean that just the British, Monaco and Italian GPs would remain from the original rota of six grands prix for the inaugural World Championship of 1950. Now that Silverstone has cemented its future until 2027 through comprehensively upgrading its facilities with an all-new pit and paddock complex, with further development work being undertaken for this year, at least the British GP's future is secure.

The Italian GP, due to F1's eternal leaning toward Ferrari, is also safe so long as environmental protesters do not kick up a fuss again about Monza being used on the grounds of noise and other pollution. And that just leaves Monaco of the original sextet. No race should feel more secure because although the track itself is an anachronism, its pits and paddock no better than a poor compromise, the principality has the glamorous image and all the star-studded appeal desired by both fans and sponsors, and therefore the teams.

Against this turning of the tide the re-establishment of a grand prix in the United States of America for the first time since Indianapolis last hosted one in 2007 was seen as a really good thing, especially for the teams' sponsors. The circuit near Austin in Texas is a brand new one and has been built by the Hellmund family, who are dyed-in-the-wool racing people. There were setbacks last year as the contract was batted around, with construction work even being stopped for a while in the autumn. Yet all came back on the tracks to avoid its debut being delayed by a year as news broke that it will be joined in 2013 by a second American race on a new street circuit in New Jersey. It would really help if a rising American star was ready to race in F1, but Alexander Rossi might need yet another year before he gets there to draw extra thousands through the turnstiles.

Encouraging spectators to attend new or revived races is essential to the future of any grand prix for this is the key way to draw in the revenue required to host F1. However, some countries have notably failed to achieve this. Bahrain's race crowd has always been shaky and the Shanghai International Circuit's gargantuan grandstands never anything approaching full, while Turkey – despite having one of F1's best circuits in the Istanbul Otodrom – has never attracted crowds and therefore lost its race for 2012.

For decades, Australia had to make do without a grand prix,
but this sports-mad nation is now firmly on the F1 calendar,
although it could really do with some more overtaking spots.

The teams like going to Melbourne's Albert Park circuit as the event has a sense of occasion helped by being close to the centre of one of the most sports-crazy cities on earth. Melbournites turn out in their droves for cricket, tennis and Australian Rules Football – and they've welcomed F1 warmly since 1996, producing good crowds to enjoy a packed race programme.

Built around a lake in a municipal park just a tram-ride away from the city centre, the Albert Park circuit offers flow, even if this is interrupted by chicanes. However, although Turn 1 on the opening lap plus Turn 3 (and perhaps Turn 13 thereafter)

tempt drivers into thinking they might have a shot at overtaking, there is precious little passing action.

With concrete walls acting as barriers just feet from the circuit's edge, any slip-up can be punished, although mercifully few have ever got it wrong through the left-hand sweeper from Turn 10 to Turn 11.

While blue skies and sunshine often with a blast of heat are the norm, rain has been known to hit Melbourne in March and this always has a way of shuffling the order. The other factor to produce results that can later look unusual is the Australian GP is often first of the season and the order has yet to settle down.

> "I love Melbourne, but not only the track. The atmosphere around the Grand Prix is fantastic. All the people here enjoy the whole weekend, as there are more events on the Sunday." **Fernando Alonso**

68

INSIDE TRACK
AUSTRALIAN GRAND PRIX

Date:	**18 March**
Circuit name:	**Albert Park**
Circuit length:	**3.295 miles/5.300km**
Number of laps:	**58**
Email:	**enquiries@grandprix.com.au**
Website:	**www.grandprix.com.au**

PREVIOUS WINNERS

2002	**Michael Schumacher** FERRARI
2003	**David Coulthard** McLAREN
2004	**Michael Schumacher** FERRARI
2005	**Giancarlo Fisichella** RENAULT
2006	**Fernando Alonso** RENAULT
2007	**Kimi Räikkönen** FERRARI
2008	**Lewis Hamilton** McLAREN
2009	**Jenson Button** BRAWN
2010	**Jenson Button** McLAREN
2011	**Sebastian Vettel** RED BULL

Key race: If incident is key to a race being good, then the 1999 Australian GP was great. Both Stewarts caught fire on the grid; Jacques Villeneuve had a spectacular accident, leader Mika Hakkinen retired his McLaren with throttle problems on the restart and through it all came Eddie Irvine.

Key corner: Turn 1 is top for overtaking manoeuvres, but speed carried through the tricky right flick at Turn 12 is what can improve a lap time the most.

Best view: There is a limited number of grandstand seats by Turn 3, but these afford a good view of the short straight under the trees from Turn 2 and the numerous outbraking attempts that occur into this 100-degree right as well as the changes of line drivers take down to Turn 4 in the mêlée.

Closest finish: When teams are in the enviable position of having their cars finish first and second, often they cross the finish line almost as one. In 1998, McLaren ushered Mika Hakkinen back ahead of team-mate David Coulthard after he had fallen to second when he thought he heard a signal to pit, thus allowing Coulthard to honour a pre-race agreement that whichever of them led into the first corner would win the race. The Finn finished just 0.702s in front.

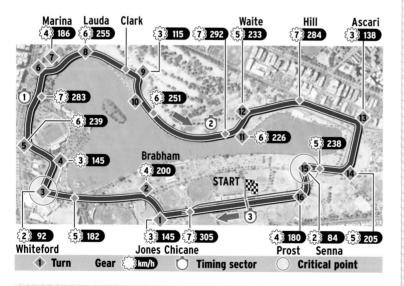

2011 POLE TIME: VETTEL (RED BULL), 1M23.529S, 142.011MPH/228.544KPH
2011 WINNER'S AVERAGE SPEED: 128.117MPH/206.184KPH

2011 FASTEST LAP: MASSA (FERRARI), 1M28.947S, 133.360MPH/214.623KPH
LAP RECORD: M SCHUMACHER (FERRARI), 1M24.125S, 141.016MPH/226.933KPH, 2004

SEPANG

The climate is hot and humid, making life tough for the drivers and pit crews, while the rain (when it comes) arrives in storms, not showers. Despite this, Sepang is a great place to go racing.

There have been some washouts since the Malaysian GP was moved from an October slot to one at the start of the championship, being in the monsoon season. Yet this has not spoilt the racing because the circuit is of such a clever design that it offers both spectacle and excitement. As its straights are long and then wide at the entry of the hairpins at their far ends, it's made for racing. In essence, they are designed for overtaking. Indeed, it makes you wonder why other circuits since created by the same architect, Hermann Tilke, have not been so effective.

Indeed, Sepang's first corner is a great way to start a race as it not only turns the cars back on themselves, but faces the drivers with the immediate decision of where to place their cars for the second bend that it almost directly feeds into. Always there is incident, with inspired gambles paying off and innocent moves becoming unravelled as others spill into their path.

Where Sepang scored last year was that its long straight leading to the final corner presented an opportunity for drivers to try and tow themselves onto the tail of the car ahead to then be close enough to use their DRS on the corresponding straight past the pits in a bid to make a passing move into Turn 1.

"This is a circuit that makes me smile, as it's very flowing. It's one of those circuits where you can really have a good tussle as corners flow into each other." **Jenson Button**

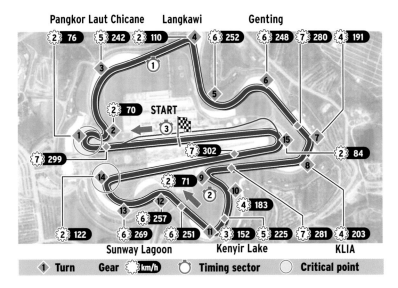

2011 POLE TIME: VETTEL (RED BULL), 1M34.870S, 130.688MPH/210.323KPH
2011 WINNER'S AVERAGE SPEED: 118.495MPH/190.700KPH

2011 FASTEST LAP: WEBBER (RED BULL), 1M40.571S, 123.295MPH/198.424KPH
LAP RECORD: JUAN PABLO MONTOYA (WILLIAMS), 1M34.223S, 131.991MPH/212.419KPH, 2004

INSIDE TRACK
MALAYSIAN GRAND PRIX

Date:	25 March
Circuit name:	Sepang Circuit
Circuit length:	3.444 miles/5.542km
Number of laps:	56
Email:	inquiries@sepangcircuit.com.my
Website:	www.malaysiangp.com.my

PREVIOUS WINNERS

2002	**Ralf Schumacher** WILLIAMS
2003	**Kimi Raïkkönen** McLAREN
2004	**Michael Schumacher** FERRARI
2005	**Fernando Alonso** RENAULT
2006	**Giancarlo Fisichella** RENAULT
2007	**Fernando Alonso** McLAREN
2008	**Kimi Raïkkönen** FERRARI
2009	**Jenson Button** BRAWN
2010	**Sebastian Vettel** RED BULL
2011	**Sebastian Vettel** RED BULL

Key race: Downpours have shaped many a race here and it was the one on lap 3 of 2001 that produced the greatest "save". Ferrari's Michael Schumacher and Rubens Barrichello were first and second when they spun off at the same corner. At the end of lap 4, David Coulthard took the lead and pitted for rain tyres. Ferrari elected to fit intermediates instead and this proved spot-on, enabling their drivers to race on to first and second.
Key corner: Now that DRS is being used, a super-quick exit from the lap's final corner – Turn 15 – is essential if a driver is to be as close as possible to the car ahead when entering the zone in which the slot in the pursuer's rear wing may be opened to offer extra straightline speed.
Best view: Now that DRS boosts overtaking at circuits with a long straight, the Turn 1 grandstand (outside Turn 1 and looking back up the straight) is the best one for action.
Closest finish: Rain has intervened on so many occasions since Sepang's first Grand Prix of 1999 that there have been few really close finishes. However, Eddie Irvine headed home Ferrari team-mate Michael Schumacher by 1.040s in 1999, then Schumacher resisted McLaren's David Coulthard by only 0.732s in 2000.

SHANGHAI

Here is a circuit with all the ingredients for enthralling racing, a mixture of every type of corner and a lengthy straight into a hairpin. All that spoils the show is the weather, which is so often gloomy.

Shanghai is a city with a new face on an old ethos of commerce, a place that has reinvented itself and is thriving on the change. The Shanghai International Circuit is not the same, however, being a new face on something that did not exist before. Though ultra-modern and made for purpose, as yet it has failed to turn the Chinese into a nation of motorsport lovers.

Built to a considerable scale and ready for racing in 2004, the Hermann Tilke -designed track made all others look small and frankly, insignificant. With more grandstand seats than any other track to host F1, save Indianapolis, it also offers the

teams villas surrounded by ponds instead of pit offices and has a media centre the size of an aircraft hangar. Everything is outsize except for the crowd, something that has not changed over the interim.

The race organizers deserve better as the circuit offers some serious opportunities for overtaking, with the right, right, left of the first-corner sequence up and over a ridge the first of these, the braking area for Turn 6 always presents an opportunity for passing, as does the tight Turn 11 at the end of the inner straight. Of course, the best passing place of all is into Turn 14 at the end of the back straight, which is why the grandstand there is the only full one.

"The track has very long right handers, where you have to get everything right to gain an advantage. There are different lines, so there are many ways to approach a lap." **Adrian Sutil**

70

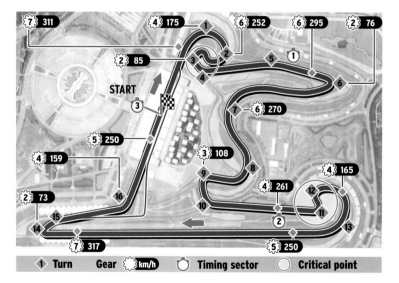

| Turn | Gear | km/h | Timing sector | Critical point |

2011 POLE TIME: VETTEL (RED BULL),
1M33.706S, 130.237MPH/209.597KPH
2011 WINNER'S AVERAGE SPEED:
117.294MPH/188.767KPH

2011 FASTEST LAP: WEBBER (RED BULL),
1M34.893S, 123.181MPH/198.241KPH
LAP RECORD: M SCHUMACHER (FERRARI),
1M32.238S, 132.202MPH/212.759KPH, 2004

INSIDE TRACK
CHINESE GRAND PRIX

Date:	**8 April**
Circuit name:	**Shanghai International Circuit**
Circuit length:	**3.390 miles/5.450km**
Number of laps:	**56**
Email:	**f1@china-sss.com**
Website:	**www.f1china.com.cn**

PREVIOUS WINNERS	
2004	**Rubens Barrichello** FERRARI
2005	**Fernando Alonso** RENAULT
2006	**Michael Schumacher** FERRARI
2007	**Kimi Räikkönen** FERRARI
2008	**Lewis Hamilton** McLAREN
2009	**Sebastian Vettel** RED BULL
2010	**Jenson Button** McLAREN
2011	**Lewis Hamilton** McLAREN

Key race: Last year's Chinese GP was particularly exciting for Lewis Hamilton, but the race in 2007, where the McLaren driver famously beached his car in the pit entrance gravel trap was more of a competition, with his slip-up on worn-out tyres handing victory to Kimi Räikkönen, who would go on to pip him to the title by a point.

Key corner: As with other circuits in 2011, following the advent of the DRS rear wing, the corner that became the most important was the one before the DRS zone. This final corner of the lap is a tricky one in fourth gear, with many running wide on the exit. However, if a driver gets it right with KERS pumping out extra power before the rear wing slot opens, it's game on for a passing move into Turn 1.

Best view: The grandstand down at Turn 14 can pretty much see only that corner, but this hairpin at the end of the back straight is where the vast majority of passing happens, so it's the place to be.

Closest finish: With the long back straight followed by a hairpin, drivers can get close for a final dash to the line and the driver with the smallest winning margin so far is Rubens Barrichello, who won in 2004 for Ferrari by just 1.035s from Jenson Button's BAR, with Kimi Räikkönen's McLaren only a further 0.434s adrift.

SAKHIR

Back after a year's break following the political unrest of last spring, the Sakhir circuit must be hoping for a strong race as it has been overshadowed by neighbouring Abu Dhabi's facility.

An experiment with an extra loop of the circuit failed to work in 2010 and so the original track layout will be used, just as it was meant to be last year. The uprisings that swept from North Africa to the Middle East last spring, however, never gave the teams the chance to prove the original layout offered better racing as the Grand Prix was postponed and then, with little support from the teams (who were happy to lose a race from their busy schedule) cancelled.

Built on scrubby desert outside the capital of Manama, the Sakhir circuit was seen as intriguing and cutting-edge when it made its bow in 2004. Since then,

standards have moved on, though, and Abu Dhabi's Yas Marina circuit certainly made it clear which was the region's biggest player. Furthermore, combined with a lack of spectators, this is an event that has failed to capture the imagination and subsequently makes for a less than inspiring atmosphere. If the same circuit was placed in a verdant setting, however, it might be viewed in a more positive light as it has an interesting combination of corners, ranging from a series of sweepers to hairpins and decently long straights in between, with the devilment of sand blowing onto the track to keep drivers on their toes.

"It's a good circuit for overtaking, especially into Turn 1 after the long straight, where you brake very hard from over 190mph, coming all the way down to first gear." **Jenson Button**

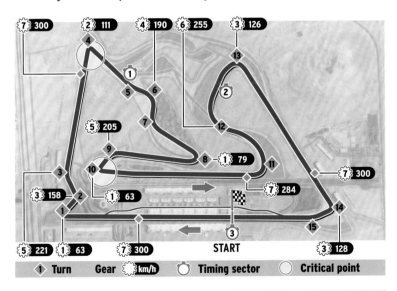

Turn   **Gear**   **km/h**   **Timing sector**   **Critical point**

Circuit gear/speed markers:
- 7 / 300
- 2 / 111
- 4 / 190
- 6 / 255
- 3 / 126
- 5 / 205
- 3 / 158
- 1 / 63
- 1 / 79
- 7 / 300
- 7 / 284
- 5 / 221
- 1 / 63
- 7 / 300
- 3 / 128

START

2010 POLE TIME: **VETTEL (RED BULL),** 1M54.101S, 123.491MPH/198.739KPH
2010 WINNER'S AVERAGE SPEED: 115.744MPH/186.272KPH

2010 FASTEST LAP: **ALONSO (FERRARI),** 1M58.287S, 119.216MPH/191.715KPH
LAP RECORD: **M SCHUMACHER (FERRARI),** 1M30.252S, 134.262MPH/216.061KPH, 2004

INSIDE TRACK
BAHRAIN GRAND PRIX

Date:	**4 November**
Circuit name:	**Bahrain International Circuit**
Circuit length:	**3.363 miles/5.412km**
Number of laps:	**57**
Email:	**info@bic.com.bh**
Website:	**www.bahraingp.com.bh**

PREVIOUS WINNERS

2004	**Michael Schumacher**	FERRARI
2005	**Fernando Alonso**	RENAULT
2006	**Fernando Alonso**	RENAULT
2007	**Felipe Massa**	FERRARI
2008	**Felipe Massa**	FERRARI
2009	**Jenson Button**	BRAWN
2010	**Fernando Alonso**	FERRARI

Key race: The 2009 Bahrain GP was an interesting one because Toyota came good to fill the front row of the grid by going out to qualify with extremely light fuel loads. Timo Glock and then Jarno Trulli took turns at the front, but reality was regained when they dropped down the order after pitting early, allowing man of the moment Jenson Button to take a lead for Brawn that he would hold to the finish, resisting all that Red Bull's Sebastian Vettel could offer.

Key corner: Being quick, the sweepers that are Turns 5, 6 and 7 represent a real challenge and a mistake in the first part of this sequence is magnified all the way through. Sand on the track remains a problem in this "desert" section, just to add a few surprises.

Best view: In the heat of the desert, you must watch from a grandstand to be sure of some welcome shade and the pick of the grandstands is the one at Turn 1, providing the added benefit of offering views over the kickback to Turn 2 and beyond, thus almost all of the lap's overtaking.

Closest finish: Fernando Alonso made it two Bahrain GP wins on the trot by winning the 2006 World Championship opener, but his second Bahrain victory for Renault was far from relaxing, with Michael Schumacher's Ferrari sitting right on his tail to cross the finish line just 1.246s behind.

Spain may not enjoy the coveted position of hosting two grands prix for much longer, but racing fans are unlikely to be upset by any alternation as the circuit offers few overtaking places.

The Circuit de Catalunya is a great driving circuit, with a wide range of corners to entertain the driver - short only of many long, fast ones. However, it is not and never has been a great racing circuit, instead being a circuit on which really the drivers only have the entry to Turn 1 to offer them a chance of passing the car ahead. Yet even this opportunity has been hampered, with the use of KERS combined with DRS still not offering the chasing driver the chance he ought to have because Turns 14/15 - the corner sequence before the final corner - is a chicane demanding a single-file approach, so removing any hope the chasing driver will be close enough under acceleration to catch a tow down the long, sloping start/finish straight.

It seems strange now that Spain was once seen as motorbike racing crazy, with little interest in F1. Of course all that changed with the rise and rise of Fernando Alonso, when tens of thousands more fans made their pilgrimage to the Circuit de Catalunya for the Spanish GP. Better still, each year they had a second chance with the European GP moving to Valencia's street circuit. With the Spanish economy in an increasingly precarious state, however, race attendance has slumped so the future of both races now hangs in the balance.

"This track is very special for me as I have the crowd, the environment they give and the weather. I live in Barcelona, so it's cool to drive here." **Jaime Alguersuari**

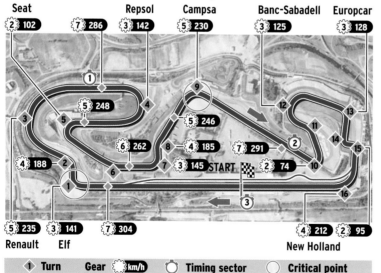

Seat **2** 102   Repsol **7** 286   **3** 142   Campsa **5** 230   Banc-Sabadell **3** 125   Europcar **3** 128

5 248   **5** 246   **6** 262   **4** 185   **7** 291   **2**   **4** 188   **3** 145 START   **2** 74   **3**

5 235   **3** 141   **7** 304   **4** 212   **2** 95

Renault   Elf   New Holland

◆ **Turn**   **Gear** 🔧**km/h**   ◯ **Timing sector**   ◯ **Critical point**

2011 POLE TIME: **WEBBER (RED BULL),** 1M20.981S, 128.563MPH/206.903KPH
2011 WINNER'S AVERAGE SPEED: 115.616MPH/186.067KPH

2011 FASTEST LAP: **HAMILTON (MCLAREN),** 1M26.727S, 120.071MPH/193.236KPH
LAP RECORD: **RAÏKKÖNEN (FERRARI),** 1M21.670S, 127.500MPH/205.192KPH, 2008

INSIDE TRACK
SPANISH GRAND PRIX

Date:	**13 May**
Circuit name:	**Circuit de Catalunya**
Circuit length:	**2.892 miles/4.654km**
Number of laps:	**66**
Email:	**N/A**
Website:	**www.circuitcat.com**

PREVIOUS WINNERS

2002	**Michael Schumacher** FERRARI
2003	**Michael Schumacher** FERRARI
2004	**Michael Schumacher** FERRARI
2005	**Kimi Raïkkönen** McLAREN
2006	**Fernando Alonso** RENAULT
2007	**Felipe Massa** FERRARI
2008	**Kimi Raïkkönen** FERRARI
2009	**Jenson Button** BRAWN
2010	**Mark Webber** RED BULL
2011	**Sebastian Vettel** RED BULL

Best race: Spanish GPs at the Circuit de Catalunya tend to supply incident rather than cut-and-thrust racing packed with overtaking due to the restrictive nature of the lap. However, perhaps the most enthralling race since the circuit made its grand prix debut in 1991 was in 1996, when Michael Schumacher produced a masterclass in how to drive in streaming wet conditions. Early on in the race, he passed Jacques Villeneuve's Williams and then pulled ever further away to win by 45s.

Best corner: From a driver's viewpoint, Turn 9 (Campsa) must offer the most satisfaction when you get it right as this fifth-gear right uphill over a blind brow feeds cars onto the lap's secondary straight and any speed carried through here reaps dividends down the straight as it drops gently to the tight lefthander at Turn 10.

Best view: As Turn 1 remains pretty much the only corner with a chance of overtaking, a grandstand seat is the one to secure. Those in attendance in 1991 - when Ayrton Senna and Nigel Mansell flashed downhill toward them, wheels interlocked - will never forget it.

Closest finish: With Lewis Hamilton getting his head down in his McLaren in 2011, he was just 0.630s behind Sebastian Vettel's Red Bull when they passed the checkered flag.

MONACO

It's tight, it's steep, it's twisty and almost impossible to pass on, yet it's wonderful! Monaco is entirely different to the other F1 circuits... and all the better for it.

To understand Monaco's eternal place on the F1 calendar, you should ask a friend, even one not interested in F1, to pick a grand prix they'd like to attend. Monaco would win this poll as it offers something not easy to find anywhere else: a stunning setting, glamour, sporting excitement and hopefully, a sunny Mediterranean climate to make you feel like a millionaire.

There are yachts in the harbour, celebrities strutting about, a casino if you want to feel lucky and nightclubs that could relieve you of a week's wages. However, this venerable (and outmoded) street circuit is imbued with a history like nowhere else, with its first grand prix dating back to 1929.

As a consequence of Monaco's history and prestige, it is *the* Grand Prix other than their home grand prix that all drivers long to win. To do so, they really need to qualify on pole position, as the track is so narrow that overtaking happens more through crafty race strategy than on-track inspiration. Look down the list, though, and it's a race that has almost always yielded only to the best as Ayrton Senna's record tally of six wins reflects. For the record, Michael Schumacher has triumphed on five occasions.

"You have to be very aggressive on a street circuit like this and at the same time you cannot afford any mistakes. You need to be very precise with the way you are putting the car." **Nico Rosberg**

INSIDE TRACK
MONACO GRAND PRIX

Date:	**27 May**
Circuit name:	**Monte Carlo Circuit**
Circuit length:	**2.075 miles/3.339km**
Number of laps:	**78**
Email:	**info@acm.mc**
Website:	**www.acm.mc**

PREVIOUS WINNERS

2002	**David Coulthard**	McLAREN
2003	**Juan Pablo Montoya**	WILLIAMS
2004	**Jarno Trulli**	RENAULT
2005	**Kimi Raïkkönen**	McLAREN
2006	**Fernando Alonso**	RENAULT
2007	**Fernando Alonso**	McLAREN
2008	**Lewis Hamilton**	McLAREN
2009	**Jenson Button**	BRAWN
2010	**Mark Webber**	RED BULL
2011	**Sebastian Vettel**	RED BULL

Key race: Nigel Mansell's pursuit of Ayrton Senna in 1992 was TV gold, but perhaps the greatest Monaco drive came 22 years earlier, when Jochen Rindt worked his way up from eighth to give chase to Jack Brabham. Ten seconds down with 10 laps to go, he was still over 1s down going onto the final lap. Incredibly, his Lotus was first to the finish after Brabham slithered into the straw bales at Rascasse, known then as Gasworks Bend.

Key corner: The harbourfront chicane is key to a quick lap and last year saw two huge spins there when Nico Rosberg dropped his Mercedes after coming over the crest of the descent and missed everything. Sergio Pérez had a similar accident but slammed his Sauber into the tyrewall.

Best view: Looking back up the hill from the Tip Top bar and seeing the cars fire out from behind the barriers across Casino Square remains one of F1's hallmark shots, the cars skittering for grip as the track drops away from them before they fire down the slope to Mirabeau.

Closest finish: The tight nature of the final run of corners dictates against really close finishes, but the closest came in 1992, when McLaren's Ayrton Senna hung on to beat Nigel Mansell's Williams by 0.215s.

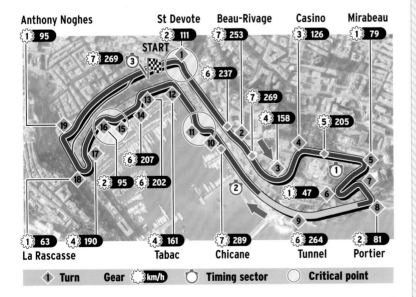

Anthony Noghes · St Devote · Beau-Rivage · Casino · Mirabeau · La Rascasse · Tabac · Chicane · Tunnel · Portier

START

◆ Turn · Gear · km/h · ○ Timing sector · ○ Critical point

2011 POLE TIME: VETTEL (RED BULL),
1M13.556S, 101.555MPH/163.438KPH
2011 WINNER'S AVERAGE SPEED:
74.921MPH/120.574KPH

2011 FASTEST LAP: WEBBER (RED BULL),
1M16.234S, 98.008MPH/157.729KPH
LAP RECORD: M SCHUMACHER (FERRARI),
1M14.439S, 100.373MPH/161.527KPH, 2004

Over the years, Montreal's Circuit Gilles Villeneuve has proved that anything can happen when F1 comes to town and frantic on-track action is all but guaranteed, especially if it rains.

Built on an island that appears to possess more water than land and sited out toward the far bank of the St Lawrence River from the city, the circuit is one with a difference: it literally does not have an infield and its pit and paddock area is larger only than the one in Monaco. Yet this track is extremely popular with those treading the F1 beat as it has a strong identity, passionate fans and the city of Montreal is also a wonderfully hospitable place to stay, eat and party.

Despite almost the whole of its length being surrounded by concrete walls, the circuit offers scope for overtaking. Where the track tightens into Turn 2 is always exciting on the opening lap, with Turn 3 also the scene of passing while drivers sort themselves out. However, the main excitement comes either at the far hairpin, L'Epingle, or after the drag down the long back straight into the chicane to complete a lap where entry is all but blind and "Champions' Wall" waits to claim those who slide wide on the exit.

Since Jacques Villeneuve's departure from F1, the home fans have not had a Canadian driver to cheer on, but they still come. It is hoped Robert Wickens will graduate to F1 in the next year or so to offer them more to shout about.

"This track has a great history and it's a bit like a street circuit as it's quite bumpy. It's like a go-kart track too as we have to take the kerbs." **Lewis Hamilton**

74

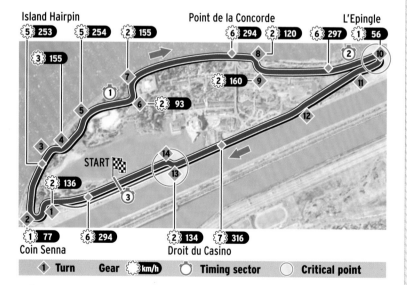

Island Hairpin · 5 253 · 5 254 · 2 155 · Point de la Concorde · 6 294 · 2 120 · 6 297 · 1 56 · L'Epingle

3 155 · 8 · 2 · 10

7 · 2 160 · 9 · 11

1 · 6 · 2 93 · 12

5 · 4 · 14

3 · START · 13

2 136 · 3

2 · 1 · 1 77 · 6 294 · 2 134 · 7 316

Coin Senna · Droit du Casino

◆ **Turn** · **Gear** ❄ **km/h** · ○ **Timing sector** · ○ **Critical point**

2011 POLE TIME: **VETTEL (RED BULL),** 1M13.014S, 133.618MPH/215.038KPH
2011 WINNER'S AVERAGE SPEED: 46.518MPH/74.864KPH

2011 FASTEST LAP: **BUTTON (MCLAREN),** 1M16.956S, 126.767MPH/204.012KPH
LAP RECORD: **BARRICHELLO (FERRARI),** 1M13.622S, 132.511MPH/213.246KPH, 2004

INSIDE TRACK
CANADIAN GRAND PRIX

Date:	**10 June**
Circuit name:	**Circuit Gilles Villeneuve**
Circuit length:	**2.710 miles/4.361km**
Number of laps:	**70**
Email:	**info@circuitgillesvilleneuve.ca**
Website:	**www.circuitgillesvilleneuve.ca**

PREVIOUS WINNERS	
2001	**Ralf Schumacher** WILLIAMS
2002	**Michael Schumacher** FERRARI
2003	**Michael Schumacher** FERRARI
2004	**Michael Schumacher** FERRARI
2005	**Kimi Raïkkönen** McLAREN
2006	**Fernando Alonso** RENAULT
2007	**Lewis Hamilton** McLAREN
2008	**Robert Kubica** BMW SAUBER
2010	**Lewis Hamilton** McLAREN
2011	**Jenson Button** McLAREN

Key race: Few local fans would name the 1979 Canadian GP as the circuit's best, as their hero Gilles Villeneuve got beaten, but it was nonetheless an epic encounter. Villeneuve got the jump on Alan Jones's pole-sitting Williams to lead the first 50 laps but then the Ferrari driver fumbled at the chicane, leaving Jones to power past into Island Hairpin.

Key corner: On this car-breaker of a circuit, the pick of the twists is the right/left chicane that completes the lap as a decent entry and exit from here can fire a driver to a good lap time, while a poor line can lead to the car slamming into "Champions' Wall" at its exit.

Best view: A grandstand seat with a clear view of the Turn 1/2/3 sequence is the best place to observe the scene, especially on the opening lap of the race where many an overambitious passing bid into the lefthander at Turn 2 is followed by all sorts of evasive action into Turn 3.

Closest finish: Michael Schumacher headed Rubens Barrichello home by just 0.174s in 2000, but they were Ferrari teammates attempting to fix a photo finish. In out-and-out racing, the tightest finish came in 2003 when Schumacher won again for Ferrari, this time beating his brother Ralf's Williams by just 0.784s.

VALENCIA

As this street circuit hosts a grand prix for the fifth time, it would take an intrepid gambler to back it for a long-term future for the venue has yet to draw in the crowds or produce an exciting race.

Valencia initially sought global recognition through hosting the America's Cup sailing regatta in the middle of the last decade. Then, avariciously, and with an eye on Fernando Alonso's success in becoming World Champion in 2005 and 2006, it made a bid for some of the World Championship action. Now the city is paying the price, though, as it has cost a fortune to erect and dismantle the temporary circuit around the docks and it has not proved to be a popular place for the teams to visit. Furthermore, the crowds are staying away, so revenues are not so great as planned. Meanwhile, the Spanish economy is also in a nosedive.

Considering the circuit itself, it's one of several Hermann Tilke-penned circuits that simply do not deliver. Observe the circuit map and the long, arcing straight after the bridge down to Turn 12 ought to provide scope for passing, but the slow corner onto this straight probably scuppers that. It's the same story for the run to Turn 17 and the blast through the kink at Turn 1 down to the heavy braking for Turn 2. Only on the opening lap does this tight righthander produce any passing for the surrounding walls urge the drivers to display caution or risk wrecking their race. Thus far, they have heeded their concerns and the racing at Valencia has suffered accordingly.

> "The circuit has long straights with a fair amount of slow corners, so good braking ability and traction are very important. Like Monaco, it rubbers in as the meeting progresses." **Jarno Trulli**

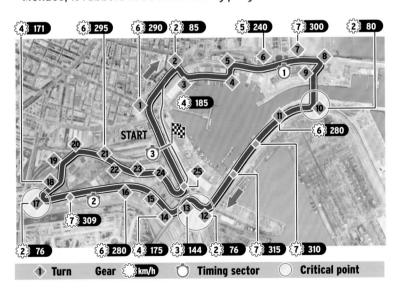

◇ **Turn**　**Gear** ⚙**km/h** ◯ **Timing sector** ◯ **Critical point**

2011 POLE TIME: **VETTEL (RED BULL),** 1M36.975S, 126.255MPH/203.188KPH
2011 WINNER'S AVERAGE SPEED: 115.617MPH/186.068KPH

2011 FASTEST LAP: **VETTEL (RED BULL),** 1M41.852S, 119.015MPH/191.563KPH
LAP RECORD: **GLOCK (TOYOTA), 1M38.683S,** 122.837MPH/197.687KPH, 2009

INSIDE TRACK
EUROPEAN GRAND PRIX

Date:	**24 June**
Circuit name:	**Valencia Circuit**
Circuit length:	**3.401 miles/5.474km**
Number of laps:	**57**
Email:	info@valenciastreetcircuit.com
Website:	**www.valenciastreetcircuit.com**

PREVIOUS WINNERS

2008	**Felipe Massa** FERRARI	
2009	**Rubens Barrichello** BRAWN	
2010	**Sebastian Vettel** RED BULL	
2011	**Sebastian Vettel** RED BULL	

Key race: It was only later in the season that the full worth of Felipe Massa's victory in the inaugural race here in 2008 was felt. His pole-to-flag victory for Ferrari moved him ahead of team-mate Kimi Räikkönen and brought momentum his way, which came within one place of taking the title in the finale in Brazil before Lewis Hamilton prevailed. When gifted victory in the next race, however – at Spain, when Hamilton was penalized – Massa's challenge came alive.

Key corner: On the opening lap, Turn 2 is the one that counts for this is many a driver's best chance to make a passing move when the field is bunched. Thereafter, Turn 12 is the driver's greatest opportunity for a late-braking dive past a rival as it is approached down the circuit's longest straight.

Best view: For anyone who has watched the coverage before, the finest observation point must surely be from the hotel with a swimming pool on its roof with a view down over the track at Turn 1. There might be next to no overtaking there, but it's perfect for the opening lap and the views are panoramic across the harbour.

Closest finish: In the quartet of grands prix held on Valencia's street circuit to date, Rubens Barrichello's breakthrough win for Brawn GP in 2009 – his first for almost five years – has proved to be the closest one so far, as Lewis Hamilton was but 2.358s behind when the chequered flag fell, the McLaren driver left frustrated by a pitstop blunder that cost him a likely victory.

SILVERSTONE

To turn up at Silverstone these days is exciting, if a little confusing, because new pit buildings and a revised start line location are continuously added to as the circuit reinvents itself.

Knowing Silverstone's future as the home of the British GP is safe is a good feeling after British fans were kept on edge for years while F1 chief executive Bernie Ecclestone criticized the venue and constantly undermined its right to host a round of the World Championship.

His criticism was aimed in an attempt to encourage the British government to invest in the circuit as so many of the governments in countries new to hosting grands prix had in theirs. Despite Britain being the hub of the motorsport industry and eight of the 12 teams being based in England, successive governments have resisted this opportunity. However, the changes demanded have been made and no longer can Silverstone's facilities be described as out of date. Instead they will be augmented for 2012 with some of the infrastructure that was not ready for last year's first running of a grand prix using the new pit complex between Club and Abbey.

A hotel and large grandstands opposite The Wing, as the pit building is called, are next up - Silverstone will then be head and shoulders above all but a handful of rivals. In terms of being a total motorsport facility, it's out front, with multiple circuit variations, accommodation and a diverse selection of industries in its technology park reflecting Britain's position as head of the motorsport pack.

"It's a great lap and a place where you can feel an F1 car excel through the quick corners. There is also a high-speed end of the lap so you need the tyres to last in qualifying." **Paul di Resta**

INSIDE TRACK
BRITISH GRAND PRIX

Date:	**8 July**
Circuit name:	**Silverstone**
Circuit length:	**3.666 miles/5.900km**
Number of laps:	**52**
Email:	**sales@silverstone-circuit.co.uk**
Website:	**www.silverstone-circuit.co.uk**

PREVIOUS WINNERS

2002	**Michael Schumacher** FERRARI
2003	**Rubens Barrichello** FERRARI
2004	**Michael Schumacher** FERRARI
2005	**Juan Pablo Montoya** McLAREN
2006	**Fernando Alonso** RENAULT
2007	**Kimi Raïkkönen** FERRARI
2008	**Lewis Hamilton** McLAREN
2009	**Sebastian Vettel** RED BULL
2010	**Mark Webber** RED BULL
2011	**Fernando Alonso** FERRARI

Key race: One of the most exciting British GPs at Silverstone was in 1969 when good friends Jackie Stewart and Jochen Rindt became locked in a duel for 63 of the 84 laps. Rindt led away from pole in his Lotus, but Stewart hounded him with his Matra and took the lead on lap 6. Ten laps later, Rindt took over again and as if tied together, the two lapped every other driver. Sadly, Rindt had to pit with rear-wing damage while Stewart raced on, unchallenged.

Key corner: Brooklands has been given a new lease of life with the recent reshaping of the circuit and the long run down from the Arena section makes it an overtaking spot again.

Best view: The grandstand at Club is now the place to be, as Lewis Hamilton proved last year when he hung on around the outside of Felipe Massa on the last lap.

Closest finish: Although Silverstone has provided some really close and competitive racing over the years, many of the battles have come to an end before the chequered flag, leaving Ferrari driver Alberto Ascari's win by just 1s over Juan Manuel Fangio's Maserati in 1953 the closest ever. In recent years, Mark Webber's 1.360s victory for Red Bull Racing over Lewis Hamilton's McLaren of 2010 proved the tightest finish.

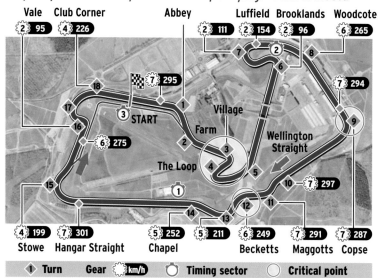

Vale | **Club Corner** | **Abbey** | **Luffield** | **Brooklands** | **Woodcote**
2 95 | 4 226 | 2 111 | 2 154 | 2 96 | 6 265

7 295
18
17
16 | 3 START
6 275 | 1
2 | Village
Farm
The Loop
3
4 | 5
Wellington
Straight
10 7 297
7 294
9
15 | 12
14 | 13 | 11

Stowe | **Hangar Straight** | **Chapel** | **Becketts** | **Maggotts** | **Copse**
4 199 | 7 301 | 5 252 | 5 211 | 6 249 | 7 291 | 7 287

◆ **Turn** ⚙ **Gear** 🕐 **km/h** ○ **Timing sector** ○ **Critical point**

2011 POLE TIME: WEBBER (RED BULL),
1M30.399S, 145.993MPH/234.953KPH
2011 WINNER'S AVERAGE SPEED:
128.720MPH/207.155KPH

2011 FASTEST LAP: ALONSO (FERRARI),
1M34.908S, 138.848MPH/223.455KPH
LAP RECORD: ALONSO (FERRARI), 1M30.874S,
145.018MPH/233.384KPH, 2010

HOCKENHEIM

The alternation in hosting the German GP between Hockenheim and the Nürburging continues and this year it's Hockenheim's turn, with Sebastian Vettel offering the fans every chance of a home victory.

Sebastian Vettel, Nico Rosberg, Michael Schumacher, Nick Heidfeld and Adrian Sutil, the F1 grid is packed with German drivers at present, so this country's fans really have no excuse but to turn out at Hockenheim in their droves, as they used to. Let's hope they do, too, for the future of the German GP looks ever shakier since the crowds began dwindling.

The Hockenheim circuit is a good place to watch racing, especially for those sitting in the vast grandstands overlooking the first corner, Nordkurve, or the Spitzkehre hairpin at the end of the arcing back straight. And the racing can get a little exciting into the tight left at Turn 8, too - at the end

of the kinked straight from Spitzkehre.

One thought that will be running through everyone's mind is that we want a real grand prix this time around, as the World Championship's last visit here was spoilt by Ferrari suggesting that Felipe Massa might like to cede victory to his team-mate Fernando Alonso, to which he acquiesced.

Although Hockenheim has been halved in length in recent years, and lost its entire forest loop in order to bring the cars past the grandstands more times in the course of a race, the intimacy of the stadium section remains, along with the deafening noise from the fans' airhorns, making this very much a venue of substance.

INSIDE TRACK
GERMAN GRAND PRIX

Date:	**22 July**
Circuit name:	**Hockenheim**
Circuit length:	**2.842 miles/4.574km**
Number of laps:	**67**
Email:	**Info@hockenheimring.de**
Website:	**www.hockenheimring.de**

PREVIOUS WINNERS	
1999	**Eddie Irvine** FERRARI
2000	**Rubens Barrichello** FERRARI
2001	**Ralf Schumacher** WILLIAMS
2002	**Michael Schumacher** FERRARI
2003	**Juan Pablo Montoya** WILLIAMS
2004	**Michael Schumacher** FERRARI
2005	**Fernando Alonso** RENAULT
2006	**Michael Schumacher** FERRARI
2008	**Lewis Hamilton** McLAREN
2010	**Fernando Alonso** FERRARI

Key race: There have been some brilliant races here, but it's the ones on the full circuit through the forest up to 2001 that really stand out. The pick of these was in 2000, when Rubens Barrichello scored his first grand prix win in a race destined to be McLaren's until a spectator ran out onto the track which brought out the safety car and this played into the Brazilian Ferrari driver's hands.

Key corner: Speed carried through Turn 12 is vital as it means that a driver can travel into the stadium section with perhaps a fraction more speed than the one ahead and so make a bid at overtaking into lightly banked Turn 13. With a concrete grid under the grass at the exit, running wide is not too costly, so it's worth a try.

Best view: A seat in the grandstand at the last corner, Turn 17, offers a view across the entire stadium section, from Turn 12 down to Turn 1. Better still, the atmosphere can be truly electric as tens of thousands of fans make their feelings known.

Closest finish: The first German GP held here, in 1970, was won by Jochen Rindt, with his Lotus 72 finishing just 0.7s ahead of Jacky Ickx's Ferrari, but David Coulthard was just 0.426s down on his McLaren team-mate Mika Hakkinen in 1998.

"I love the track as it's quite challenging and has some good overtaking opportunities. I also have good memories of it as I won in here in all the junior categories." **Nico Rosberg**

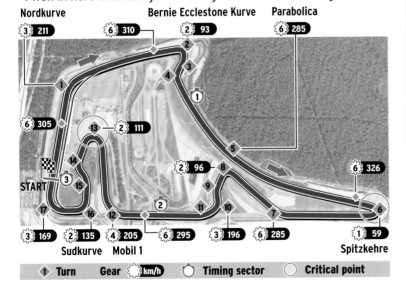

Nordkurve 3 211 6 310 | **Bernie Ecclestone Kurve** 2 93 | **Parabolica** 6 285
6 305 | 2 111 | 6 326
2 96
3 196 6 295 4 205 2 135 3 169
Sudkurve **Mobil 1** | 3 196 6 295 | 6 285 | 1 59 **Spitzkehre**

◆ **Turn** **Gear** ✱ **km/h** ○ **Timing sector** ○ **Critical point**

2010 POLE TIME: **VETTEL (RED BULL)**, 1M13.791S, 138.651MPH/223.138KPH
2010 WINNER'S AVERAGE SPEED: 130.356MPH/209.788KPH

2010 FASTEST LAP: **VETTEL (RED BULL)**, 1MM15.824S, 134.940MPH/217.165KPH
LAP RECORD: **RAÏKKÖNEN (McLAREN)**, 1M14.917S, 136.567MPH/219.784KPH, 2004

Overtaking is extremely tricky around the Hungaroring, but it makes the teams work all the harder to produce a race strategy that will have their drivers running at the front on the final lap.

Jenson Button has won twice at the Hungaroring and his win for Honda in 2006 and last year for McLaren both owe a huge amount to his uncanny ability to interpret changeable track conditions and save his tyres accordingly. On a circuit that offers few passing opportunities, this is vital – as is the ability to stay out of trouble.

Indeed, many drivers have had their race ruined after just the first couple of corners because it can get extremely crowded as the field streams down the hill into Turn 1 at the start of the Grand Prix, then jostles its way along the short blast to Turn 2, with many taking risks to ensure

they're on the inside line for the downhill lefthander. With overtaking so difficult around this stream of twists and turns, the thought of not only making a pit stop for a new nose but trying to work back past the tailenders afterward should be enough to encourage some caution.

Temperatures here can be extremely high in the height of summer and this may bring thunderstorms or a rate of tyrewear way in excess of the norm, both of which add to the excitement of the meeting as teams hope that the knowledge of Pirelli's latest compounds gained in practice will enable them to select the optimum tyre strategy.

> "The Hungaroring is a very good, technical and slow circuit, for which traction and braking stability are very important. Off the track, I like the city a lot as it's a very nice and enjoyable place to be." **Sergio Pérez**

78

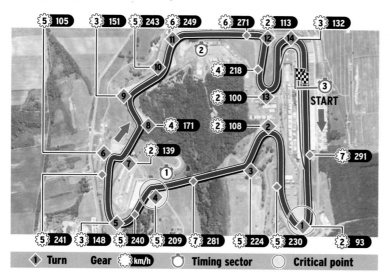

2011 POLE TIME: **VETTEL (RED BULL)**, 1M19.815S, 122.774MPH/197.586KPH
2011 WINNER'S AVERAGE SPEED: **107.134MPH/172.416KPH**

2011 FASTEST LAP: **MASSA (FERRARI)**, 1M23.415S, 117.475MPH/189.058KPH
LAP RECORD: **M SCHUMACHER (FERRARI)**, 1M19.041S, 123.828MPH/199.282KPH, 2004

INSIDE TRACK
HUNGARIAN GRAND PRIX

Date:	**29 July**
Circuit name:	**Hungaroring**
Circuit length:	**2.722 miles/4.381km**
Number of laps:	**70**
Email:	**office@hungaroring.hu**
Website:	**www.hungaroring.hu**

PREVIOUS WINNERS	
2002	**Rubens Barrichello** FERRARI
2003	**Fernando Alonso** RENAULT
2004	**Michael Schumacher** FERRARI
2005	**Kimi Raïkkönen** McLAREN
2006	**Jenson Button** HONDA
2007	**Lewis Hamilton** McLAREN
2008	**Heikki Kovalainen** McLAREN
2009	**Lewis Hamilton** McLAREN
2010	**Mark Webber** RED BULL
2011	**Jenson Button** McLAREN

Key race: Last year's victory was special as McLaren's Lewis Hamilton and Jenson Button fought over the lead before Button's precise style and cool approach won the day. Probably the most exciting race, however, was in 1989, when Nigel Mansell seized his moment in traffic to pass Ayrton Senna for the lead.

Key corner: Turn 4 is the one the drivers look to when trying to trim their lap time. It's approached via the second-longest straight that drops from Turn 3, then rises into and through the fourth-gear corner. Not running wide on the exit is vital because drivers need to haul their cars over to the left to take Turn 5.

Best view: The finest viewing comes from either the spectator banking overlooking the start/finish straight into the valley below, or the view back from the opposite side over the level run between Turns 5 and 9, with the chicane at Turns 6/7 a good place to watch cars being manhandled.

Closest finish: With so little overtaking possible, many races are run with cars running line astern. One such race was in 1990, when Thierry Boutsen qualified his Williams on pole – which is so important at such a twisting track – and kept Ayrton Senna's McLaren behind him to win by just 0.288s.

SPA-FRANCORCHAMPS

Thoughts that the future of the Belgian GP might be in jeopardy are almost too much to countenance as this is one of the world's great circuits and F1 would be all the poorer without it.

Spa-Francorchamps has it all: great corners, wonderful sweeping sections of track. It has terrain, it has weather and oh yes, to add an extra twist to proceedings, a long and rich history, too.

That its long-term future is far from secure is worrying indeed, so F1 fans the world over must be praying a solution may be found to keep it on the F1 calendar. To many, it is an annual fix, a race at a venue that stands out as somewhere truly special. Mention corners like Eau Rouge, Pouhon and Blanchimont and any driver's eyebrows will rise for these are corners of note. Then there is the climb from Raidillon to

Les Combes, ripe for slipstreaming, a blast of KERS and use of the DRS to attempt a passing move into the chicane at the top.

The terrain is special, too as the track threads a course through the forests covering the slopes of the Ardennes hills, with a viewpoint on the outside of the second part of Les Combes offering not only a clear view of the descent from Rivage to Pouhon but also snatches of the circuit appearing in gaps between the trees as far away as the Bus Stop and even the hairpin at La Source.

Some wonderful races have taken place here so let's hope there will be a great many more.

> "I've had lots of great times at Spa. It's been the place virtually every highlight of my career took place: my first race, my first win, my seventh world title. That's why I often call it my living room."

Michael Schumacher

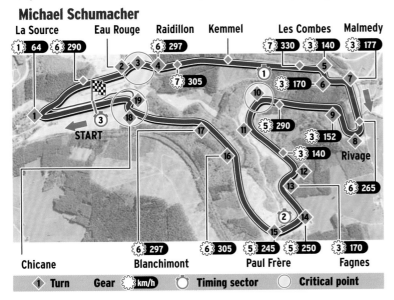

Legend: ◆ Turn · Gear · ⚙ km/h · ◯ Timing sector · ◯ Critical point

2011 POLE TIME: VETTEL (RED BULL), 1M48.298S, 144.667MPH/232.820KPH
2011 WINNER'S AVERAGE SPEED: 132.393MPH/213.066KPH

2011 FASTEST LAP: WEBBER (RED BULL), 1M49.883S, 142.583MPH/229.466KPH
LAP RECORD: VETTEL (RED BULL), 1M47.263S, 146.065MPH/235.069KPH, 2009

INSIDE TRACK
BELGIAN GRAND PRIX

Date:	**2 September**
Circuit name:	**Spa-Francorchamps**
Circuit length:	**4.352 miles/7.004km**
Number of laps:	**44**
Email:	secretariat@spa-francorchamps.be
Website:	**www.spa-francorchamps.be**

PREVIOUS WINNERS

2000	**Mika Hakkinen** McLAREN
2001	**Michael Schumacher** FERRARI
2002	**Michael Schumacher** FERRARI
2004	**Kimi Raïkkönen** McLAREN
2005	**Kimi Raïkkönen** McLAREN
2007	**Kimi Raïkkönen** FERRARI
2008	**Felipe Massa** FERRARI
2009	**Kimi Raïkkönen** FERRARI
2010	**Lewis Hamilton** McLAREN
2011	**Sebastian Vettel** RED BULL

Key race: One of the great races was in 2000 when two drivers on top of their game, Michael Schumacher and Mika Hakkinen, fought hard for honours. Schumacher led for Ferrari, but the McLaren driver closed in after an early spin. His first attempt to pass was chopped by Schumacher. Next time around he got by, diving to one side of Ricardo Zonta as they lapped the BAR driver while Schumacher went past on the other side.

Key corner: The Eau Rouge/Raidillon combination of left into a compression, right on the rise and left again over the top remains not just difficult but vital for carrying as much speed as possible onto the long straight up the slope to Les Combes. Every extra rev carried through this seventh-gear sweeper pays big dividends.

Best view: To observe cars at speed and under loading, the double downhill double left at Pouhon takes some beating.

Closest finish: Ferrari was in a class of its own for much of 1961, the first year for 1.5-litre engines; it filled the first four places at the finish, with Wolfgang von Trips edging out team-mate Phil Hill by 0.7s after leading all 75 laps. More recently, Damon Hill claimed Jordan's first win in 1998 by 0.932s from his disgruntled team-mate Ralf Schumacher.

As F1 casts its net ever wider, venues with a powerful history such as Monza feel all the more venerable and essential to the mix. That it provides some great action is a bonus.

Back in 1922, Monza opened for racing and remarkably, little has changed in format or feel since then. Built in a Royal Park outside the town of Monza to the north of Milan, the circuit is set among mature trees towering over the giant grandstands and all but enclosing the track on the run from the Lesmos back to the Ascari chicane. A flat-out blast this may be along its straights, but it's no Silverstone as it offers speed in confinement rather than wide, open spaces.

Although chicanes were inserted at three points around the lap in 1972 to break up the groups of cars that once hunted in slipstreaming packs, Monza still has a flat-out feel and continues to offer plenty of 200mph motoring. The first chicane is something of a nuisance on the opening lap, but repeated warnings from officials have led to fewer of the rash moves that have in the past spoilt the races of more than the driver who was that touch overambitious.

Always, the atmosphere is one of anticipation – especially if a Ferrari driver has a good chance of winning – but the mood can turn nasty if a rival team gets in the way, as McLaren's Mika Hakkinen discovered in the 1990s, with Italian charm fast disappearing and a sharper edge becoming apparent from the home fans.

> "Having good brakes and traction are important factors here so setting the car up becomes crucial for a good race. The tifosi also make it feel very special." **Rubens Barrichello**

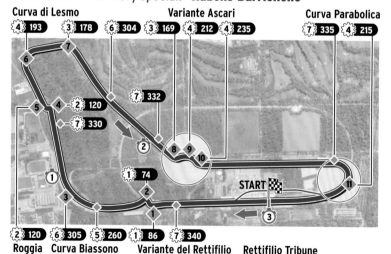

Curva di Lesmo · **Variante Ascari** · **Curva Parabolica**

Roggia · **Curva Biassono** · **Variante del Rettifilio** · **Rettifilio Tribune**

START

◆ Turn   Gear   km/h   ○ Timing sector   ○ Critical point

2011 POLE TIME: **VETTEL (RED BULL),** 1M22.275S, 157.,502MPH/253.476KPH
2011 WINNER'S AVERAGE SPEED: 141.578MPH/227.848KPH

2011 FASTEST LAP: **HAMILTON (MCLAREN),** 1M26.187S, 150.354MPH/241.971KPH
LAP RECORD: **BARRICHELLO (FERRARI),** 1M21.046S, 159.909MPH/257.349KPH, 2004

INSIDE TRACK
ITALIAN GRAND PRIX

Date:	**9 September**
Circuit name:	**Monza Circuit**
Circuit length:	**3.600 miles/5.793km**
Number of laps:	**53**
Email:	**infoautodromo@monzanet.it**
Website:	**www.monzanet.it**

PREVIOUS WINNERS

2002	**Rubens Barrichello** FERRARI
2003	**Michael Schumacher** FERRARI
2004	**Rubens Barrichello** FERRARI
2005	**Juan Pablo Montoya** McLAREN
2006	**Michael Schumacher** FERRARI
2007	**Fernando Alonso** McLAREN
2008	**Sebastian Vettel** TORO ROSSO
2009	**Rubens Barrichello** BRAWN
2010	**Fernando Alonso** FERRARI
2011	**Sebastian Vettel** RED BULL

Key race: Juan Manuel Fangio holds 24 grands prix, but the 1953 Italian GP is the only race that he won coming out of the final corner. There had been 19 lead changes before Alberto Ascari led a five-car pack onto the final lap. Ferrari team-mate Giuseppe Farina challenged him into the final corner but Ascari spun, Farina drove onto the grass in avoidance, Onofre Marimon collected Ascari and Fangio dived by to win for Maserati.

Key corner: For such a high-speed circuit, there are remarkably few fast corners but the pick is Curva Parabolica, which completes the lap, with drivers giving their all to gain maximum exit speed to blast past the pits.

Best view: There are few grandstands out around the lap because it is not permitted for trees to be chopped down through the wooded section to accommodate them. So, the best place to watch for overtaking action is by the first chicane.

Closest finish: As if the first two cars crossing the finish line in 1971, with Peter Gethin's BRM nosing ahead of Ronnie Peterson's March by 0.01s was not enough, the next three were all within just 0.61s of the winner after a slipstreaming classic. The next time they visited, chicanes had been inserted to break them up.

MARINA BAY

Of the new circuits that joined the World Championship over the past decade, this has to be the one that makes Bernie Ecclestone most proud as it offers something completely different.

Street racing really brings something special to F1's party, but run the race after nightfall so that all the city's smartest buildings are illuminated as a backdrop and therei s instantly a new arena, a whole new flavour.

In fact, Singapore's street circuit might be used as a template for how to do street racing. Not only does it include some notable landmarks such as crossing the Anderson Bridge but it offers an interesting challenge, too - unlike some other street circuits that have fallen by the wayside. The straights are long enough to give scope for overtaking, although that curse of so many street circuits - 90-degree bends around

corners - does break the flow in places.

The circuit certainly gave the teams cause for concern before the inaugural Singapore GP in 2008 as they were worried about how much the drivers would be able to see between the illuminated corners. But all was fine. What was not so good, of course, was the furore marring that first race over whether Nelson Piquet Jr had been asked to spin off and bring out the safety car to help Renault team-mate Fernando Alonso take victory.

It's strange for the teams to have to while away the day and then work evenings at the circuit, but they welcome the drop in temperature.

> "As it's a night race, I try to sleep until the afternoon. The lap has 23 corners, so it's important to find a good rhythm without touching the walls." **Sebastian Vettel**

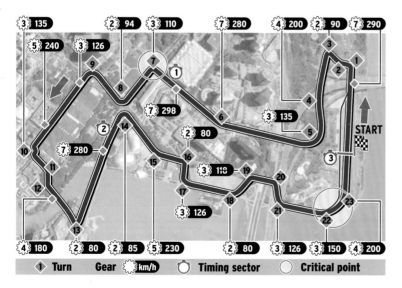

2011 POLE TIME: VETTEL (RED BULL), 1M44.381S, 108.716MPH/174.962KPH
2011 WINNER'S AVERAGE SPEED: 96.816MPH/155.810KPH

2011 FASTEST LAP: BUTTON (MCLAREN), 1M48.454S, 104.634MPH/168.392KPH
LAP RECORD: RAÏKKÖNEN (FERRARI), 1M45.599S, 107.358MPH/172.776KPH, 2008

INSIDE TRACK
SINGAPORE GRAND PRIX

Date:	**23 September**
Circuit name:	**Marina Bay Circuit**
Circuit length:	**3.152 miles/5.073km**
Number of laps:	**61**
Email:	**info@singaporegp.sg**
Website:	**www.singaporegp.sg**

PREVIOUS WINNERS

2008	**Fernando Alonso** RENAULT
2009	**Lewis Hamilton** McLAREN
2010	**Fernando Alonso** FERRARI
2011	**Sebastian Vettel** RED BULL

Key race: The inaugural Singapore GP in 2008 was of vital importance as this was the first time when F1 cars raced under cover of darkness. You might say it was a resounding success as everything worked from an operational point of view and there were no accidents caused by drivers not being able to see clearly. However, there was one accident that affected the outcome and this was Nelson Piquet Jr's, which brought out the safety car at a timely moment after Renault team-mate Fernando Alonso had been first to pit - from eleventh place - and this put him into a position from where he was able to advance to the lead and subsequent victory.

Key corner: Good track position into Turn 2 is crucial on the first lap as this dictates how drivers will be placed to double back through Turn 3 and also whether they will be exposed to collisions.

Best view: The grandstand by Turn 18 is unique in F1 as this is where the track disappears beneath the seats before turning right through Turn 19 under the grandstand, then soon afterwards right again through Turn 20 to emerge from under the grandstand for Turn 21.

Closest finish: When Fernando Alonso flashed across the finish line under the street lights in 2010, it could hardly have been closer as his Ferrari was just 0.293s clear of Sebastian Vettel's Red Bull, with the German frustrated to be bottled up behind on this circuit, which makes it so hard to pull off an overtaking move.

SUZUKA

This is a circuit that yields only to the best, being incredibly technical and demanding, as well as no stranger to tremendous downpours - just to make it that little bit more tricky!

Suzuka has always been packed with fans for the Japanese GP, many of them sitting all day in the grandstands while holding up banners displaying their allegiance to one driver. The crowds are not so big these days, but the spectacular showing of Kamui Kobayashi in 2010 and again last year has given them someone new to cheer on, one of their own.

In many ways the circuit is an anachronism, its pits and paddock cramped and access to the infield a bottleneck. However, the key part - the racing surface - is probably still the best there is. The circuit uses its position on a hillside to

good effect, with the descent to Turns 1 and 2 matched by the uphill Esses as the cars come back in the opposite direction. Indeed, the hairpin after the track crosses under its return leg is a definite place for the bold to overtake. However, if drivers get a clear run through Spoon Curve at the far end of the circuit and then carry any extra speed down the long back straight, it's 130R that they all think about. Not so fearsome as it was in the past, now the wall on the outside has been moved back, it's through here that they can stretch their advantage and get into position to try and line up a pass into the Casio Triangle.

> "Suzuka is one of my favourite circuits, and I think one of the best tracks, too. Racing there is exciting and cool. It's really enjoyable to drive if you get in the right rhythm." **Kamui Kobayashi**

82

INSIDE TRACK
JAPANESE GRAND PRIX

Date:	**7 October**
Circuit name:	**Suzuka**
Circuit length:	**3.608 miles/5.806km**
Number of laps:	**53**
Email:	**info@suzukacircuit.com.jp**
Website:	**www.suzukacircuit.co.jp**

PREVIOUS WINNERS	
2000	**Michael Schumacher** FERRARI
2001	**Michael Schumacher** FERRARI
2002	**Michael Schumacher** FERRARI
2003	**Rubens Barrichello** FERRARI
2004	**Michael Schumacher** FERRARI
2005	**Kimi Raïkkönen** McLAREN
2006	**Fernando Alonso** RENAULT
2009	**Sebastian Vettel** RED BULL
2010	**Sebastian Vettel** RED BULL
2011	**Jenson Button** McLAREN

Key race: The Japanese GP was the penultimate race in 2005 and while Fernando Alonso had a good points lead, McLaren was looking to topple Renault in the constructors' championship and Kimi Raïkkönen performed miracles to help them. After being hit with a 10-place penalty for an engine change, he started seventeenth and charged, coming out of his pitstop second with just eight laps to go. He then hauled in Renault's Giancarlo Fisichella and passed him around the outside at Turn 1 on the final lap.

Key corner: For overtaking, there can be a possibility into the chicane but the more important part is the exit from the chicane's final righthander as this dictates speed down the straight to Turn 1.

Best view: To see an F1 car being wrung by the neck with precision, spectators head for the banking above the Esses.

Closest finish: Records show Suzuka's tightest finish was in 1991, when Ayrton Senna let his McLaren team-mate Gerhard Berger through to win, finishing just 0.344s apart. However, the closest true racing finish was in 1997, when Michael Schumacher won for Ferrari after resisting a strong challenge by Heinz-Harald Frentzen, whose Williams finished 1.358s adrift.

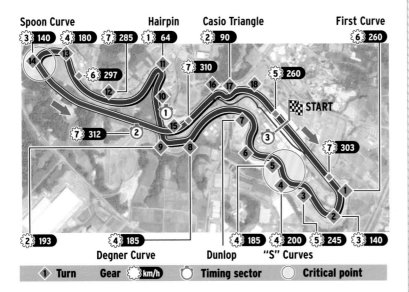

Spoon Curve   Hairpin   Casio Triangle   First Curve

Degner Curve   Dunlop   "S" Curves

◆ **Turn**   **Gear**   **km/h**   ○ **Timing sector**   ○ **Critical point**

2011 POLE TIME: VETTEL (RED BULL),
1M30.466S, 143.588MPH/231.083KPH
2011 WINNER'S AVERAGE SPEED:
126.121MPH/202.972KPH

2011 FASTEST LAP: BUTTON (MCLAREN),
1M36.568S, 134.515MPH/216.481KPH
LAP RECORD: RAÏKKÖNEN (MCLAREN),
1M31.540S, 141.904PH/228.373KPH, 2005

YEONGAM

Last year, the weather was unkind to race organizers as it hampered the rush to complete their circuit in time for the inaugural Korean GP. It offered a real challenge to the drivers, though.

A complex like the Korea International Circuit would never be built in Europe, being just part of a massive, built-from-scratch project. In fact, it's a circuit within a government-financed tourism and leisure city, one of six in remote regions. Built on land reclaimed from the sea, this new city in Yeongam will also include: a resort hotel complex, a cruise-ship terminal, a marina, a casino, a university, medical school and business parks.

The finished project – and it was still to be completed at the time of its 2010 debut – is impressive and the circuit has an identity of its own. A key difference is

that it runs in an anticlockwise direction, whereas most other F1 circuits run clockwise, thus putting pressure on the right side of the drivers' necks, whereas this one tests their left.

Another feature is that the run from Turn 2 to Turn 3 is, at 0.74 miles/1.19km, F1's longest straight. Feeding into a tight corner, it then offers another potential passing place into Turn 4 before the track feeds into a sequence of sweepers and tight bends that tend to make the cars run line astern. Of course there are bumps to be ironed out but this is a circuit with a reputation that will only grow.

"The track is nice to drive and very interesting as it has three different sectors, each of which are very different to each other."
Fernando Alonso

2011 POLE TIME: **HAMILTON (MCLAREN),**
1M35.820S, 131.083MPH/210.958KPH
2011 WINNER'S AVERAGE SPEED:
117.372MPH/188.893KPH

2011 FASTEST LAP: **VETTEL (RED BULL),**
1M39.605S, 126.101MPH/202.941KPH
LAP RECORD: **VETTEL (RED BULL),**
1M39.605S, 126.101MPH/202.941KPH, 2011

INSIDE TRACK
KOREAN GRAND PRIX

Date:	**14 October**
Circuit name:	**Korea International Circuit**
Circuit length:	**3.489 miles/5.615km**
Number of laps:	**57**
Email:	**N/A**
Website:	**www.koreangp.kr**

PREVIOUS WINNERS

2010	**Fernando Alonso** FERRARI
2011	**Sebastian Vettel** RED BULL

Key race: Everything seemed to militate against the circuit's inaugural grand prix of 2010 running smoothly. First, the construction work was way behind schedule. Diabolical weather then strafed the circuit and the race had to be started behind a safety car, though it was soon red-flagged as it was simply too wet. At the second attempt the safety car led around again. Moments later, it was needed once more as Mark Webber had crashed at Turn 12 and taken out Nico Rosberg. Finally, leader Sebastian Vettel's Red Bull's engine failed and so Fernando Alonso was able to win for Ferrari.

Key corner: Turn 3 stands out as the key corner for two reasons. First, because it's the chief overtaking spot on the circuit being at the end of the long straight from Turn 2. Second, because a good exit from here affords drivers the chance to perhaps grab a slipstream from a rival on the blast down the next straight to Turn 4 for another look at passing before the circuit feeds into a seemingly endless run of twists and turns back around to the start/finish straight, which dictate almost all driving must be single-file.

Best view: The grandstands are impressive and the one at Turn 1 offers the finest observation point for the start, with clear sight of the kink at Turn 2 as the field of cars, then accelerates hard up the longest straight to Turn 3.

Closest finish: The inaugural Korean GP was all but a washout with poor visibility. The second running of the race, last year, was several seconds closer at the finish, with Lewis Hamilton beating Vettel by 12.019s.

BUDDH INTERNATIONAL

With India apparently on the slide in cricket, it was great timing when the country hosted a grand prix for the first time last November to shift the nation's focus onto a sport in which it plays an increasing role.

The Buddh International Circuit proved a hit when the World Championship rolled into New Delhi for the first time last year and made the short journey out to the circuit at Greater Noida. Like so many all-new circuits before it, the construction work seemed to be getting nowhere fast, with expanses of bare earth being seen in the months before its eventual debut. Images of unfinished facilities for the 2010 Commonwealth Games in New Delhi abounded, yet although the tidying up of the infield will take years as trees grow and grass is laid down, the circuit was widely applauded.

One of its key elements is the gradient it possesses, with a marked climb from Turn 2 to Turn 3, followed by a plunging exit onto the circuit's longest straight down to Turn 4. Actually, that should say "up to Turn 4" as the straight kicks up to this tight right before dropping toward Turn 5. Other points of elevation come at the loop through Turns 10 and 11, plus the penultimate corner: Turn 15.

The circuit is not the only sporting element of this leisure complex, with world-class stadia being built for cricket and hockey in addition to a championship-standard golf course.

There has been talk of a shifting of the race date to April in the future, but that would be in very hot weather.

> **"It's not like any other track, but it's probably closest to Sakhir as it has one straight that is very long, at 1.2km." Karun Chandhok**

84

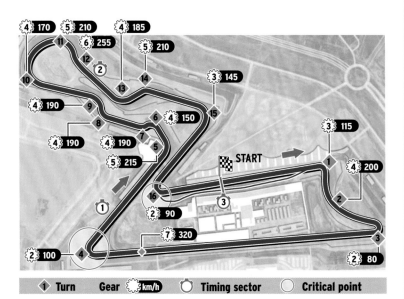

◆ **Turn**　**Gear**　km/h　○ **Timing sector**　○ **Critical point**

2011 POLE TIME: VETTEL (RED BULL), 1M24.178S, 136.191MPH/219.178KPH
2011 WINNER'S AVERAGE SPEED: 126.457MPH/203.513KPH

2011 FASTEST LAP: VETTEL (RED BULL), 1M27.249S, 131.387MPH/211.463KPH
LAP RECORD: VETTEL (RED BULL), 1M27.249S, 131.387MPH/211.463KPH, 2011

INSIDE TRACK
INDIAN GRAND PRIX

Date:	**22 April**
Circuit name:	**Buddh International Circuit**
Circuit length:	**3.190 miles/5.134km**
Number of laps:	**61**
Email:	**jaypee.sports@jalindia.co/in**
Website:	**www.jaypeesports.com**

PREVIOUS WINNERS
2011	**Sebastian Vettel**	RED BULL

Key race: This is an extremely easy one to select since only one grand prix has been held here. And that was last year, when the impressive new Buddh International Circuit was inaugurated in style with Sebastian Vettel racing to an almost effortless victory for Red Bull Racing in a race overshadowed by the deaths the previous weekend of Indycar racer Dan Wheldon and Moto GP rider Marco Simoncelli.

Key corner: The open hairpin of Turn 4 is the most important of the 16 corners around the lap because this is where the drivers have their best chance of overtaking on the rising entry to the tight righthander after racing down the circuit's longest straight. However, drivers who dive for the inside line in a passing move may find themselves slow on the exit as a result of this, thus allowing the driver they've just passed to move back ahead again as they accelerate down the hill toward Turn 5.

Best view: For a spectacular backdrop, as well as an exciting view of the track right at their feet, those fans heading for the grandstands at Turn 4 have chosen well. They'll enjoy the arrival uphill of the pack on the opening lap, the heavy braking and attempted passing manoeuvres right in front of their eyes. In addition, helping to keep them in on the action, this grandstand offers views across to the final corner onto the start/finish straight.

Closest finish: As above, this can only be the result from the 2011 Indian GP, when Sebastian Vettel brought his Red Bull RB7 home 8.433s in front of Jenson Button's McLaren MP4-26.

YAS MARINA

When Abu Dhabi decided that it wanted to become part of the World Championship, it thought big and opulent, and it's safe to say there is no other circuit like Yas Marina anywhere else in the world.

In theory, the Yas Marina circuit has it all – a fast section, a "street" section, even a marina lined with yachts. And as the race slides from day to evening, it has a building spanning the track that lights up spectacularly. Despite all the best considerations at the design stage, however, the circuit somehow lacked many places to do the one thing all fans like so much: overtaking.

In order to boost the chances for drivers to overtake here, before last year's Grand Prix changes were made to three corners. The first were to the chicane before the first hairpin in the Turns 5/6/7 complex. Next came the end of the back straight and finally, at the end of the following straight, Turns 11 to 14 – and they worked well in conjunction with timely applications of DRS.

Yas Marina is fortunate that Abu Dhabi is one of the few countries seemingly not to have been affected by the global recession as it sits atop considerable oil reserves and oil has certainly not gone out of fashion, so at least infrastructure changes can be made at will. Some drivers may even hope that the tight lefthander as they reach the bottom of the pit exit tunnel might be made less severe as many have almost wrecked their chances by coming close to the wall there.

> "This is a track I like very much. It's a fantastic setting with the track winding around the harbour and hotel, and there's always a great atmosphere there with so many fans." **Nico Rosberg**

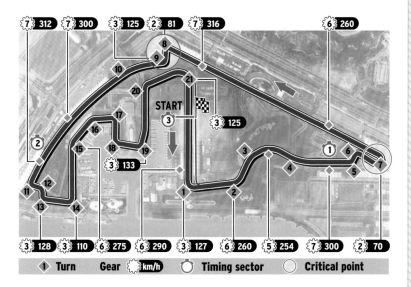

Turn ◆ | Gear | km/h | ⌾ Timing sector | ○ Critical point

2011 POLE TIME: **VETTEL (RED BULL),** 1M38.481S, 126.155MPH/203.207KPH
2011 WINNER'S AVERAGE SPEED: 117.125MPH/188.494KPH

2011 FASTEST LAP: **WEBBER (RED BULL),** 1M42.612S, 121.076MPH/194.854KPH
LAP RECORD: **VETTEL (RED BULL),** 1M40.279S, 123.893MPH/199.383KPH, 2009

INSIDE TRACK
ABU DHABI GRAND PRIX

Date:	**28 October**
Circuit name:	**Yas Marina Circuit**
Circuit length:	**3.451 miles/5.554km**
Number of laps:	**56**
Email:	
customerservice@yasmarinacircuit.com	
Website:	**www.yasmarinacircuit.com**

PREVIOUS WINNERS		
2009	**Sebastian Vettel** RED BULL
2010	**Sebastian Vettel** RED BULL
2011	**Lewis Hamilton** McLAREN

Key race: With just three grands prix under its belt so far, there are few to choose from, but the 2010 race at Yas Marina held the most excitement. This was the championship finale and the 2009 race winner Sebastian Vettel arrived with it all to do. He was third, seven points behind Red Bull team-mate Mark Webber and 15 down on Ferrari's Fernando Alonso. Yet he stuck his car on pole and resisted all McLaren's Lewis Hamilton could throw at him to race clear to win, while the other pair got on the wrong end of strategy calls. They were caught out in emerging from their pit stops behind slower cars, with Alonso particularly frustrated to be stuck behind Vitaly Petrov, so they could finish only eighth and seventh, allowing Vettel to become champion by four points.

Key corner: Traction out of Turn 7 onto the long, long main straight is vital if a driver is to stand any chance of tucking in behind another in the hope of overtaking into Turn 8.

Best view: The grandstand above Turn 8 still offers the best location for watching the action, with cars powering down the circuit's longest straight toward them before breaking out of their slipstreaming position and making a dive inside, or even occasionally outside, for this tight lefthander.

Closest finish: In the three Abu Dhabi Grands Prix to date, the closest finish has been the one in 2011, in which McLaren's Lewis Hamilton earned a late-season fillip in beating Fernando Alonso's Ferrari by the margin of 8.457s.

America has a checkered history in Formula One, with the US GP dotting around the country from the 1980s. Perhaps the new Circuit of the Americas will provide a lasting home, though.

The US GP has been held at Sebring (Florida), Riverside (California), Watkins Glen (New York), Long Beach (California), Las Vegas (Nevada), Detroit (Michigan), Dallas (Texas), Phoenix (Arizona) and Indianapolis (Indiana). Promoter Tavo Hellmund hopes it will settle in Austin.

Mexican, but brought up in Austin, Tavo is the son of Gustavo Hellmund, who redeveloped Autódromo Hermanos Rodríguez in the 1970s. Before turning promoter, he was a racing driver. To build a circuit from scratch takes finance and he was helped in this through teaming up with Red McCombs, an investor who made his fortune through car dealerships.

Circuit of the Americas was designed by Hermann Tilke to include the best corners from classic tracks around the world, including an esses sequence between Turn 6 and Turn 9 reminiscent of those at Suzuka. One of the most exciting sections of the lap, however, will be the climb to the first corner – rising some 131ft/40m before the plunging exit down toward Turn 2. Unusually, the circuit runs in an anti-clockwise direction, so the drivers' necks will get a workout.

Being just 8 miles/12.8km from downtown Austin, the crowds should throng and one can only wonder how many more might be heading to Texas, should an American driver be racing.

> **"There's 160-feet elevation change and Turn 1 is like the first corner at the Red Bull Ring (formerly A1-Ring), which will make it feel like riding a rollercoaster in one of the fastest cars in the world."**
> **David Coulthard**

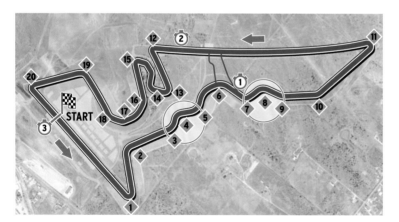

↓ Turn **Gear 🏁km/h** **○ Timing sector** **○ Critical point**

2011 POLE TIME: **NOT APPLICABLE**	2011 FASTEST LAP: **NOT APPLICABLE**
2011 WINNER'S AVERAGE SPEED:	LAP RECORD: **NOT APPLICABLE**
NOT APPLICABLE	

INSIDE TRACK
UNITED STATES GRAND PRIX

Date:	**18 November**
Circuit name:	**Circuit of the Americas**
Circuit length:	**3.400 miles/5.472km**
Number of laps:	**56**
Email:	**info@circuitoftheamericas.com**
Website:	**www.circuitoftheamericas.com**

Key race: Obviously, this is still to come but the first key race for the revamped United States GP will be to sell the tickets for this autumn's inaugural event in Texas as this will be key to the circuit's long-term future. If ticket sales are good, it will prove that the United States still has the stomach for Formula One after a history of its race being dotted round this vast country.

Key corner: While a driver's ability to carry momentum through the esses (Turns 6-9) will be vital for a quick lap, speed carried through Turn 19 and particularly the final corner, Turn 20, will be essential to a fast lap time as it feeds onto the main straight.

Best view: With its unusually lofty position, the grandstand at Turn 1 will not only offer a view back down the start/finish straight and over the braking (overtaking) zone at its feet, but also out across much of the rest of the circuit. Expect this to be the first sell-out grandstand.

Closest finish: It would have to be the finish to the race to take the circuit from a scrub-covered site to a sporting facility ready for this autumn's inaugural race, especially as there was a period when work stopped because of contract negotiation. At least in Texas rain is not a problem for most of the year, so enabling construction to proceed without interruption.

First experience: Amazingly, the first F1 car around the Circuit of the Americas was last August, when David Coulthard took a Red Bull F1 car for a blast on the newly graded circuit, scrabbling for grip on a loose surface. With the laying of tarmac still months away, it was more rally cross than racing circuit but gave the Grand-Prix-winner-turned-BBC-commentator the chance to get a feel for its flow.

INTERLAGOS

Nips and tucks keep Interlagos's infrastructure from appearing ancient, although the gloss is only skin deep. Fortunately, this undulating stretch of tarmac remains one of the best circuits.

Spend a day at Interlagos and you'll understand why atmosphere is so vital for any sporting event. If this tricky circuit was placed in a sterile location, it would still be a good one, but the sheer passion of the Brazilian fans and the cacophony they emit make the place somewhere truly special.

Naturally, Brazil is still looking for a driver to excite them as Ayrton Senna once did, but they have been in love with Formula One since the Fittipaldi brothers gave them someone to cheer on in the early 1970s.

Hacked back from its original looping format around some lakes for F1's return in 1990, the circuit still offers thrills aplenty, with the dipping first corner a real challenge and the twisting uphill and downhill section from Ferradura to Juncao keeping drivers right on the edge if they want to press for that ultimate lap. It's a circuit on which drivers can really race and although both pit and paddock facilities are woeful, that is what counts when it comes to making the sport look its best.

The fact that Interlagos now occupies the slot of the season's finale only adds to the allure of the Brazilian GP. Just ask Lewis Hamilton the difference between how he felt on the Sunday night in 2007 and how much better it felt there in 2008, when he was crowned champion.

> "The Brazilian GP means to me traffic, strange weather and nice-looking women. A lap of Interlagos has four high-speed stretches, two slow turns and three spots for overtaking." **Mark Webber**

INSIDE TRACK
BRAZILIAN GRAND PRIX

Date:	**25 November**
Circuit name:	**Interlagos**
Circuit length:	**2.667 miles/4.292km**
Number of laps:	**71**
Email:	**info@gpbrazil.com**
Website:	**www.gpbrazil.com**

PREVIOUS WINNERS

2002	**Michael Schumacher** FERRARI
2003	**Giancarlo Fisichella** JORDAN
2004	**Juan Pablo Montoya** WILLIAMS
2005	**Juan Pablo Montoya** McLAREN
2006	**Felipe Massa** FERRARI
2007	**Kimi Raïkkönen** FERRARI
2008	**Felipe Massa** FERRARI
2009	**Mark Webber** RED BULL
2010	**Sebastian Vettel** RED BULL
2011	**Mark Webber** RED BULL

Key race: The 2008 title decider between Felipe Massa and Lewis Hamilton was a race of unbelievable tension, but for sheer emotional release for the partisan fans, 1993 remains the zenith. This was the occasion when Ayrton Senna used his Ford-powered McLaren to show true grit in overcoming a stop-go penalty, the arrival of rain and Damon Hill's more powerful Honda-engined Williams.

Key corner: In terms of contributing to a fast lap, Turn 12 – Juncao – is critical, for if a driver is off balance through this uphill lefthander and unable to get the power down going onto the start/finish "straight", then they stand the risk of being passed rather than doing any passing.

Best view: There can be no better place to watch than the Senna S, a beguiling twist into which drivers know they must find an advantage but all too often brake just too late as they dive over the blind brow beyond the apex-obscuring pit wall and run wide. The spectators get to see overtaking and fumbling, too.

Closest finish: Though there were cries of complaint that he had not been trying hard to take the lead, Ralf Schumacher tucked his Williams into the wake of brother Michael's Ferrari to finish just 0.588s behind in 2002.

Senna "S" Subida dos Boxes Juncao
START Curva do Sol Reta Oposta Descida do Lago

◆ **Turn**   ⚙ **Gear**   ⚙ **km/h**   ○ **Timing sector**   ○ **Critical point**

2011 POLE TIME: VETTEL (RED BULL),
1M11.918S, 134.026MPH/215.695KPH
2011 WINNER'S AVERAGE SPEED:
123.576MPH/198.876KPH

2011 FASTEST LAP: WEBBER (RED BULL),
1M15.324S, 127.966MPH/205.942KPH
LAP RECORD: MONTOYA (WILLIAMS),
1M11.473S, 134.837MPH/217.000KPH, 2004

The official TV cameramen capture the emotion as the teams gather beneath the podium at the Nürburgring to wait for Hamilton, Alonso and Webber to be given their trophies.

REVIEW OF
THE 2011 SEASON

With 15 poles and 11 wins, it came as no surprise when Sebastian Vettel became World Champion for the second year in succession. Indeed, such was the German's dominance that Red Bull Racing team-mate Mark Webber failed to win until the final round of the year. McLaren proved best of the rest, with Jenson Button coming out on top from his internal battle with Lewis Hamilton.

If Red Bull Racing did well to win its first drivers' and constructors' titles in 2010, its Adrian Newey-penned RB7 chassis was better still in 2011 and proved more than just the supreme machine for grabbing pole position, which it took at every round bar one, proving fabulous in race trim, too. Indeed, with Sebastian Vettel taking six wins, as well as three second places in the first nine rounds, the drivers' title would clearly be his.

Red Bull Racing team-mate Mark Webber, on the other hand, collected just one second place and four thirds in the same races, which suggests that the Australian veteran was not liking his car's behaviour on the new Pirellis to the extent that Vettel was. Meanwhile, the German ace just kept on winning and earning ever more plaudits.

Even though 2008 World Champion Lewis Hamilton was able to win as early as round three in China, both McLaren and Ferrari were left floundering for form. Hamilton's team-mate Jenson Button was also victorious before mid-season, albeit with an extraordinary drive in wet/dry conditions in Canada rather than a flat-out sprint in standard, dry conditions. Ferrari then looked to have made progress when Fernando Alonso won at Silverstone

but this proved to be something of a false dawn and his best efforts could add no more. Team-mate Felipe Massa got nowhere and even put his long-term future at Ferrari in doubt.

McLaren at least kept advancing, with Hamilton winning at the Nürburgring and in Abu Dhabi, Button at the Hungaroring and Suzuka to finish the year as runner-up behind Vettel, impressing many more than he did even in his title-winning year with Brawn GP in 2009. Conversely, Hamilton could not wait for the season to end, having been involved in more on-track incidents than during the rest of his career combined, almost invariably with Ferrari's Felipe Massa. Some questioned Hamilton's state of mind, saying that his focus appeared to be elsewhere, but he has vowed to use the close-season to get himself back on an even keel.

The gap from the top three teams back to the other nine teams was a big one, with Mercedes GP winning the battle to rank fourth. All Nico Rosberg and Michael Schumacher could hope to do, though, was to pick up scraps, with Schumacher's fourth place in the topsy-turvy Canadian GP their best. The seven-time World Champion continued to struggle for form in his second season back, but from midway through the year was back to something approaching his best although he found running in midfield made collisions more of a factor than running at the front as he had done before.

Renault started better, with third place for Vitaly Petrov in the Australian opener, but its forward-facing exhausts hampered development and the team dropped away – Force India in particular coming on strong to outpace it. The biggest blow, however, was the loss of inspirational lead driver Robert Kubica after he suffered terrible arm injuries in an incident while contesting a rally in the close-season. Scuderia Toro Rosso's drivers also outran the Renaults but fell off the pace in the closing races to slip behind unspectacular Sauber, who ranked eighth overall. Yet again the Swiss team had cause to consider how it can maintain the strong form with which it starts most seasons before it falls away.

One of the saddest sights of 2011 was the continued fall from grace of Williams, with this once-great team scoring just five points all year. Indeed, had the points been awarded down only to eighth place (as they were until 2009), Williams would have come away with none at all despite the best efforts of Rubens Barrichello and rookie Pastor Maldonado, who at least brought a healthy cash injection. A deal with Renault for engines in 2012 ought to be a step in the right direction.

Then came the three teams that had been new to F1 in 2010: Lotus, Virgin and HRT. Lotus was easily the best of these, with Heikki Kovalainen heroic in his pursuit of any finish higher than eighteenth. However, most of its headlines centred on boss Tony Fernandes' constant legal battles with the Renault team over the use of the Lotus name, which Renault had bestowed on it by the car manufacturer, Group Lotus.

Virgin gave up on taking a CFD-only design approach, its chassis proving to be far from the best, while HRT simply lacked the finances to do anything more than prop up the tail of the field while it sought financing to continue.

Sebastian Vettel arrived in Melbourne as reigning World Champion and left with rivals wondering what they might have to do to prevent him from making it two in a row as Red Bull Racing looked to be completely in a class of its own.

The opening race was supposed to be in Bahrain but street protests there led to its postponement and eventual cancellation. So it was on the Albert Park circuit that F1 fans were able to discover how accurate testing form had been. As expected, Red Bull Racing came out on top, but McLaren got far closer than expected, even after they had decided at the eleventh hour to abandon their complex exhaust system, yet were able to place their cars second and fourth on the grid for Lewis Hamilton and Jenson Button as they outpaced Ferrari's best, Fernando Alonso.

Tellingly, Vettel's pole time was fastest by 0.778s, so all rivals could hope for was that they might be able to get close enough to use their drag reduction system rear wing on the main straight to haul him back in. Yet perhaps because the DRS activation zone on the start/finish straight was short, it did not produce many extra passes.

Thus Vettel was left under no pressure into the opening turn as Hamilton's McLaren was slow off the line and then ran untroubled in the lead, pulling clear at will. Mark Webber settled into third ahead of Renault's Vitaly Petrov, who benefited from a tussle into Turn 1 between Button and Alonso. Alonso's woes increased when team-mates Felipe Massa, Nico Rosberg and Sauber's Kamui Kobayashi all passed him.

The greatest excitement in the early laps came when Button attempted to get back past Massa, but this was spoilt after he was given a drive-through penalty for going off the track to gain an advantage.

Another driver in trouble was Webber, who dropped away from the leading duo as his Red Bull consumed its rear tyres and fell to an eventual fifth. Then Hamilton broke a floor stay, ending any hopes he might have had of keeping Vettel in sight. With Webber's worsening pace, Petrov took third.

One of the drives of the race came from rookie Sergio Pérez, who ran a one-stop strategy and managed to make it work well

Sebastian Vettel began his title defence in style by winning the opening race from pole.

MELBOURNE ROUND 1

DATE: **27 MARCH 2011**

Laps: **58** • Distance: **191.117 miles/307.574km** • Weather: **Sunny and dry**

Pos	Driver	Team	Result	Stops	Qualifying Time	Grid
1	Sebastian Vettel	Red Bull	1h29m30.259s	2	1m23.529s	1
2	Lewis Hamilton	McLaren	1h29m52.556s	2	1m24.307s	2
3	Vitaly Petrov	Renault	1h30m00.819s	2	1m25.247s	6
4	Fernando Alonso	Ferrari	1h30m02.031s	3	1m24.974s	5
5	Mark Webber	Red Bull	1h30m08.430s	3	1m24.395s	3
6	Jenson Button	McLaren	1h30m24.563s	2	1m24.779s	4
DQ	Sergio Pérez	Sauber	1h30m36.104s	1	1m26.108s	13
DQ	Kamui Kobayashi	Sauber	1h30m47.131s	2	1m25.626s	9
7	Felipe Massa	Ferrari	1h39m55.445s	3	1m25.599s	8
8	Sebastien Buemi	Toro Rosso	57 laps	2	1m27.066s	10
9	Adrian Sutil	Force India	57 laps	2	1m31.407s	16
10	Paul di Resta	Force India	57 laps	2	1m26.739s	14
11	Jaime Alguersuari	Toro Rosso	57 laps	3	1m26.103s	12
12	Nick Heidfeld	Renault	57 laps	2	1m27.239s	18
13	Jarno Trulli	Lotus	56 laps	2	1m29.342s	20
14	Jérôme d'Ambrosio	Virgin	54 laps	2	1m30.822s	22
NC	Timo Glock	Virgin	49 laps	2	1m29.858s	21
R	Rubens Barrichello	Williams	48 laps/transmission	3	No time	17
R	Nico Rosberg	Mercedes	22 laps/crash damage	1	1m25.421s	7
R	Heikki Kovalainen	Lotus	19 laps/water leak	1	1m29.254s	19
R	Michael Schumacher	Mercedes	19 laps/crash damage	1	1m25.971s	11
R	Pastor Maldonado	Williams	9 laps/transmission	0	1m26.768s	15

FASTEST LAP: MASSA, 1M28.947S, 133.568MPH/214.957KPH ON LAP 55 • RACE LEADERS: VETTEL 1-13, 17-58; HAMILTON 14-16

enough not only to outpace highly-rated team-mate Kobayashi, but to finish seventh, up from thirteenth. Kobayashi finished eighth, but both drivers were disqualified for an irregularity in the top flap of their rear wings, elevating Force India's Adrian Sutil and Paul di Resta into the points.

The HRTs of Vitantonio Liuzzi and Narain Karthikeyan ended up outside the 107% qualifying rule.

MALAYSIAN GP

As expected, this was a case of round two, win number two for Sebastian Vettel as Red Bull Racing's reigning World Champion had everything under control at Sepang, leaving his rivals with little hope in the heat and humidity of Malaysia.

Sebastian Vettel was on pole again, but this time his margin of advantage was just 0.1s. Once again, McLaren's Lewis Hamilton was the German's closest challenger. So, with a longer straight on which drivers could harness their KERS in combination with the DRS rear wing, plus the likelihood of more extreme tyre wear, there was less certainty that Vettel would have things his own way.

It was not Hamilton who led the chase, though, but his team-mate Jenson Button, a driver whose ultra-smooth style is allied with an exceptional level of sensitivity. Just 0.226s down on Hamilton in qualifying fourth behind Mark Webber in the other Red Bull, Button gained a place at the start as Webber's KERS was not working. The Australian was swamped and completed lap 1 in ninth, behind both Ferraris, fighting with the Mercedes and Saubers. However, as the challengers battled into Turn 1, Nick Heidfeld passed them around the outside in his black-and-gold Renault to slot into second, giving Vettel a buffer between himself and the fastest of his pursuers.

Hamilton advanced to second after the first of his pit stops, helped by Heidfeld's Renault being delayed when a wheel jammed. But he knew that his pace would suffer later: in qualifying, he'd flat-spotted one of his sets of Prime tyres and was forced to do two stints on Pirelli's harder compound Options. He'd already noticed a chink in Red Bull's armour, however, and this was the failure of Vettel's KERS, with the team instructing the race leader not to use it from lap 29.

As the race went on, Button became the faster McLaren driver, moving into second at the third round of pit stops to leave Hamilton battling Fernando Alonso. This proved his undoing as he was adjudged to have weaved in front of Alonso and so hit with a 20s penalty, which dropped him from seventh after having to make a fourth pit stop for tyres, to eighth. Alonso was penalized 20s for clipping Hamilton

SEPANG ROUND 2

DATE: **10 APRIL 2011**

Laps: **56** • Distance: **192.888 miles/310.424km** • Weather: **Hot and humid**

Pos	Driver	Team	Result	Stops	Qualifying Time	Grid
1	Sebastian Vettel	Red Bull	1h37m39.832s	3	1m34.870s	1
2	Jenson Button	McLaren	1h37m43.093s	3	1m35.200s	4
3	Nick Heidfeld	Renault	1h38m04.907s	3	1m36.124s	6
4	Mark Webber	Red Bull	1h38m06.216s	4	1m35.179s	3
5	Felipe Massa	Ferrari	1h38m16.790s	3	1m36.251s	7
6	Fernando Alonso	Ferrari	1h38m37.080s*	4	1m35.802s	5
7	Kamui Kobayashi	Sauber	1h38m46.271s	2	1m36.820s	10
8	Lewis Hamilton	McLaren	1h38m49.789s*	4	1m34.974s	2
9	Michael Schumacher	Mercedes	1h39m04.728s	3	1m37.035s	11
10	Paul di Resta	Force India	1h39m11.395s	3	1m37.370s	14
11	Adrian Sutil	Force India	1h39m21.211s	3	1m37.593s	17
12	Nico Rosberg	Mercedes	55 laps	3	1m36.809s	9
13	Sebastien Buemi	Toro Rosso	55 laps	3	1m37.160s	12
14	Jaime Alguersuari	Toro Rosso	55 laps	2	1m37.347s	13
15	Heikki Kovalainen	Lotus	55 laps	2	1m38.645s	19
16	Timo Glock	Virgin	54 laps	2	1m40.648s	21
17	Vitaly Petrov	Renault	52 laps/steering	3	1m36.324s	8
R	Vitantonio Liuzzi	HRT	46 laps/handling	3	1m41.549s	23
R	Jérôme d'Ambrosio	Virgin	42 laps/electrical	2	1m41.001s	22
R	Jarno Trulli	Lotus	31 laps/clutch	1	1m38.791s	20
R	Sergio Pérez	Sauber	23 laps/electrical	1	1m37.528s	16
R	Rubens Barrichello	Williams	22 laps/hydraulics	2	1m37.496s	15
R	Narain Karthikeyan	HRT	14 laps/overheating	0	1m42.574s	24
R	Pastor Maldonado	Williams	8 laps/misfire	0	1m38.276s	18

FASTEST LAP: WEBBER, 1M40.571S, 123.295MPH/198.424KPH ON LAP 46 • **RACE LEADERS:** VETTEL 1–13, 15–25, 27–56; ALONSO 14, 26
* TWENTY-SECOND POST-RACE PENALTY

Sebastian Vettel was on pole again for the second round and led away from the two McLarens.

but this failed to alter his position as he was led home by team-mate Felipe Massa.

Up front, Vettel came under increasing pressure in the final stint as they raced on the Options, with his gap to Button falling from 8.8s to 3.2 by flagfall. In the closing laps, Webber hoped to usurp Heidfeld but had to settle for fourth place.

Lewis Hamilton drove an exceptional race in Shanghai, overhauling Sebastian Vettel for victory by pitting three times to the German's two and making the most of the difference between new tyres and old to hit the front and race on to victory.

When Sebastian Vettel claimed his third pole in three races it looked as though he was set fair for win number three, especially as he had a margin of 0.715s over the next fastest qualifier: McLaren's Jenson Button. A Vettel win seemed even more likely on race day as there was not the usual spectre of rain hanging over the circuit. However, Button got the jump at the start and Hamilton demoted Vettel to third.

Had fortune been different, Hamilton would not have been there to pass him as his engine only managed to fire up within 30s of being too late to leave the pitlane. As it was, Hamilton was second and Nico Rosberg made a bid to pass Vettel for third at Turn 6. But the attempt did not work and the first three were able to make their escape while Rosberg was left fighting Ferrari's Felipe Massa and Fernando Alonso.

So, the next big question was, who would be pitting first? Rosberg, as it transpired: on lap 12. Button and Vettel were called in on lap 13, though both failed to hear. With Rosberg lapping 3s per lap faster on new tyres, this proved expensive. Furthermore, Button then pulled in at Red Bull by mistake, which enabled Vettel to rejoin ahead, though not back into the effective lead as Rosberg had already claimed that.

On lap 15, Hamilton was thus forced to pit and the extra time on worn tyres lost him a place to Massa. After that, McLaren switched its drivers to three-stop strategies.

Rosberg led until his second stop, leaving Vettel in front. And there he stayed, albeit with his KERS not working, until he pitted on lap 30. He now had to make his remaining set of tyres last to the finish, as did Massa, and the race was one that would only reveal the final outcome in the last few laps. And so it was that Hamilton passed Vettel at Turn 7 on lap 52 to race to a deserved win.

Mark Webber had had a nightmare in qualifying and missed the first cut. So,

Good strategy helped Hamilton to prevent Vettel from making it three wins from three races.

SHANGHAI ROUND 3
DATE: **17 APRIL 2011**

Laps: **56** • Distance: **189.568 miles/305.081km** • Weather: **Overcast and cool**

Pos	Driver	Team	Result	Stops	Qualifying Time	Grid
1	**Lewis Hamilton**	McLaren	1h36m58.226s	3	1m34.463s	3
2	**Sebastian Vettel**	Red Bull	1h37m03.424s	2	1m33.706s	1
3	**Mark Webber**	Red Bull	1h37m05.781s	3	1m36.468s	18
4	**Jenson Button**	McLaren	1h37m08.226s	3	1m34.421s	2
5	**Nico Rosberg**	Mercedes	1h37m11.674s	3	1m34.670s	4
6	**Felipe Massa**	Ferrari	1h37m14.066s	2	1m35.145s	6
7	**Fernando Alonso**	Ferrari	1h37m28.848s	2	1m35.119s	5
8	**Michael Schumacher**	Mercedes	1h37m29.252s	3	1m36.457s	14
9	**Vitaly Petrov**	Renault	1h37m55.630s	2	No time	10
10	**Kamui Kobayashi**	Sauber	1h38m01.499s	2	1m36.236s	13
11	**Paul di Resta**	Force India	1h38m06.983s	2	1m36.190s	8
12	**Nick Heidfeld**	Renault	1h38m10.965s	2	1m36.611s	16
13	**Rubens Barrichello**	Williams	1h38m28.415s	2	1m36.465s	15
14	**Sebastien Buemi**	Toro Rosso	1h38m28.897s	3	1m36.203s	9
15	**Adrian Sutil**	Force India	55 laps	3	1m35.874s	11
16	**Heikki Kovalainen**	Lotus	55 laps	2	1m37.894s	19
17	**Sergio Pérez**	Sauber	55 laps	3	1m36.053s	12
18	**Pastor Maldonado**	Williams	55 laps	3	1m36.956s	17
19	**Jarno Trulli**	Lotus	55 laps	2	1m38.318s	20
20	**Jérôme d'Ambrosio**	Virgin	54 laps	2	1m39.119s	21
21	**Timo Glock**	Virgin	54 laps	3	1m39.708s	22
22	**Vitantonio Liuzzi**	HRT	54 laps	2	1m40.212s	23
23	**Narain Karthikeyan**	HRT	54 laps	1	1m40.445s	24
R	**Jaime Alguersuari**	Toro Rosso	9 laps/lost wheel	1	1m36.158s	7

FASTEST LAP: WEBBER, 1M38.993S, 123.181MPH/198.241KPH ON LAP 42 • RACE LEADERS: BUTTON 1-13; HAMILTON 14, 52-56; ALONSO 15-16; ROSBERG 17-24, 34-39; VETTEL 25-30, 40-51; MASSA 31-33

from eighteenth on the grid, it was decided that he would run a three-stop strategy. His progress was slow in the first stint, being on hards while everyone else was on

softs. Thereafter, always on softs, he tore up the order to pass Rosberg for fourth with two laps to go, and then Button on the penultimate lap.

TURKISH GP

After the blip of being beaten in China, Sebastian Vettel made it business as usual again in Turkey in claiming his fourth pole of the season and racing clear of team-mate Mark Webber for the first Red Bull Racing one-two of the season.

After the race, the merits of DRS were very much a matter for discussion as, get this: some believed there had been too much overtaking. Yes, after seasons in which all those involved were of the view that it had become too difficult to pass, it was now thought the drag reduction system in which the chasing car had a slot open between the two planes of its rear wing to provide greater straightline speed in a specified area was making it too easy.

Certainly, the shape of the circuit and the length of the straight from Turn 10 through the kink at Turn 11 down to the hairpin at Turn 12 helped. However, none of this affected the outcome of the race in which Sebastian Vettel was simply dominant. What this glut of passing did do, however, was to keep the fans excited if they were overlooking the back straight and - along with most of the drivers making four tyre stops and a set of fresh tyres slash lap times by as much as 4s - confuse the TV director.

Vettel had team-mate Mark Webber diagonally behind him in second on the grid and then Nico Rosberg's Mercedes as the best of the rest, with Lewis Hamilton fourth and Fernando Alonso fifth. However, by Turn 1, Vettel lost his protection from behind as Webber had been slow away and Rosberg raced straight into second place. Hamilton then made a bid to pass Webber at Turn 3, got it wrong and so Alonso and Jenson Button dived by him as he regained control. Hamilton then battled for several laps to pass Button and their tyres suffered.

If Michael Schumacher's F1 return in 2010 had not been a success, his Turkish GP was marked by an air of desperation; he clumsily clouted Vitaly Petrov after the Renault driver passed him into Turn 12. Up front, though, Vettel had no such trouble. Behind him, Rosberg found his rear tyres going off and so Webber and Vettel closed onto his tail.

With all frontrunners bar Button electing to pit four times, there was a significant

ISTANBUL PARK ROUND 4

DATE: **8 MAY 2011**

Laps: **58** • Distance: **192.257 miles/309.408km** • Weather: **Dry and bright**

Pos	Driver	Team	Result	Stops	Qualifying Time	Grid
1	**Sebastian Vettel**	Red Bull	1h30m17.558s	4	1m25.049s	1
2	**Mark Webber**	Red Bull	1h30m26.365s	4	1m25.454s	2
3	**Fernando Alonso**	Ferrari	1h30m27.633s	4	1m25.851s	5
4	**Lewis Hamilton**	McLaren	1h30m57.790s	4	1m25.595s	4
5	**Nico Rosberg**	Mercedes	1h31m05.097s	4	1m25.574s	3
6	**Jenson Button**	McLaren	1h31m16.989s	3	1m25.982s	6
7	**Nick Heidfeld**	Renault	1h31m18.415s	4	1m26.659s	9
8	**Vitaly Petrov**	Renault	1h31m25.726s	4	1m26.296s	7
9	**Sebastien Buemi**	Toro Rosso	1h31m26.952s	3	1m27.255s	16
10	**Kamui Kobayashi**	Sauber	1h31m35.579s	3	No time	24
11	**Felipe Massa**	Ferrari	1h31m37.381s	4	No time	10
12	**Michael Schumacher**	Mercedes	1h31m43.002s	4	1m26.646s	8
13	**Adrian Sutil**	Force India	57 laps	3	1m27.027s	12
14	**Sergio Pérez**	Sauber	57 laps	4	1m27.244s	15
15	**Rubens Barrichello**	Williams	57 laps	3	1m26.764s	11
16	**Jaime Alguersuari**	Toro Rosso	57 laps	4	1m27.572s	17
17	**Pastor Maldonado**	Williams	57 laps	3	1m27.236s	14
18	**Jarno Trulli**	Lotus	57 laps	3	1m29.673s	19
19	**Heikki Kovalainen**	Lotus	56 laps	3	1m28.780s	18
20	**Jérôme d'Ambrosio**	Virgin	56 laps	2	1m30.445s	23*
21	**Narain Karthikeyan**	HRT	55 laps	3	1m31.564s	22
22	**Vitantonio Liuzzi**	HRT	53 laps	4	1m30.692s	20
R	**Paul di Resta**	Force India	44 laps/loose wheel	4	1m27.145s	13
NS	**Timo Glock**	Virgin	0 laps/gearbox	-	1m30.813s	21

FASTEST LAP: WEBBER, 1M29.703S, 133.416MPH/214.713KPH ON LAP 48 • RACE LEADERS: VETTEL 1-11, 13-58; BUTTON 12
* FIVE-PLACE GRID PENALTY

Vettel leads the pack into the first corner. Game over already - he was in winning form.

amount of place changing, but Vettel's pace was always enough to see him return into the lead and, as Rosberg lost ground, Webber assumed second place with the Ferrari (Alonso) third. Hamilton had to settle for fourth, rueing his failed move on Webber and the battle with Button that took so much out of their tyres.

SPANISH GP

A fourth win from five starts for Sebastian Vettel began to convince rivals that there would be no stopping the German in his attempt to claim a second consecutive drivers' title. Lewis Hamilton, however, at least felt that there might still be hope.

There was one change at the top and this came in qualifying, when Sebastian Vettel was beaten to pole with team-mate Mark Webber outpacing him. However, it was what happened at the start that shocked him more, as Fernando Alonso sent the home fans wild when he passed not only Lewis Hamilton (who started from third), but both Red Bulls, too.

Vettel had at least passed Webber on the run to Turn 1, so slotted in to second. On this circuit that offers next to no scope for overtaking, though, his planned first stint was compromised, even with DRS, as the operating zone for this was not long enough to give the pursuing driver the chance to complete a passing move. The answer was to bring Vettel's first pit stop forward and thus enable him to run at his own pace to be sure of being in the lead after the first round of stops. So it was that Vettel pitted after nine laps. This might have worked in getting him out ahead of Alonso when the Spaniard pitted a lap later, but he came out into traffic. Although Vettel was quick to pass Jenson Button and Felipe Massa, the delay was enough for Alonso to emerge still ahead. One thing it did do, however, was to prove both Red Bull and Ferrari were planning four stops.

Hamilton gained a position as Webber came out behind Button – on tyres more worn as he'd been squeezed at the start and fell from fifth to ninth behind Vitaly Petrov, both Mercedes and Massa's Ferrari. Thereafter, the team put Button onto a three-stop strategy; this delay was enough for Hamilton to grab third. Button then gained places when he passed both Massa and Nico Rosberg.

At the second round of stops, Vettel was first in, but this time around came out into clear air, which was enough for him to be ahead when Alonso re-emerged. Hamilton stayed out four laps longer and lapped fast enough to rejoin second. He then set about

Vettel, whose KERS became intermittent. Hopes of Hamilton getting close enough to use his DRS to pass came to naught because Vettel had so much downforce through the

final corner. Button hauled himself first past Webber, then Alonso to finish third.

The show was great, and lasted all the way to the chequered flag.

Sebastian Vettel notched up his fourth win of 2011, but Hamilton's McLaren was not far behind.

CIRCUIT DE CATALUNYA ROUND 5   DATE: 22 MAY 2011
Laps: 66 • Distance: 190.834 miles/307.118km • Weather: Dry and sunny

Pos	Driver	Team	Result	Stops	Qualifying Time	Grid
1	Sebastian Vettel	Red Bull	1h39m03.301s	4	1m21.181s	2
2	Lewis Hamilton	McLaren	1h39m03.931s	4	1m21.961s	3
3	Jenson Button	McLaren	1h39m38.998s	3	1m21.996s	5
4	Mark Webber	Red Bull	1h39m51.267s	4	1m20.981s	1
5	Fernando Alonso	Ferrari	65 laps	4	1m21.964s	4
6	Michael Schumacher	Mercedes	65 laps	3	No time	10
7	Nico Rosberg	Mercedes	65 laps	3	1m22.599s	7
8	Nick Heidfeld	Renault	65 laps	3	No time	24
9	Sergio Pérez	Sauber	65 laps	3	1m23.367s	12
10	Kamui Kobayashi	Sauber	65 laps	3	1m23.702s	14
11	Vitaly Petrov	Renault	65 laps	3	1m22.471s	6
12	Paul di Resta	Force India	65 laps	3	1m26.126s	16
13	Adrian Sutil	Force India	65 laps	3	1m26.571s	17
14	Sebastien Buemi	Toro Rosso	65 laps	3	1m23.231s	11
15	Pastor Maldonado	Williams	65 laps	4	1m22.952s	9
16	Jaime Alguersuari	Toro Rosso	64 laps	4	1m23.694s	13
17	Rubens Barrichello	Williams	64 laps	4	1m26.910s	19
18	Jarno Trulli	Lotus	64 laps	3	1m26.521s	18
19	Timo Glock	Virgin	63 laps	3	1m27.315s	20
20	Jérôme d'Ambrosio	Virgin	62 laps	3	1m28.556s	23
21	Narain Karthikeyan	HRT	61 laps	3	1m27.908s	22
R	Felipe Massa	Ferrari	58 laps/gearbox	3	1m22.888s	8
R	Heikki Kovalainen	Lotus	48 laps/accident	3	1m25.403s	15
R	Vitantonio Liuzzi	HRT	28 laps/gearbox	1	1m27.809s	21

FASTEST LAP: HAMILTON, 1M26.727S, 120.071MPH/193.236KPH ON LAP 52 • RACE LEADERS: ALONSO 1-10, 12-18; HAMILTON 11, 19-23, 34-35, 48-49; VETTEL 24-33, 36-47, 50-66

96

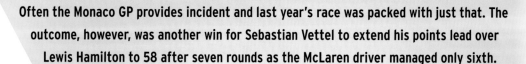

MONACO GP

Often the Monaco GP provides incident and last year's race was packed with just that. The outcome, however, was another win for Sebastian Vettel to extend his points lead over Lewis Hamilton to 58 after seven rounds as the McLaren driver managed only sixth.

Pole at Monaco is more vital than any other circuit: a decent start from there should all but guarantee the polesitter leads into the first corner. So it was with dejection that Sebastian Vettel's rivals acknowledged he had taken pole for the sixth time in 2011. Most upset was Lewis Hamilton, who had not set a banker time in the final session after being fastest in Q1 and Q2 and was caught out when Sergio Pérez crashed, leaving him with no time set.

The Mexican driver had lost control on the slope down from the tunnel to the harbourfront and hit the barriers sideways and hard at the chicane. Concussed, he was kept in hospital for observation until the Monday.

Vettel was duly first into Ste Devote as Jenson Button held off Fernando Alonso for second, with Mark Webber tucking into fourth. Even using KERS in conjunction with DRS proved of little use since the circuit does not offer the space for passing. Button was first to pit and Vettel followed in the next lap, but a misheard signal led to the readied supersoft tyres being swapped for softs; enough time was lost to send him out behind Button, who was on the supersofts and pulling away. Worse still, Webber came in on the same lap and no tyres were ready, with the delay dropping him to fourteenth.

Felipe Massa then clipped Webber, bent a wing and crashed in the tunnel, bringing out the safety car. Button, who'd pulled 15s clear and just pitted for a third set of supersofts, would have been cursing for he still had to pit for the harder tyre. With Vettel hanging on from Alonso and Button, all was set for an intriguing finish when, with nine laps to go, the red flag was flown. Vitaly Petrov had crashed at Piscine after Adrian Sutil hit the barriers and slowed. Hamilton lifted to avoid him but was hit by Jaime Alguersuari, who veered into Petrov's path. This meant everyone was able to fit fresh tyres and

MONACO ROUND 6

DATE: **29 MAY 2011**

Laps: **78** • Distance: **161.884 miles/260.528km** • Weather: **Sunny and dry**

Pos	Driver	Team	Result	Stops	Qualifying Time	Grid
1	Sebastian Vettel	Red Bull	2h09m38.373s	1	1m13.556s	1
2	Fernando Alonso	Ferrari	2h09m39.511s	2	1m14.483s	4
3	Jenson Button	McLaren	2m09m40.751s	3	1m13.997s	2
4	Mark Webber	Red Bull	2h10m01.474s	2	1m14.019s	3
5	Kamui Kobayashi	Sauber	2h10m05.289s	1	1m15.973s	12
6	Lewis Hamilton	McLaren	2h10m25.583s*	3	No time	9
7	Adrian Sutil	Force India	77 laps	2	1m16.121s	14
8	Nick Heidfeld	Renault	77 laps	2	1m16.214s	15
9	Rubens Barrichello	Williams	77 laps	2	1m15.826s	11
10	Sebastien Buemi	Toro Rosso	77 laps	2	1m16.300s	16
11	Nico Rosberg	Mercedes	76 laps	3	1m15.766s	7
12	Paul di Resta	Force India	76 laps	3	1m16.118s	13
13	Jarno Trulli	Lotus	76 laps	2	1m17.381s	18
14	Heikki Kovalainen	Lotus	76 laps	2	1m17.343s	17
15	Jérôme d'Ambrosio	Virgin	75 laps	2	1m18.736s	21
16	Vitantonio Liuzzi	HRT	75 laps	1	No time	23
17	Narain Karthikeyan	HRT	74 laps	2	No time	22
18	Pastor Maldonado	Williams	73 laps/accident	2	1m16.528s	8
R	Vitaly Petrov	Renault	67 laps/accident	1	1m15.815	10
R	Jaime Alguersuari	Toro Rosso	66 laps/accident	2	1m17.820s	19
R	Felipe Massa	Ferrari	32 laps/accident	1	1m14.877s	6
R	Michael Schumacher	Mercedes	32 laps/airbox fire	1	1m14.682s	5
R	Timo Glock	Virgin	30 laps/suspension	1	1m17.914s	20
NS	Sergio Pérez	Sauber	-/driver injury	-	1m15.482s	-

FASTEST LAP: WEBBER, 1M16.234S, 98.008MPH/157.729KPH ON LAP 78 • RACE LEADERS: VETTEL 1-15, 33-78; ALONSO 16; BUTTON 17-32
* TWENTY-SECOND PENALTY FOR CAUSING AN AVOIDABLE ACCIDENT

The safety car came out after Felipe Massa clipped Mark Webber and crashed in the tunnel.

so Vettel could rid himself of those he had been using for 53 laps to defend his lead from Alonso and Button.

Webber passed Kamui Kobayashi for fourth, but Hamilton hit Pastor Maldonado at Ste Devote as he passed him for sixth. Although given a 20s penalty, this failed to alter his position.

Jenson Button took four hours to complete a rain-struck Canadian GP. It was more than double the norm and he dropped to last, but a scintillating drive that displayed all his skills in adapting to changing conditions brought him the most unlikely of wins.

The spectators might have been wet, but they were thrilled by one of the most remarkable drives in F1 history. It was produced by Jenson Button and included more incident than most drivers fit into a season. Indeed, he qualified seventh, with Sebastian Vettel on pole ahead of Ferrari's Fernando Alonso and Felipe Massa.

Vettel led away on a wet track, but Lewis Hamilton dived inside Mark Webber and spun him around, allowing Nico Rosberg, Button and Michael Schumacher past. Schumacher and Hamilton demoted Button further around the lap, then Hamilton tried to pass Schumacher at the hairpin and went wide to allow Button back through. A few laps later, Button was slow out of the chicane so Hamilton jinked left as they accelerated, but Button kept coming across. Hamilton clipped the pitwall and bounced into his sidepod. As Button drove to the pits to change from rain tyres to intermediates, Hamilton was out.

Button was subsequently hit with a drive-through penalty for going too fast behind the safety car. Once served, he started to fly on his inters while others pitted for the same just as the rain began to fall, leaving Vettel leading from Massa and Kamui Kobayashi. Then, as the rain became heavier and Button pitted for wets, the safety car came out. Six laps later, the race was stopped because of too much sitting water.

After a two-hour delay, the race restarted behind the safety car. Schumacher went for inters, while Button did the same on the next lap. Alonso rejoined in front of Button, who tried to pass him at Turn 4, but they touched to leave the Ferrari stuck on a kerb. This brought out the safety car and gave Vettel the opportunity to change to inters as Button limped pitward with a puncture. What happened next was remarkable as Button passed car after car on a greasy track before following Webber's lead to change to dry tyres. Even though others also fitted dries, he was the man on the

move and was given a helping hand when Kobayashi and Nick Heidfeld clashed and brought out the safety car.

Restarting fourth, Button passed Webber

and then Schumacher on the next lap to leave only Vettel, who was 3s ahead. With a lap to go, however, Button got onto his tail, Vettel slipped at Turn 6 and Button was by.

Jenson Button proved the master of proceedings in the wet to track and pass Vettel to win.

MONTREAL ROUND 7

DATE: **12 JUNE 2011**

Laps: **70** • Distance: **189.691 miles/305.279km** • Weather: **Wet, then drying**

Pos	Driver	Team	Result	Stops	Qualifying Time	Grid
1	**Jenson Button**	McLaren	4h04m39.537s	6	1m13.838s	7
2	**Sebastian Vettel**	Red Bull	4h04m42.246s	3	1m13.014s	1
3	**Mark Webber**	Red Bull	4h04m53.365s	3	1m13.429s	4
4	**Michael Schumacher**	Mercedes	4h04m53.756s	4	1m13.864s	8
5	**Vitaly Petrov**	Renault	4h04m59.932s	2	1m14.085s	10
6	**Felipe Massa**	Ferrari	4h05m12.762s	4	1m13.217s	3
7	**Kamui Kobayashi**	Sauber	4h05m12.807s	2	1m15.285s	13
8	**Jaime Alguersuari**	Toro Rosso	4h05m15.501s	3	1m16.294s	18
9	**Rubens Barrichello**	Williams	4h05m24.654s	4	1m15.361s	16
10	**Sebastien Buemi**	Toro Rosso	4h05m26.593s	4	1m15.334s	15
11	**Nico Rosberg**	Mercedes	4h05m29.991s	4	1m13.814s	6
12	**Pedro de la Rosa**	Sauber	4h05m43.144s	2	1m15.587s	17
13	**Vitantonio Liuzzi**	HRT	69 laps	3	1m18.424s	21
14	**Jérôme d'Ambrosio**	Virgin	69 laps	5	1m19.414s	24
15	**Timo Glock**	Virgin	69 laps	2	1m18.537s	22
16	**Jarno Trulli**	Lotus	69 laps	4	1m16.745s	19
17	**Narain Karthikeyan**	HRT	69 laps	2	1m18.574s	23
18	**Paul di Resta**	Force India	67 laps/accident	4	1m14.752s	11
R	**Pastor Maldonado**	Williams	61 laps/accident	5	1m15.043s	12
R	**Nick Heidfeld**	Renault	55 laps/accident	2	1m14.062s	9
R	**Adrian Sutil**	Force India	49 laps/suspension	4	1m15.287s	14
R	**Fernando Alonso**	Ferrari	36 laps/accident	3	1m13.199s	2
R	**Heikki Kovalainen**	Lotus	28 laps/driveshaft	1	1m16.786s	20
R	**Lewis Hamilton**	McLaren	7 laps/accident damage	0	1m13.565s	5
NS	**Sergio Pérez**	Sauber	Driver unwell	-	No time	-

FASTEST LAP: BUTTON, 1M16.956S, 126.767MPH/204.012KPH ON LAP 69 • RACE LEADERS: VETTEL 1-19, 21-69; MASSA 20; BUTTON 70

EUROPEAN GP

After the drama and excitement of the Canadian GP, this proved a let-down as all races on the Valencia street circuit have been to date. Sebastian Vettel qualified on pole for the seventh time in eight races to secure his sixth victory.

There is a vital ingredient missing from races on Valencia's circuit that snakes around the docks: overtaking. Sure, there are usually blue skies and sunshine but it lacks the glamour of Monaco and the opportunity for drivers to display their skills in combat. So, when Vettel qualified on pole yet again, this hampered rivals' chances of making a dent in his vast points lead. Team-mate Mark Webber started second on the grid and though Vettel was none too quick off the mark, was unable to make a pass into Turn 2, the first likely passing place, so that was that.

That is not to say the German did not come under pressure but he was safely in the lead throughout. Indeed, he led every lap bar the 14th, when Felipe Massa held the lead while Vettel made the first of three pit stops.

Lewis Hamilton had lined up third, but got bogged down at the start and this let both Ferraris past, with Massa powering past Fernando Alonso. Naturally, the Spaniard refused to lose face in front of the home fans and so seized the chance to re-pass Massa when his team-mate lost momentum after a failed move on Webber. As Vettel broke clear, Alonso obviously had the appetite for a fight and put Webber under pressure, though getting past was another matter. Behind them, Massa fell away but was able to resist all that Hamilton threw at him, with Jenson Button some way adrift after losing time getting past Nico Rosberg, who passed him at the start.

Although most teams had hoped to run a two-stop strategy, tyre wear on the day was such that three stops were clearly required. Vettel and his pursuers all pitted and rejoined, with Hamilton's early stop and superior pace on new rubber taking him ahead of Massa for fourth. Two rounds of pit stops later, the order was still the same and remained so to the flag.

Jaime Alguersuari was one of the few participants to produce a notable drive

VALENCIA ROUND 8

DATE: **26 JUNE 2011**

Laps: **57** • Distance: **191.340 miles/307.932km** • Weather: **Hot and sunny**

Pos	Driver	Team	Result	Stops	Qualifying Time	Grid
1	Sebastian Vettel	Red Bull	1h39m36.169s	3	1m36.975s	1
2	Fernando Alonso	Ferrari	1h39m47.060s	3	1m37.454s	4
3	Mark Webber	Red Bull	1h40m03.424s	3	1m37.163s	2
4	Lewis Hamilton	McLaren	1h40m22.359s	3	1m37.380s	3
5	Felipe Massa	Ferrari	1h40m27.874s	3	1m37.535s	5
6	Jenson Button	McLaren	1h40m36.234s	3	1m37.645s	6
7	Nico Rosberg	Mercedes	1h41m14.259s	3	1m38.231s	7
8	Jaime Alguersuari	Toro Rosso	56 laps	2	1m40.232s	18
9	Adrian Sutil	Force India	56 laps	3	No time	10
10	Nick Heidfeld	Renault	56 laps	3	No time	9
11	Sergio Pérez	Sauber	56 laps	1	1m39.657s	16
12	Rubens Barrichello	Williams	56 laps	3	1m39.489s	13
13	Sebastien Buemi	Toro Rosso	56 laps	3	1m39.711s	17
14	Paul di Resta	Force India	56 laps	3	1m39.422s	12
15	Vitaly Petrov	Renault	56 laps	3	1m39.068s	11
16	Kamui Kobayashi	Sauber	56 laps	2	1m39.525s	14
17	Michael Schumacher	Mercedes	56 laps	3	1m38.240s	8
18	Pastor Maldonado	Williams	56 laps	3	1m39.645s	15
19	Heikki Kovalainen	Lotus	55 laps	3	1m41.664s	19
20	Jarno Trulli	Lotus	55 laps	2	1m42.234s	20
21	Timo Glock	Virgin	55 laps	2	1m42.553s	21
22	Jérôme d'Ambrosio	Virgin	55 laps	2	1m43.735s	23
23	Vitantonio Liuzzi	HRT	54 laps	3	1m43.584s	22
24	Narain Karthikeyan	HRT	54 laps	3	1m44.363s	24

FASTEST LAP: VETTEL, 1M41.852S, 119.020MPH/191.544KPH ON LAP 53 • RACE LEADERS: VETTEL 1-13, 15-57; MASSA 14

Qualifying on pole at Valencia remains a huge advantage and set Vettel up for another win.

as he delighted the home crowd by using a two-stop strategy to help him drive his Toro Rosso from eighteenth on the grid to eighth as the first of the lapped runners.

Remarkably, especially on a street circuit, every one of the 24 starters made it to the finish, albeit with the HRTs three laps down at the finish.

Conditions in Montreal could hardly have been worse for teams and spectators alike. With stoppages and safety car periods, the Grand Prix took just over four hours from start to finish. This is Sergio Pérez's Sauber waiting on the starting grid.

Ferrari's form fluctuated in the early rounds but on the 60th anniversary of its
first victory in a World Championship grand prix – fittingly here at Silverstone –
Fernando Alonso was in fighting form and put one over the pace-setting Red Bulls.

Rain has affected grands prix at Silverstone before but this occasion proved a welcome intervention as it offered those not driving Red Bulls a chance to topple the dark-blue cars.

Mark Webber had outpaced Sebastian Vettel in final qualifying but the German was faster away when the race began on a damp track, for the first time powering off from a starting grid in front of the new pit building rather than the old one before Copse. Luckily there was no more rain and so Fernando Alonso, Jenson Button, Felipe Massa et al. were faced with ever less spray as the early laps ticked by. Button lost ground, however, being passed by Massa and then team-mate Lewis Hamilton, who set about Massa as if he had completely forgotten that McLaren struggled for grip through qualifying.

Conversely, a new rear wing and revised bodywork worked wonders for Ferrari and Alonso closed in on Webber for second. At this point Michael Schumacher clouted Kamui Kobayashi's Sauber. Having damaged his nose, he pitted and elected to have slicks fitted. Others then decided that they too would fit them. Massa proved the main loser in this sequence, being passed by Hamilton when in the pits and Button after rejoining.

Hamilton caught and passed Alonso at Copse but Alonso returned to third with a good move into Brooklands, then making Webber his next target. Unfortunately for the Australian, his second stop was slowed by a sticking wheelnut, dropping him behind Alonso. Vettel came in from the lead and Red Bull's fortunes took a further dive as the rear jack broke, gifting Alonso the lead.

Though straight onto Alonso's tail, Hamilton was consuming too much fuel and had to back off, bottling up Vettel as Alonso pulled clear. Red Bull deflected in making Vettel come in early for his third stop to emerge ahead of Hamilton. Meanwhile, Button's hopes of jumping Webber were thwarted when his right front wheel was not attached before he left the pits.

Fernando Alonso and Ferrari made the most of rule changes and incidents to come out on top.

SILVERSTONE ROUND 9

DATE: 10 JULY 2011

Laps: 52 • Distance: 190.271 miles/306.212km • Weather: **Wet start, then dry**

Pos	Driver	Team	Result	Stops	Qualifying Time	Grid
1	**Fernando Alonso**	Ferrari	1h28m41.196s	3	1m30.516s	3
2	**Sebastian Vettel**	Red Bull	1h28m57.707s	3	1m30.431s	2
3	**Mark Webber**	Red Bull	1h28m58.143s	3	1m30.399s	1
4	**Lewis Hamilton**	McLaren	1h29m10.182s	3	1m32.376s	10
5	**Felipe Massa**	Ferrari	1h29m10.206s	3	1m31.124s	4
6	**Nico Rosberg**	Mercedes	1h29m41.861s	2	1m32.209s	9
7	**Sergio Pérez**	Sauber	1h29m46.786s	2	1m32.624s	12
8	**Nick Heidfeld**	Renault	1h29m56.738s	2	1m33.805s	16
9	**Michael Schumacher**	Mercedes	1h29m59.108s	2	1m32.656s	13
10	**Jaime Alguersuari**	Toro Rosso	1h30m00.304s	2	1m35.245s	18
11	**Adrian Sutil**	Force India	1h30m00.908s	3	1m32.617s	11
12	**Vitaly Petrov**	Renault	1m30m01.877s	2	1m32.734s	14
13	**Rubens Barrichello**	Williams	51 laps	2	1m33.119s	15
14	**Pastor Maldonado**	Williams	51 laps	3	1m31.933s	7
15	**Paul di Resta**	Force India	51 laps	3	1m31.929s	6
16	**Timo Glock**	Virgin	50 laps	2	1m36.203s	20
17	**Jérôme d'Ambrosio**	Virgin	50 laps	2	1m37.154s	22
18	**Vitantonio Liuzzi**	HRT	50 laps	2	1m37.484s	23
19	**Daniel Ricciardo**	HRT	49 laps	2	1m38.059s	24
R	**Jenson Button**	McLaren	39 laps/loose wheel	3	1m31.898s	5
R	**Sebastien Buemi**	Toro Rosso	25 laps/puncture	2	1m35.749s	19
R	**Kamui Kobayashi**	Sauber	23 laps/oil leak	1	1m32.128s	8
R	**Jarno Trulli**	Lotus	10 laps/oil leak	0	1m36.456s	21
R	**Heikki Kovalainen**	Lotus	2 laps/gearbox	0	1m34.821s	17

FASTEST LAP: ALONSO, 1M34.908S, 138.854MPH/223.464KPH ON LAP 41 • RACE LEADERS: VETTEL 1-27; ALONSO 28-52

Still in fuel-saving mode, Hamilton was forced to cede third to Webber and only a remarkable piece of driving through Club kept Massa behind him at the finish. After qualifying sixth, rookie Paul di Resta's hopes of a strong result were ruined in finding team-mate Adrian Sutil in his pit with a puncture only to end up fifteenth.

GERMAN GP

After disappointments at Silverstone, Lewis Hamilton put McLaren firmly back on the map with an immaculate drive at the Nürburgring on a cool day when the rear tyres of his MP4-26 refused to wear out at the same rate as before.

After a welter of criticism for overly aggressive driving, Hamilton needed this win to put him back into the championship mix. That is to say the mix for the quartet of drivers fighting over second place behind runaway leader Sebastian Vettel. Indeed, even on an off-day the reigning champion still managed to collect 10 points for fourth place to leave him with a lead of 77 points after 10 of 19 rounds.

Placing his McLaren second on the grid, 0.055s behind Mark Webber, was seen as being much about Hamilton driving an inspired lap as team-mate Jenson Button's best was 1.154s slower, and seventh.

Assuming his car might not be so fast as the Red Bulls or Ferraris in race trim, Hamilton wanted a strong start – and that is what he got, taking the lead after Webber was slow away. As the Ferrari attacked, Vettel had to fight hard to hold on to third. He failed in this attempt, though, as Fernando Alonso forced his way ahead at tight Turn 4 on lap 2.

For once, Vettel appeared to have no answers as Hamilton, Webber and Fernando Alonso all left him in their wake. Then Alonso made a mistake on lap 2, while Vettel regained third. Delayed by the Red Bull, Alonso fought back on lap 8, passing him into Turn 1. Vettel then had a big moment at Turn 10, one he was lucky to correct.

Webber, meanwhile, had no such concerns and closed in on Hamilton. Getting past was another matter until Hamilton slipped up at the chicane. Webber dived past, but Hamilton had a better exit from the final corner to re-pass him into Turn 1. As they fought, Alonso closed in to put Webber under pressure but in pitting first, Webber led after the first round of pit stops. At the second round of stops, Hamilton took the lead. A lap later, Alonso came in and then pulled back out just in front of Hamilton. However, the McLaren driver was determined to get past and did so in Turn 3.

NÜRBURGRING ROUND 10

DATE: 24 JULY 2011

Laps: 60 • **Distance:** 191.940 miles/308.898km • **Weather: Overcast, but dry**

Pos	Driver	Team	Result	Stops	Qualifying Time	Grid
1	**Lewis Hamilton**	McLaren	1h37m30.334s	3	1m30.134s	2
2	**Fernando Alonso**	Ferrari	1h37m34.314s	3	1m30.442s	4
3	**Mark Webber**	Red Bull	1h37m40.112s	3	1m30.079s	1
4	**Sebastian Vettel**	Red Bull	1h38m18.255s	3	1m30.216s	3
5	**Felipe Massa**	Ferrari	1h38m22.586s	3	1m30.910s	5
6	**Adrian Sutil**	Force India	1h38m56.542s	2	1m32.010s	8
7	**Nico Rosberg**	Mercedes	59 laps	3	1m31.263s	6
8	**Michael Schumacher**	Mercedes	59 laps	3	1m32.482s	10
9	**Kamui Kobayashi**	Sauber	59 laps	2	1m33.786s	17
10	**Vitaly Petrov**	Renault	59 laps	2	1m32.187s	9
11	**Sergio Pérez**	Sauber	59 laps	2	1m33.176s	15
12	**Jaime Alguersuari**	Toro Rosso	59 laps	2	1m33.698s	16
13	**Paul di Resta**	Force India	59 laps	2	1m32.560s	12
14	**Pastor Maldonado**	Williams	59 laps	2	1m32.635s	13
15	**Sebastien Buemi**	Toro Rosso	59 laps	2	No time	24
16	**Heikki Kovalainen**	Lotus	58 laps	3	1m35.599s	18
17	**Timo Glock**	Virgin	57 laps	2	1m36.400s	19
18	**Jérôme d'Ambrosio**	Virgin	57 laps	2	1m36.641s	21
19	**Daniel Ricciardo**	HRT	57 laps	2	1m37.036s	22
20	**Karun Chandhok**	Lotus	56 laps	3	1m36.422s	20
R	**Vitantonio Liuzzi**	HRT	37 laps/electronics	1	1m37.011s	23*
R	**Jenson Button**	McLaren	35 laps/hydraulics	1	1m31.288s	7
R	**Rubens Barrichello**	Williams	16 laps/engine	0	1m33.043s	14
R	**Nick Heidfeld**	Renault	9 laps/accident	0	1m32.215s	11

FASTEST LAP: HAMILTON, 1M34.302S, 122.119MPH/196.532KPH ON LAP 59 • **RACE LEADERS:** HAMILTON 1–11, 13–16, 30, 33–50, 57–60; WEBBER 12, 17–29, 54–56; ALONSO 31–32, 51–53
* FIVE-PLACE GRID PENALTY FOR GEARBOX CHANGE

Lewis Hamilton is mobbed by McLaren team members after putting his season back on track.

The timing of their third stops was critical and Hamilton got it right after a series of fast laps to make his and still emerge ahead of Alonso to go on and win the race. Webber was slightly adrift in third, while a further 38s back, Vettel made it past Massa for fourth, when both pitted with two laps to go.

Jenson Button has great affection for the Hungaroring as it was here that he scored his very first grand prix win in 2006. This visit marked his 200th grand prix start and he celebrated in style by mastering changing conditions for his eleventh F1 victory.

Apart from the first half of his extraordinary title-winning season with Brawn GP in 2009, Jenson Button has not exactly made a habit of planting his car on pole and racing off, untroubled, to victory. Instead, crafty wins of great subtlety on a wet or drying track have been his hallmark and this one was no different.

Button began the race from third on the grid behind Sebastian Vettel and his own McLaren team-mate Lewis Hamilton. Suitably for him, the track was damp at the start and although he got alongside Hamilton out of Turn 1, he failed to advance from there. A few laps in, Hamilton did gain ground when he passed Vettel for the lead into Turn 2, then pulled away. It might have been his day but as light rain grew heavier, he spun two-thirds of the way through the race and almost clouted Paul di Resta's Force India, while booting his car back to face in the right direction. At that same moment, Button flashed past into the lead.

Hamilton's team-mate moved past Vettel into second on his second stint, then closed in as Hamilton's own car ate its front-left tyre at a greater rate, moving on to a four-stop strategy. Being smoother, Button was able to remain on a three-stop run, which started to yield dividends as Hamilton pressed on through traffic, trying to build up a large enough gap to enable him to make that extra stop without falling behind Button.

Having lost a lead of more than 5s, Hamilton was determined to get the place back, which he did by using his DRS on the start/finish straight, going on to lap 51 in an entertaining battle. The pair then swapped places a couple of times more before Hamilton pitted on lap 52 and had intermediate tyres fitted. But the rain eased and like Mark Webber, he too had to pit once more for slicks.

Hamilton was then hit with a drive-through penalty for the way he almost put

Jenson Button continued his habit of winning races run in the most difficult of conditions.

HUNGARORING ROUND 11

DATE: **31 JULY 2011**

Laps: **70** • Distance: **190.340 miles/306.323km** • Weather: **Wet, then dry**

Pos	Driver	Team	Result	Stops	Qualifying Time	Grid
1	**Jenson Button**	McLaren	1h46m42.337s	3	1m20.024s	3
2	**Sebastian Vettel**	Red Bull	1h46m45.925s	3	1m19.815s	1
3	**Fernando Alonso**	Ferrari	1h47m02.156s	4	1m20.365s	5
4	**Lewis Hamilton**	McLaren	1h47m30.675s	5	1m19.978s	2
5	**Mark Webber**	Red Bull	1h47m32.079s	5	1m20.474s	6
6	**Felipe Massa**	Ferrari	1h48m05.513s	4	1m20.350s	4
7	**Paul di Resta**	Force India	69 laps	3	1m22.256s	11
8	**Sebastien Buemi**	Toro Rosso	69 laps	3	1m24.070s	23*
9	**Nico Rosberg**	Mercedes	69 laps	4	1m21.098s	7
10	**Jaime Alguersuari**	Toro Rosso	69 laps	3	1m22.979s	16
11	**Kamui Kobayashi**	Sauber	69 laps	3	1m22.435s	13
12	**Vitaly Petrov**	Renault	69 laps	4	1m22.284s	12
13	**Rubens Barrichello**	Williams	68 laps	5	1m22.684s	15
14	**Adrian Sutil**	Force India	68 laps	4	1m21.445s	8
15	**Sergio Pérez**	Sauber	68 laps	3	No time	10
16	**Pastor Maldonado**	Williams	68 laps	4	No time	17
17	**Timo Glock**	Virgin	66 laps	3	1m26.294s	20
18	**Daniel Ricciardo**	HRT	66 laps	3	1m26.479s	22
19	**Jérôme d'Ambrosio**	Virgin	65 laps	4	1m26.510s	24
20	**Vitantonio Liuzzi**	HRT	65 laps	5	1m26.323s	21
R	**Heikki Kovalainen**	Lotus	55 laps/water leak	5	1m24.362s	18
R	**Michael Schumacher**	Mercedes	26 laps/gearbox	2	1m21.907s	9
R	**Nick Heidfeld**	Renault	23 laps/engine fire	2	1m22.470s	14
R	**Jarno Trulli**	Lotus	17 laps/water leak	1	1m24.534s	19

FASTEST LAP: MASSA, 1M23.415S, 117.490MPH/189.082KPH ON LAP 61 • RACE LEADERS: VETTEL 1-4, 28; HAMILTON 5-26, 29-40, 43-46, 51; BUTTON 27, 41-42, 47-50, 52-70
* FIVE-PLACE GRID PENALTY FOR CAUSING CONTACT IN GERMAN GP

di Resta off as he rejoined from his spin. Not only had the race now become Button's but Hamilton fell from the podium reckoning to make way for the Red Bull duo, Vettel ahead of Webber as he tumbled to fourth. It could have been Hamilton's day, but Button's greater caution saved his tyres and he deservedly reaped the reward.

BELGIAN GP

This was a proper race on a proper circuit, with incident and lead changes aplenty when the drivers – especially the Red Bull Racing ones – were forced to cope with blistering. At flagfall, Sebastian Vettel recorded his seventh win of the year.

It had been predicted this would be one of a handful of circuits on which Red Bull's rivals might stand a chance as its long, fast corners were not best suited to its RB7 – tyre wear had been a problem at the Nürburgring. Over the short blasts required in qualifying, though, Sebastian Vettel pipped McLaren's Lewis Hamilton to take pole on a drying circuit. However, the race was always likely to be more of a challenge for Vettel and Mark Webber, with tyre degradation a concern.

There was a great deal of first-corner action triggered by Renault new boy Bruno Senna, who outbraked himself and hit Jaime Alguersuari's Toro Rosso into Fernando Alonso's path. Further back, Timo Glock hit Paul di Resta, with Jenson Button receiving damage in the mêlée while the Lotus duo collided.

Webber's anti-stall had kicked in and left him in the pack but he did well to avoid the collisions as Vettel led out of the hairpin, chased by fast-starting Nico Rosberg. The Mercedes took the lead on the run-up to Les Combes, with Felipe Massa third ahead of Hamilton and Alonso to stay there for two laps before Vettel assumed control into Les Combes. Vettel's front tyres were blistering, though, and Webber, running eighth, elected to pit and swap his option tyres for harder primes. Vettel stayed out for another two laps before ceding the lead to Rosberg when he pitted before being passed by both Alonso and Hamilton.

The move of the race came after Alonso pitted from the lead, with Webber passing him into Eau Rouge after the Spaniard rejoined. This left Hamilton out front, though he made a mistake after pitting when he passed Kamui Kobayashi into Les Combes but pulled left across and his McLaren was turned across the Sauber's nose before thumping into the barriers. This brought out the safety car and Vettel seized the moment, pitting, which gained him track position so that he was in place to pass Webber once the

SPA-FRANCORCHAMPS ROUND 12 DATE: 27 AUGUST 2011
Laps: 44 • Distance: 191.488 miles/308.171km • Weather: Overcast and cool

Pos	Driver	Team	Result	Stops	Qualifying Time	Grid
1	Sebastian Vettel	Red Bull	1h26m44.893s	3	1m48.298s	1
2	Mark Webber	Red Bull	1h26m48.634s	2	1m49.376s	3
3	Jenson Button	McLaren	1h26m54.562s	3	2m05.150s	13
4	Fernando Alonso	Ferrari	1h26m57.915s	2	1m51.251s	8
5	Michael Schumacher	Mercedes	1h27m32.357s	3	No time	24
6	Nico Rosberg	Mercedes	1h27m33.567s	2	1m50.552s	5
7	Adrian Sutil	Force India	1h27m44.606s	2	2m07.777s	15
8	Felipe Massa	Ferrari	1h27m50.969s	3	1m50.256s	4
9	Vitaly Petrov	Renault	1h27m56.810s	2	1m52.303s	10
10	Pastor Maldonado	Williams	1h28m02.508s	2	2m08.106s	21*
11	Paul di Resta	Force India	1h28m08.887s	2	2m07.758s	17
12	Kamui Kobayashi	Sauber	1h28m16.869s	2	2m04.757s	12
13	Bruno Senna	Renault	1h28m17.878s	3	1m51.121s	7
14	Jarno Trulli	Lotus	43 laps	2	2m08.773s	18
15	Heikki Kovalainen	Lotus	43 laps	3	2m08.354s	16
16	Rubens Barrichello	Williams	43 laps	3	2m07.349s	14
17	Jérôme d'Ambrosio	Virgin	43 laps	2	2m11.601s	20
18	Timo Glock	Virgin	43 laps	4	2m09.566s	19
19	Vitantonio Liuzzi	HRT	43 laps	2	2m11.616s	22
R	Sergio Pérez	Sauber	27 laps/damage	3	1m51.374s	9
R	Daniel Ricciardo	HRT	13 laps/vibration	1	2m13.077s	23
R	Lewis Hamilton	McLaren	12 laps/accident	1	1m48.730s	2
R	Sebastien Buemi	Toro Rosso	6 laps/rear wing	0	2m04.692s	11
R	Jaime Alguersuari	Toro Rosso	1 lap/accident	0	1m50.773s	6

FASTEST LAP: WEBBER, 1M49.883S, 142.583MPH/229.466KPH ON LAP 33 • RACE LEADERS: ROSBERG 1-2, 6, VETTEL 3-5, 11-13, 18-30, 32-44, ALONSO 7, 14-17, HAMILTON 8-10, BUTTON 31
* FIVE-PLACE GRID PENALTY FOR CAUSING AN AVOIDABLE ACCIDENT

Mercedes GP's Nico Rosberg challenges Vettel on the climb to Les Combes on the first lap.

safety car withdrew. A lap later, he passed Alonso for the lead and the race was won.

With the Ferraris struggling on the harder tyre, Button – who'd had to pit early for a new nose – was flying on the softer tyres. He passed Massa for fifth on lap 24, then Rosberg. Finally, on lap 42, he passed Alonso but ran out of time to catch Webber.

This was a race in which Red Bull Racing thought they could be toppled, with McLaren's cars better suited to Monza. But no one told Sebastian Vettel that as he raced clear to win from a delayed Jenson Button and moved to the brink of his second title.

Although before arriving at Monza it was felt that the high-speed bends might make the Red Bull RB7s suffer severe tyre wear as the race progressed, Vettel achieved what he could expect and claimed pole. His margin of nigh on half a second over Lewis Hamilton's McLaren was truly impressive.

At the start, Fernando Alonso made a getaway every bit as good as the one made to the Spanish GP to pull level with Vettel before diving down the inside line into the right-hander. However, passage through this tricky chicane was not a smooth ride for those behind as Vitantonio Liuzzi became overambitious from last grid position only to find himself edged wide and he gyrated down the grass before slamming into cars that were already setting themselves up for the second part of the chicane. As the HRT hit Vitaly Petrov's Renault, so others behind were forced to take evasive action but Liuzzi, Nico Rosberg and Petrov were out.

The safety car was deployed and protected Alonso's lead but after this withdrew, almost immediately the Spaniard lost out to Vettel, with the German passing the Ferrari driver around the outside at Curva Biassono.

Hamilton, running third, was caught napping at the restart and lost third place to Michael Schumacher. This ruined Hamilton's race for he could not get back past, failing, even with DRS deployed, to match the Mercedes down the straights.

On lap 5, Mark Webber was over-optimistic into the first chicane as he tried to pass Felipe Massa but hit a kerb when he backed out and tipped the Ferrari into a spin. Driving back to the pits as fast as he dared, Webber was pitched straight on at Parabolica after his broken wing folded under the car. This clash gave Button – slow away at the start due to a clutch problem – the chance to move ahead of both. He then set off after the Schumacher/ Hamilton tussle, with Schumacher becoming increasingly desperate in holding Hamilton back and being warned by his team to allow

Monza was scene of Vettel's first win. Victory this time put him close to a second title.

MONZA ROUND 13

DATE: **11 SEPTEMBER 2011**

Laps: **53** • Distance: **190.800 miles/307.063km** • Weather: **Dry and bright**

Pos	Driver	Team	Result	Stops	Qualifying Time	Grid
1	**Sebastian Vettel**	Red Bull	1h20m46.172s	2	1m22.275s	1
2	**Jenson Button**	McLaren	1h20m55.762s	2	1m22.777s	3
3	**Fernando Alonso**	Ferrari	1h21m03.081s	2	1m22.841s	4
4	**Lewis Hamilton**	McLaren	1h21m03.589s	2	1m22.725s	2
5	**Michael Schumacher**	Mercedes	1h21m18.849s	2	1m23.777s	8
6	**Felipe Massa**	Ferrari	1h21m29.165s	2	1m23.188s	6
7	**Jaime Alguersuari**	Toro Rosso	52 laps	2	1m25.334s	18
8	**Paul di Resta**	Force India	52 laps	2	1m24.163s	11
9	**Bruno Senna**	Renault	52 laps	3	No time	10
10	**Sebastian Buemi**	Toro Rosso	52 laps	2	1m24.932s	16
11	**Pastor Maldonado**	Williams	52 laps	2	1m24.726s	14
12	**Rubens Barrichello**	Williams	52 laps	2	1m24.648s	13
13	**Heikki Kovalainen**	Lotus	51 laps	2	1m27.184s	20
14	**Jarno Trulli**	Lotus	51 laps	2	1m26.647s	19
15	**Timo Glock**	Virgin	51 laps	2	1m27.591s	21
NC	**Daniel Ricciardo**	HRT	39 laps	2	1m28.054s	23
R	**Sergio Pérez**	Sauber	32 laps/gearbox	0	1m24.845s	15
R	**Kamui Kobayashi**	Sauber	21 laps/gearbox	2	1m25.065s	17
R	**Adrian Sutil**	Force India	9 laps/hydraulics	0	1m24.209s	12
R	**Mark Webber**	Red Bull	4 laps/accident	0	1m22.972s	5
R	**Jérôme d'Ambrosio**	Virgin	1 lap/gearbox	0	1m27.609s22	
R	**Vitaly Petrov**	Renault	0 laps/accident	0	1m23.530s	7
R	**Nico Rosberg**	Mercedes	0 laps/accident	0	1m24.477s	9
R	**Vitantonio Liuzzi**	HRT	0 laps/accident	0	1m28.231s	24

FASTEST LAP: HAMILTON, 1M26.187S, 150.371MPH/241.999KPH ON LAP 52 • RACE LEADERS: ALONSO 1-4; VETTEL 5-53

space. Then, on lap 16, when Hamilton had just been chopped, Button dived past his team-mate at the second chicane and then Schumacher, too, at Ascari. This became

second on lap 36, when he passed Alonso at Curva Biassono.

Although Button closed in on Vettel, the German coasted to his eighth win of 2011.

SINGAPORE GP

Having arrived at Marina Bay with the possibility of wrapping up his second world title, Sebastian Vettel was to leave one point short. However, no one could touch the German as he sprinted clear to claim the ninth win of his campaign.

To wrap up his second world title on the humid streets of Singapore, Sebastian Vettel had to win. More than that, either team-mate Mark Webber or McLaren's Jenson Button might delay his crowning, should they finish second while a podium finish for Ferrari's Fernando Alonso would make him wait until the next race at least. As it happened, Vettel put his Red Bull RB7 on pole by 0.35s, then disappeared into the distance, never being headed at any point in the 61-lap race distance; the rest was down to others.

Jenson Button made the best fist of it as he rocketed past Webber's RB7 while it struggled to put its power down on the dusty side of the grid. The Australian was so busy trying to resist Lewis Hamilton down to the first corner that Alonso passed him, too. Still, he was well off compared to Hamilton, who had had to lift off or risk being squeezed toward the pit wall and this loss of momentum left him eighth. It came as no surprise that this was not the last we saw of the 2008 World Champion.

While Vettel powered clear, Alonso was not able to keep up with Button as his tyres started to go off, highlighting the disadvantage in races compared to the McLaren. Further back, Hamilton was on the move. He passed Michael Schumacher's Mercedes on lap 3, then Nico Rosberg two laps later. His next target was Felipe Massa and they were right together as they pitted, but Hamilton became impatient to pass him as they left the pits and clattered into the rear of the Brazilian's Ferrari at Turn 7, losing a nose wing but slowing Massa more as he punctured his left rear. For this, Hamilton was given a drive-through penalty and did well thereafter to climb to an eventual fifth. Massa, understandably, was livid as he would collect only two points for ninth.

The order settled with Vettel leading Button and then Webber. A safety-car period was triggered by Schumacher after

MARINA BAY ROUND 14

DATE: 25 SEPTEMBER 2011

Laps: **61** • Distance: **191.972 miles/308.950km** • Weather: **Hot and humid**

Pos	Driver	Team	Result	Stops	Qualifying Time	Grid
1	Sebastian Vettel	Red Bull	1h59m06.757s	3	1m44.381s	1
2	Jenson Button	McLaren	1h59m08.494s	3	1m44.804s	3
3	Mark Webber	Red Bull	1h59m36.036s	3	1m44.732s	2
4	Fernando Alonso	Ferrari	2h00m02.206s	3	1m44.874s	5
5	Lewis Hamilton	McLaren	2h00m14.523s	4	1m44.809s	4
6	Paul di Resta	Force India	2h00m57.824s	2	no time	10
7	Nico Rosberg	Mercedes	60 laps	3	1m46.013s	7
8	Adrian Sutil	Force India	60 laps	2	no time	9
9	Felipe Massa	Ferrari	60 laps	4	1m45.800s	6
10	Sergio Pérez	Sauber	60 laps	2	1m47.616s	11
11	Pastor Maldonado	Williams	60 laps	3	1m48.270s	13
12	Sebastien Buemi	Toro Rosso	60 laps	3	1m48.634s	14
13	Rubens Barrichello	Williams	60 laps	2	1m48.082s	12
14	Kamui Kobayashi	Sauber	59 laps	4	no time	17
15	Bruno Senna	Renault	59 laps	4	1m48.662s	15
16	Heikki Kovalainen	Lotus	59 laps	3	1m50.948s	19
17	Vitaly Petrov	Renault	59 laps	3	1m49.835s	18
18	Jérôme d'Ambrosio	Virgin	59 laps	2	1m52.363s	22
19	Daniel Ricciardo	HRT	57 laps	3	1m52.404s	23
20	Vitantonio Liuzzi	HRT	57 laps	4	1m52.810s	24*
21	Jaime Alguersuari	Toro Rosso	56 laps/accident	3	1m49.862s	16
R	Jarno Trulli	Lotus	47 laps/gearbox	3	1m51.012s	20
R	Michael Schumacher	Mercedes	28 laps/accident	2	no time	8
R	Timo Glock	Virgin	9 laps/accident	0	1m52.154s	21

FASTEST LAP: BUTTON, 1M48.454S, 104.379MPH/167.982KPH ON LAP 54 • RACE LEADERS: VETTEL 1–61.
* 5-PLACE GRID PENALTY

Second place for Button was enough to leave winner Vettel still to clinch the 2011 title.

he hit and flew over Sergio Pérez's Sauber, however, but this did not pin Vettel back too much for he made a scintillating restart, helped by having lapped cars between himself and Button. Soon he was 10s clear again, but then Button closed in – as he had in Canada, but this time just ran out of time – finishing 1.7s behind.

Sebastian Vettel was desperate to clinch his second drivers' title with victory, but he had to settle for second after being bettered by Jenson Button and Fernando Alonso, showing how the leading rivals were starting to match Red Bull Racing's pace.

The Japanese GP, the 15th of the season's 19 races, was a stage set for Sebastian Vettel to make it two drivers' titles in a row. All the Red Bull driver had to do was to finish 10th, even if Jenson Button won. Typically, he refused to settle for that and raced hard, all the way to the finish. This would be in third position but he kept Fernando Alonso constantly under pressure as he tried his best to wrestle 2nd away from him.

Lewis Hamilton continued to be a magnet for incident and at Suzuka he did not even wait for the race, being caught out in the final moments of the third qualifying session. Button backed off ahead of him to make a gap for his final flier and so Hamilton backed off too, only to be passed by both Mark Webber and Michael Schumacher in the chicane in a scramble to get onto their flying laps before the chequered flag fell. Webber made it, but the other two did not. At least Hamilton had a lap in the bag that would be good enough for 3rd, but his best shot to stop Red Bull's 100% record of poles had been thwarted.

So, Vettel started from pole, but Button took a run at him on the descent to the first corner. However, claiming later that he was unsighted, Vettel kept moving across to put Button onto the grass. The English driver had to come off the throttle and team-mate Hamilton nipped by into 2nd.

It was not to be Hamilton's day, though, for a slow puncture meant Button moved past. A lap later, Vettel pitted and this showed that the Red Bulls were in tyre trouble, as they had been at Spa. Button then realized that the race could be coming to him and took the lead from Vettel when he brought the McLaren back out from his second stop.

The race rhythm was then altered when the safety car was called out while debris was cleared from the track at the chicane, debris from yet another clash between Hamilton and Felipe Massa.

Vettel wanted to be crowned with a victory, but Button spoiled this ambition by winning.

SUZUKA ROUND 15

DATE: **9 OCTOBER 2011**

Laps: **53** • Distance: **191.224 miles/307.746km** • Weather: **Sunny and dry**

Pos	Driver	Team	Result	Stops	Qualifying Time	Grid
1	**Jenson Button**	McLaren	1h30m53.427s	3	1m30.475s	2
2	**Fernando Alonso**	Ferrari	1h30m54.587s	3	1m30.886s	5
3	**Sebastian Vettel**	Red Bull	1h30m55.433s	3	1m30.466s	1
4	**Mark Webber**	Red Bull	1h31m01.498s	3	1m31.156s	6
5	**Lewis Hamilton**	McLaren	1h31m17.695s	3	1m30.617s	3
6	**Michael Schumacher**	Mercedes	1h31m20.547s	3	No time	8
7	**Felipe Massa**	Ferrari	1h31m21.667s	3	1m30.804s	4
8	**Sergio Pérez**	Sauber	1h31m32.804s	2	No time	17
9	**Vitaly Petrov**	Renault	1h31m36.034s	2	No time	10
10	**Nico Rosberg**	Mercedes	1h31m37.749s	3	No time	23
11	**Adrian Sutil**	Force India	1h31m47.874s	3	1m32.463s	11
12	**Paul di Resta**	Force India	1h31m55.753s	3	1m32.746s	12
13	**Kamui Kobayashi**	Sauber	1h31m57.132s	2	No time	7
14	**Pastor Maldonado**	Williams	1h31m57.621s	3	1m33.224s	14
15	**Jaime Alguersuari**	Toro Rosso	1h32m00.050s	2	1m33.427s	16
16	**Bruno Senna**	Renault	1h32m06.055s	2	No time	9
17	**Rubens Barrichello**	Williams	1h32m07.618s	3	1m33.059s	13
18	**Heikki Kovalainen**	Lotus	1h32m21.251s	3	1m35.454s	18
19	**Jarno Trulli**	Lotus	1h32m29.567s	3	1m35.54s	19
20	**Timo Glock**	Virgin	51 laps	3	1m36.507s	21
21	**Jérôme d'Ambrosio**	Virgin	51 laps	3	1m36.439s	20
22	**Daniel Ricciardo**	HRT	51 laps	3	1m37.846s	22
23	**Vitantonio Liuzzi**	HRT	50 laps	3	No time	24
R	**Sebastien Buemi**	Toro Rosso	11 laps/lost wheel	1	1m33.227	15

FASTEST LAP: BUTTON, 1M36.568S, 134.515MPH/216.481KPH ON LAP 52 • **RACE LEADERS:** VETTEL 1–9, 12–18; BUTTON 10, 19–20, 23–36, 41–53; MASSA 11, 22; ALONSO 21, 37; SCHUMACHER 38–40

Once the safety car withdrew, Button controlled the race from the front, but the order behind changed when Alonso waited four laps longer before making his third pit stop to emerge just ahead of Vettel. Their battle was definitely robust, but Vettel was eventually forced to settle for third place. It was enough to secure his second world title.

Already crowned champion, Sebastian Vettel did not need to win this one but did so anyway, as Red Bull Racing wrapped up the constructors' title too, while Lewis Hamilton drove manfully, resisting Mark Webber to be the best of the rest.

There was a strange look to the front of the grid for Formula One's second visit to Yeongam: a car other than a Red Bull on the pole for the first time in 2011. And the deed was done by Lewis Hamilton, not that he looked particularly happy. He continued to beat himself up about a season that had not gone his way. However, Sebastian Vettel was still on the front row, usurping Jenson Button in the dying seconds.

Hamilton led into the first corner, and the second and the third, but Vettel went past into Turn 4 to produce a display of total dominance that left him 12s clear at flagfall while rivals scrapped in his wake. Indeed, had Vettel not been involved, this might have been one of the great races, so close was the action between Hamilton, Mark Webber, Jenson Button, Felipe Massa (for a while) and Fernando Alonso.

Making Vettel's drive all the more impressive was the fact that there was a safety car period from lap 17 to 20 to wipe out his advantage. The safety car had been deployed while debris was cleared from the track after Vitaly Petrov had been so busy racing Alonso as the Spaniard fought back through the field after his first pit stop that he failed to brake in time for Turn 3, ramming Michael Schumacher's Mercedes in the process, and this meant he had to make his break all over again.

Hamilton's race was spent resisting challenges from Webber and it was made all the more interesting as their cars had performance advantages at different parts of the lap, but the Red Bull RB7 was clearly faster overall. Webber got ahead into Turn 1 on one lap, but Hamilton used his KERS and DRS to regain second down the long straight to Turn 3. It was later discovered that Hamilton's MP4-26 had lost 10 points of downforce, leaving him with obvious understeer, which made his defence all the more amazing.

Button had a terrible first lap and completed it 6th, having lost three places.

YEONGAM ROUND 16

DATE: **16 OCTOBER 2011**

Laps: **55** • Distance: **192.060 miles/309.091km** • Weather: **Warm, but overcast**

Pos	Driver	Team	Result	Stops	Qualifying Time	Grid
1	**Sebastian Vettel**	Red Bull	1h38m01.994s	2	1m36.042s	2
2	**Lewis Hamilton**	McLaren	1h38m14.013s	2	1m35.820s	1
3	**Mark Webber**	Red Bull	1h38m14.471s	2	1m36.468s	4
4	**Jenson Button**	McLaren	1h38m16.688s	2	1m36.126s	3
5	**Fernando Alonso**	Ferrari	1h38m17.683s	2	1m36.980s	6
6	**Felipe Massa**	Ferrari	1h38m27.127s	2	1m36.831s	5
7	**Jaime Alguersuari**	Toro Rosso	1h38m51.632s	2	1m38.315s	11
8	**Nico Rosberg**	Mercedes	1h38m56.047s	2	1m37.754s	7
9	**Sebastien Buemi**	Toro Rosso	1h39m04.756s	2	1m38.508s	13
10	**Paul di Resta**	Force India	1h39m10.596s	2	No time	9
11	**Adrian Sutil**	Force India	1h39m13.223s	2	No time	10
12	**Rubens Barrichello**	Williams	1h39m35.062s	2	1m39.538s	18
13	**Bruno Senna**	Renault	54 laps	2	1m38.791s	15
14	**Heikki Kovalainen**	Lotus	54 laps	2	1m40.522s	19
15	**Kamui Kobayashi**	Sauber	54 laps	3	1m38.775s	14
16	**Sergio Pérez**	Sauber	54 laps	3	1m39.443s	17
17	**Jarno Trulli**	Lotus	54 laps	2	1m41.101s	20
18	**Timo Glock**	Virgin	54 laps	2	1m42.091s	21
19	**Daniel Ricciardo**	HRT	54 laps	2	No time	24
20	**Jérôme d'Ambrosio**	Virgin	54 laps	2	1m43.483s	22
21	**Vitantonio Liuzzi**	HRT	52 laps	3	1m43.758s	23
R	**Pastor Maldonado**	Williams	30 laps/Engine	3	1m39.189s	16
R	**Vitaly Petrov**	Renault	16 laps/accident damage	1	1m38.124s	8
R	**Michael Schumacher**	Mercedes	15 laps/accident	1	1m38.354s	12

FASTEST LAP: VETTEL, 1M39.605S, 126.101MPH/202.940KPH ON LAP 55 • **RACE LEADERS:** VETTEL 1-34, 37-55; ALONSO 35-36

F1's second visit to Yeongam was infinitely drier than the first and Vettel won from Hamilton.

However, he used his tyres wisely and worked his way forward to finish 4th.

For many laps, Massa headed Ferrari team-mate Alonso, but this was reversed when Massa was delayed leaving his first pit stop; Alonso then closed on Button but could not pass him. Second to fifth places were covered by 3.6s.

Sebastian Vettel continued his domination of the 2011 World Championship when F1 made its first visit to the Buddh International circuit, but he was kept on his toes by a fine drive from Jenson Button, with Fernando Alonso jumping Mark Webber for third.

Once Sebastian Vettel had showed that he and Red Bull Racing were still the combination to beat in claiming pole at the all-new and only-just completed Buddh International circuit, he set the bar even higher and led every lap of the race, setting fastest lap as he went on to victory. No one headed him, not even during the two rounds of pit stops.

McLaren looked very competitive in India but although Lewis Hamilton had qualified second fastest, 0.3s down on Vettel, he was dropped three places on the grid for failing to heed yellow flags in practice. So Mark Webber started from the outside of the front row. He was not to stay there, though, as Button simply powered past before the end of the long straight to Turn 4.

This was nothing to what went on behind them, however, as tightening Turn 1 caught out several of the midfield runners, leading to clashes and off-track excursions at this tightening righthander. Rubens Barrichello hit the rear of Williams' team-mate Pastor Maldonado, then clattered into Kamui Kobayashi's Sauber, which ricocheted into Timo Glock's Virgin. Even though Vettel sprinted clear, the Red Bulls ate tyres and their pace slowed, allowing Button to reduce the deficit to Vettel. After the pit stops, this would expand again but Button closed in once more in his final stint to keep Vettel fighting all the way for his 11th win of 2011.

Fernando Alonso made a strong start and got briefly ahead of Button on the run to the first corner, but was on the wrong line as he challenged Webber for 2nd and was forced to slot in behind the Red Bull and the McLaren. He then tracked the Australian for 3rd and was less hard on his tyres, so found the advantage needed to move ahead at their second stops.

Unbelievably, Hamilton and Felipe Massa clashed yet again as they fought over 5th place, this time with the Brazilian given the drive-through penalty. A stop for a new nose delayed Hamilton, causing him to end up

7th behind the two Mercedes. Massa failed to finish as his left front suspension later collapsed when he hit a kerb.

In leading all 60 laps Vettel set a new

record for laps led in a season, overtaking the mark of 692 laps that Nigel Mansell had set in dominating the 16-round 1992 World Championship.

Sebastian Vettel leads the way, followed by Mark Webber, but Jenson Button was soon second.

BUDDH INTERNATIONAL ROUND 17 DATE: 30 OCTOBER 2011
Laps: 60 • Distance: 191.100 miles/307.546km • Weather: Dry and hot

Pos	Driver	Team	Result	Stops	Qualifying Time	Grid
1	Sebastian Vettel	Red Bull	1h30m35.002s	2	1m24.178s	1
2	Jenson Button	McLaren	1h30m43.435s	2	1m24.950s	4
3	Fernando Alonso	Ferrari	1h30m59.303s	2	1m24.519s	3
4	Mark Webber	Red Bull	1h31m00.531s	2	1m24.508s	2
5	Michael Schumacher	Mercedes	1h31m40.423s	2	1m26.337s	11
6	Nico Rosberg	Mercedes	1h31m41.853s	2	1m25.451s	7
7	Lewis Hamilton	McLaren	1h31m59.185s	3	1m24.474s	5*
8	Jaime Alguersuari	Toro Rosso	59 laps	2	No time	10
9	Adrian Sutil	Force India	59 laps	2	No time	8
10	Sergio Pérez	Sauber	59 laps	2	1m27.562s	20*
11	Vitaly Petrov	Renault	59 laps	2	1m26.319s	16**
12	Bruno Senna	Renault	59 laps	2	1m26.651s	14
13	Paul di Resta	Force India	59 laps	3	1m26.503s	12
14	Heikki Kovalainen	Lotus	58 laps	2	1m28.565s	18
15	Rubens Barrichello	Williams	58 laps	2	1m27.247s	15
16	Jérôme d'Ambrosio	Virgin	57 laps	2	1m30.866s	21
17	Narain Karthikeyan	HRT	57 laps	2	1m30.238s	24**
18	Daniel Ricciardo	HRT	57 laps	3	1m30.216s	23**
19	Jarno Trulli	Lotus	55 laps	3	1m28.752s	19
R	Felipe Massa	Ferrari	32 laps/suspension	3	1m25.122s	6
R	Sebastien Buemi	Toro Rosso	24 laps/engine	1	No time	9
R	Pastor Maldonado	Williams	12 laps/gearbox	0	1m26.537s	13
R	Timo Glock	Virgin	2 laps/crash damage	1	1m34.046s	22
R	Kamui Kobayashi	Sauber	0 laps/crash damage	0	1m27.876s	17

FASTEST LAP: VETTEL, 1M27.249S, 131.397MPH/211.463KPH ON LAP 60 • RACE LEADERS: VETTEL 1-60
* 3-PLACE GRID PENALTY; ** 5-PLACE GRID PENALTY

Lewis Hamilton was back to his greatest form at Yas Marina, where he scored his first win in eight rounds after he controlled proceedings in a race in which World Champion Sebastian Vettel was eliminated after a puncture on the opening lap.

Lewis Hamilton had been waiting for the 2011 World Championship to end simply so that he could start afresh following a year increasingly beset by disappointment. However, in Abu Dhabi he was setting the pace from the first day of practice. Sebastian Vettel pipped him to pole to equal Nigel Mansell's 1992 record of 14 in a season, although Hamilton went into race day with high hopes.

Hamilton's chances of victory were then boosted at the second corner of the opening lap when Vettel slowed and ceded the lead to him as his Red Bull became hard to handle after a sudden deflation of his right rear tyre pitched him into a spin. With a damaged track rod, he was unable to continue. This left Hamilton leading from team-mate Jenson Button, but not for long because Fernando Alonso had passed Mark Webber around the outside at Turn 1, then slipstreamed Button on the long run down to Turn 8 and moved past for second into the hairpin. By the end of lap 1, though, helped by having no one to fight, Hamilton was 2.5s clear. And so his race would continue all the way to the chequered flag for a 17th grand prix win, with Alonso kept a handful of seconds behind.

Webber then set about Button and although he could pass using the first of the lap's two DRS zones, Button would be able to seize the place back in the second. The frustration of this and a slow pit stop led to Red Bull changing Webber to a three-stop strategy.

Button was not having an easy time, though, as his KERS was working only intermittently but he had enough in hand to resist Webber's charge. Felipe Massa finished far adrift in 5th place after a spin but still ahead of the Mercedes GP duo, with Nico Rosberg claiming 6th.

Both Force Indias finished in the points to help cement their 6th place in the constructors' rankings, with Adrian Sutil particularly impressive in chasing Michael Schumacher to the finish line.

YAS MARINA ROUND 18

DATE: **13 NOVEMBER 2011**

Laps: **55** • Distance: **189.738 miles/305.355km** • Weather: **Sunny and dry**

Pos	Driver	Team	Result	Stops	Qualifying Time	Grid
1	**Lewis Hamilton**	McLaren	1h37m11.886s	2	1m38.622s	2
2	**Fernando Alonso**	Ferrari	1h37m20.343s	2	1m39.058s	5
3	**Jenson Button**	McLaren	1h37m37.767s	2	1m38.631s	3
4	**Mark Webber**	Red Bull	1h37m47.670s	3	1m38.858s	4
5	**Felipe Massa**	Ferrari	1h38m02.464s	2	1m39.695s	6
6	**Nico Rosberg**	Mercedes	1h38m04.203s	2	1m39.773s	7
7	**Michael Schumacher**	Mercedes	1h38m27.850s	2	1m40.662s	8
8	**Adrian Sutil**	Force India	1h38m29.008s	2	1m40.768s	9
9	**Paul di Resta**	Force India	1h38m52.973s	1	No time	10
10	**Kamui Kobayashi**	Sauber	54 laps	2	1m41.240s	16
11	**Sergio Pérez**	Sauber	54 laps	2	1m40.874s	11
12	**Rubens Barrichello**	Williams	54 laps	2	No time	23
13	**Vitaly Petrov**	Renault	54 laps	2	1m40.919s	12
14	**Pastor Maldonado**	Williams	54 laps**	2	1m41.760s	24*
15	**Jaime Alguersuari**	Toro Rosso	54 laps***	2	1m41.162s	15
16	**Bruno Senna**	Renault	54 laps	3	1m41.079s	14
17	**Heikki Kovalainen**	Lotus	54 laps	2	1m42.979s	17
18	**Jarno Trulli**	Lotus	53 laps	2	1m43.884s	18
19	**Timo Glock**	Virgin	53 laps	2	1m44.515s	19
20	**Vitantonio Liuzzi**	HRT	53 laps	1	1m45.159s	22
R	**Daniel Ricciardo**	HRT	48 laps/alternator	2	1m44.641s	20
R	**Sebastien Buemi**	Toro Rosso	19 laps/hydraulics	0	1m41.009s	13
R	**Jérôme d'Ambrosio**	Virgin	18 laps/brakes	0	1m44.699s	21
R	**Sebastian Vettel**	Red Bull	1 lap/puncture	0	1m38.481s	1

FASTEST LAP: WEBBER, 1M42.612S, 121.076MPH/194.854KPH ON LAP 51 • RACE LEADERS: HAMILTON 1-16, 18-40, 44-55; WEBBER 17; ALONSO 41-43
* X-PLACE GRID PENALTY; ** 30S PENALTY FOR IGNORING WAVED BLUE FLAGS; *** 20S PENALTY FOR IGNORING WAVED BLUE FLAGS

Lewis Hamilton was the man on the move as day turned to dusk and raced to his 17th victory.

One of the better drives down the order came from veteran Rubens Barrichello, who started 23rd after failing to set a time in qualifying yet worked his way through to 12th, three places ahead of team-mate Pastor Maldonado, who lost ground when given a drive-through penalty only to end up 14th.

To finish the season without a win while team-mate Sebastian Vettel had 11 to his name would have been too much for Mark Webber. Instead he prevented this from happening by striking when Vettel was slowed with a gearbox problem.

With McLaren unable to maintain its strong end-of-season form, Red Bull was left to dominate vices at Interlagos. Its drivers locked out the front row, with Vettel claiming 18th pole from 19 rounds. He got away cleanly at the start and was 2.2s up after two laps. Everyone else was well behaved, with Fernando Alonso demoting Lewis Hamilton into the first corner, although Rubens Barrichello blew his good qualifying position and immediately fell seven places at the start of what might have been his final grand prix.

With Vettel thus too far ahead for Mark Webber to use DRS to try and haul him when they reached the DRS zone before Turn 4 on lap 3, Vettel was able to continue to edge clear, with Jenson Button holding off Alonso for third. The first drama came when Michael Schumacher passed Bruno Senna for ninth but they touched and the German's Mercedes collected a puncture. Senna, whose front wing was damaged, was later awarded a drive-through penalty. Shortly afterwards Button was trying to resist an attack up the hill to Turn 6 from Alonso when he realized that he was about to hit Schumacher's tyre debris. He was duly forced to back off and so Alonso motored past.

In soaring track temperatures the drivers began to struggle for grip, but this proved the lesser of Vettel's problems for as early as lap 5, he began to suffer a gearbox problem and the team asked him to short shift in second; soon afterwards in third, too. Once Webber began to close, Vettel knew all hope of a twelfth win was unlikely and at the end of lap 30, he let Webber by.

The race lost Timo Glock when a wheel flew off his Virgin as he left the pits, then Pastor Maldonado spun off, but no one looked capable of stopping a Red Bull 1-2 unless Vettel's gearbox problem worsened – which it did. Alonso held onto third place, with all teams keeping an eye out for rain,

Mark Webber (right) is congratulated by Sebastian Vettel after taking his only win of 2011.

BRAZIL ROUND 19

DATE: **27 NOVEMBER 2011**

Laps: **71** • Distance: **190.067 miles/305.884km** • Weather: **Hot and bright**

Pos	Driver	Team	Result	Stops	Qualifying Time	Grid
1	**Mark Webber**	Red Bull	1h32m17.464s	3	1m12.099s	2
2	**Sebastian Vettel**	Red Bull	1h32m34.447s	3	1m11.918s	1
3	**Jenson Button**	McLaren	1h32m45.102s	3	1m12.283s	3
4	**Fernando Alonso**	Ferrari	1h32m52.512s	3	1m12.591s	5
5	**Felipe Massa**	Ferrari	1h33m24.197s	3	1m13.068s	7
6	**Adrian Sutil**	Force India	70 laps	3	1m13.298s	8
7	**Nico Rosberg**	Mercedes	70 laps	2	1m13.050s	6
8	**Paul di Resta**	Force India	70 laps	2	1m13.584s	11
9	**Kamui Kobayashi**	Sauber	70 laps	2	1m14.129s	16
10	**Vitaly Petrov**	Renault	70 laps	3	1m14.053s	15
11	**Jaime Alguersuari**	Toro Rosso	70 laps	2	1m13.804s	13
12	**Sebastien Buemi**	Toro Rosso	70 laps	2	1m13.919s	14
13	**Sergio Pérez**	Sauber	70 laps	2	1m14.182s	17
14	**Rubens Barrichello**	Williams	70 laps	3	1m13.801s	12
15	**Michael Schumacher**	Mercedes	70 laps	3	No time	10
16	**Heikki Kovalainen**	Lotus	69 laps	3	1m15.068s	19
17	**Bruno Senna**	Renault	69 laps	4	1m13.761s	9
18	**Jarno Trulli**	Lotus	69 laps	2	1m15.358s	20
19	**Jérôme d'Ambrosio**	Virgin	68 laps	2	1m17.019s	23
20	**Daniel Ricciardo**	HRT	68 laps	2	1m16.890s	22
R	**Vitantonio Liuzzi**	HRT	61 laps/alternator	2	1m16.631s	21
R	**Lewis Hamilton**	McLaren	46 laps/gearbox	3	1m12.640s	4
R	**Pastor Maldonado**	Williams	26 laps/spun off	1	1m14.625s	18
R	**Timo Glock**	Virgin	21 laps/lost wheel	1	1m17.060s	24

FASTEST LAP: WEBBER, 1M15.324S, 127.966MPH/205.942KPH ON LAP 71 • RACE LEADERS: VETTEL 1-16, 21-29, 38-39, 59; WEBBER 17-18, 30-37, 40-58, 60-71; MASSA 19-20

which never arrived. There was a thought that Button – on the harder tyres – might move ahead by making two pit stops to the Ferrari driver's three. However, Button did pit for a third time although following his final stop, he caught Alonso. After spending a few laps finding the place to pass, he pulled it off down to Turn 4 on lap 62.

Sebastian Vettel on his way to his 2011 champagne moment. Second place in Brazil brought a phenomenal season to a close.

Sebastian Vettel unleashed the winner's champagne on a total of 11 occasions during the 19-race 2011 season. It was a dominant performance by the whole of the Red Bull Racing team, who won the constructors' title as well.

FINAL RESULTS 2011

POS	DRIVER	NAT.		ENGINE	R1	R2	R3	R4
1	SEBASTIAN VETTEL	GER		RED BULL-RENAULT RB7	1P	1P	2P	1P
2	JENSON BUTTON	GBR		McLAREN-MERCEDES MP4-26	6	2	4	6
3	MARK WEBBER	AUS		RED BULL-RENAULT RB7	5	4F	3F	2F
4	FERNANDO ALONSO	SPA		FERRARI 150 ITALIA	4	6	7	3
5	LEWIS HAMILTON	GBR		McLAREN-MERCEDES MP4-26	2	8	1	4
6	FELIPE MASSA	BRA		FERRARI 150 ITALIA	7F	5	6	11
7	NICO ROSBERG	GER		MERCEDES W02	R	12	5	5
8	MICHAEL SCHUMACHER	GER		MERCEDES W02	R	9	8	12
9	ADRIAN SUTIL	GER		FORCE INDIA-MERCEDES VJM04	9	11	15	13
10	VITALY PETROV	RUS		RENAULT R31	3	17	9	8
11	NICK HEIDFELD	GER		RENAULT R31	12	3	12	7
12	KAMUI KOBAYASHI	JAP		SAUBER-FERRARI C30	D8	7	10	10
13	PAUL DI RESTA	GBR		FORCE INDIA-MERCEDES VJM04	10	10	11	R
14	JAIME ALGUERSUARI	SPA		TORO ROSSO-FERRARI STR6	11	14	R	16
15	SEBASTIEN BUEMI	SUI		TORO ROSSO-FERRARI STR6	8	13	14	9
16	SERGIO PÉREZ	MEX		SAUBER-FERRARI C30	D7	R	17	14
17	RUBENS BARRICHELLO	BRA		WILLIAMS-COSWORTH FW33	R	R	13	15
18	BRUNO SENNA	BRA		RENAULT R31	-	-	-	-
19	PASTOR MALDONADO	VEN		WILLIAMS-COSWORTH FW33	R	R	18	17
20	PEDRO DE LA ROSA	SPA		SAUBER-FERRARI C30	-	-	-	-
21	JARNO TRULLI	ITA		LOTUS-RENAULT T128	13	R	19	18
22	HEIKKI KOVALAINEN	FIN		LOTUS-RENAULT T128	R	15	16	19
23	VITANTONIO LIUZZI	ITA		HRT-COSWORTH F111	NQ	R	22	22
24	JÉRÔME D'AMBROSIO	BEL		VIRGIN-COSWORTH MVR02	14	R	20	20
25	TIMO GLOCK	GER		VIRGIN-COSWORTH MVR02	NC	16	21	NS
26	NARAIN KARTHIKEYAN	IND		HRT-COSWORTH F111	NQ	R	23	21
27	DANIEL RICCIARDO	AUS		HRT-COSWORTH F111	-	-	-	-
28	KARUN CHANDHOK	IND		LOTUS-RENAULT T128	-	-	-	-

SCORING

1st	25 points
2nd	18 points
3rd	15 points
4th	12 points
5th	10 points
6th	8 points
7th	6 points
8th	4 points
9th	2 points
10th	1 point

		R1	R2	R3	R4
1	RED BULL-RENAULT	1/5	1/4	2/3	1/2
2	McLAREN-MERCEDES	2/6	2/8	1/4	4/6
3	FERRARI	4/7	5/6	6/7	3/11
4	MERCEDES	R/R	9/12	5/8	5/12
5	RENAULT	3/12	3/17	9/12	7/8
6	FORCE INDIA-MERCEDES	9/10	10/11	11/15	13/R
7	SAUBER-FERRARI	D/D	7/R	10/17	10/14
8	TORO ROSSO-FERRARI	8/11	11/13	14/R	9/16
9	WILLIAMS-COSWORTH	R/R	R/R	13/18	15/17
10	LOTUS-RENAULT	13/R	15/R	16/19	18/19
11	HRT-COSWORTH	NQ/NQ	R/R	22/23	21/22
12	VIRGIN-COSWORTH	14/NC	16/R	20/21	20/NS

RACE RESULTS FOR BOTH DRIVERS: ie. FIRST AND SECOND LISTED AS 1/2, WITH THE TEAM'S BETTER RESULT LISTED FIRST

ROUND 1 .... AUSTRALIAN GP   ROUND 6 .... MONACO GP   ROUND 11 .... HUNGARIAN GP   ROUND 16 .... KOREAN GP
ROUND 2 .... MALAYSIAN GP   ROUND 7 .... CANADIAN GP   ROUND 12 .... BELGIAN GP   ROUND 17 .... INDIAN GP
ROUND 3 .... CHINESE GP   ROUND 8 .... EUROPEAN GP   ROUND 13 .... ITALIAN GP   ROUND 18 .... ABU DHABI GP
ROUND 4 .... TURKISH GP   ROUND 9 .... BRITISH GP   ROUND 14 .... SINGAPORE GP   ROUND 19 .... BRAZILIAN GP
ROUND 5 .... SPANISH GP   ROUND 10 .... GERMAN GP   ROUND 15 .... JAPANESE GP

D DISQUALIFIED   **F** FASTEST LAP   **NC** NON-CLASSIFIED   **NQ** NON-QUALIFIER   **NS** NON-STARTER   **P** POLE POSITION   **R** RETIRED   **W** WITHDRAWN

R5	R6	R7	R8	R9	R10	R11	R12	R13	R14	R15	R16	R17	R18	R19	TOTAL POINTS
1	1P	2P	1PF	2	4	2P	1P	1P	1P	3P	1F	1PF	RP	2P	392
3	3	1F	6	R	R	1	3	2	2F	1F	4	2	3	3	270
4P	4F	3	3	3P	3P	5	2F	R	3	4	3	4	4F	1F	258
5	2	R	2	1F	2	3	4	3	4	2	5	3	2	4	257
2F	6	R	4	4	1F	4	R	4F	5	5	2P	7	1	R	227
R	R	6	5	5	5	6F	8	6	9	7	6	R	5	5	118
7	11	11	7	6	7	9	6	R	7	10	8	6	6	7	89
6	R	4	17	9	8	R	5	5	R	6	R	5	7	15	76
13	7	R	9	11	6	14	7	R	8	11	11	9	8	6	42
11	R	5	15	12	10	12	9	R	17	9	R	11	13	10	37
8	8	R	10	8	R	R	-	-	-	-	-	-	-	-	34
10	5	7	16	R	9	11	12	R	14	13	15	R	10	9	30
12	12	18	14	15	13	7	11	8	6	12	10	13	9	8	27
16	R	8	8	10	12	10	R	7	21	15	7	8	15	11	26
14	10	10	13	R	15	8	R	10	12	R	9	R	R	12	15
9	NS	-	11	7	11	15	R	R	10	8	16	10	11	13	14
17	9	9	12	13	R	13	16	12	13	17	12	15	12	14	4
-	-	-	-	-	-	-	13	9	15	16	13	12	16	17	2
15	18	R	18	14	14	16	10	11	11	14	R	R	14	R	1
-	-	12	-	-	-	-	-	-	-	-	-	-	-	-	0
18	13	16	20	R	-	R	14	14	R	19	17	19	18	18	0
R	14	R	19	R	16	R	15	13	16	18	14	14	17	16	0
R	16	13	23	18	R	20	19	R	20	23	21	-	20	R	0
20	15	14	22	17	18	19	17	R	18	21	20	16	R	19	0
19	R	15	21	16	17	17	18	15	R	20	18	R	19	R	0
21	17	17	24	-	-	-	-	-	-	-	-	17	-	-	0
-	-	-	-	19	19	18	R	NC	19	22	19	18	R	20	0
-	-	-	-	-	20	-	-	-	-	-	-	-	-	-	0
1/4	1/4	2/3	1/3	2/3	3/4	2/5	1/2	1/R	1/3	3/4	1/3	1/4	4/R	1/2	650
2/3	3/6	1/R	4/6	4/R	1/R	1/4	3/R	2/4	2/5	1/5	2/4	2/7	1/3	3/R	497
5/R	2/R	6/R	2/5	1/5	2/5	3/6	4/8	3/6	4/9	2/7	5/6	3/R	2/5	4/5	375
6/7	11/R	4/11	7/17	6/9	7/8	9/R	5/6	5/R	7/R	6/10	8/R	5/6	6/7	7/15	165
8/11	8/R	5/R	10/15	8/12	10/R	12/R	9/13	9/R	15/17	9/16	13/R	11/12	13/16	10/17	73
12/13	7/12	18/R	9/14	11/15	6/13	7/14	7/11	8/R	6/8	11/12	10/11	9/13	8/9	6/8	69
9/10	5/NS	7/12	11/16	7/R	9/11	11/15	12/R	R/R	10/14	8/13	15/16	10/R	10/11	9/13	44
14/16	10/R	8/10	8/13	10/R	12/15	8/10	R/R	7/10	12/R	15/R	7/9	8/R	15/R	11/12	41
15/17	9/18	9/R	12/18	13/14	14/R	13/16	10/16	11/12	11/13	14/17	12/R	15/R	12/14	14/R	5
18/R	13/14	16/R	19/20	R/R	16/20	R/R	14/15	13/14	16/R	18/19	14/17	14/19	17/18	16/18	0
21/R	16/17	13/17	23/24	18/19	19/R	18/20	19/R	NC/R	19/20	22/23	19/21	17/18	20/R	20/R	0
19/20	15/R	14/15	21/22	16/17	17/18	17/19	17/18	15/R	18/R	20/21	18/20	16/R	19/R	19/R	0

MOST GRAND PRIX STARTS

DRIVERS

325	Rubens Barrichello	(BRA)
288	Michael Schumacher	(GER)
256	Riccardo Patrese	(ITA)
	Jarno Trulli	(ITA)
247	David Coulthard	(GBR)
230	Giancarlo Fisichella	(ITA)
210	Gerhard Berger	(AUT)
209	Jenson Button	(GBR)
208	Andrea de Cesaris	(ITA)
204	Nelson Piquet	(BRA)
201	Jean Alesi	FRA)
199	Alain Prost	(FRA)
194	Michele Alboreto	(ITA)
187	Nigel Mansell	(GBR)
185	Nick Heidfeld	(GER)
180	Ralf Schumacher	(GER)
178	Fernando Alonso	(SPA)
177	Mark Webber	(AUS)
176	Graham Hill	(GBR)
175	Jacques Laffite	(FRA)
171	Niki Lauda	(AUT)
165	Jacques Villeneuve	(CDN)
163	Thierry Boutsen	(BEL)
162	Mika Hakkinen	(FIN)
	Johnny Herbert	(GBR)
161	Ayrton Senna	(BRA)
159	Heinz-Harald Frentzen	(GER)
158	Martin Brundle	(GBR)
	Olivier Panis	(FRA)
157	Kimi Raïkkönen	(FIN)
153	Felipe Massa	(BRA)
152	John Watson	(GBR)
149	Rene Arnoux	(FRA)
147	Eddie Irvine	(GBR)
	Derek Warwick	(GBR)
146	Carlos Reutemann	(ARG)
144	Emerson Fittipaldi	(BRA)
135	Jean-Pierre Jarier	(FRA)
132	Eddie Cheever	(USA)
	Clay Regazzoni	(SUI)
128	Mario Andretti	(USA)
126	Jack Brabham	(AUS)
123	Ronnie Peterson	(SWE)
119	Pierluigi Martini	(ITA)
116	Damon Hill	(GBR)
	Jacky Ickx	(BEL)
	Alan Jones	(AUS)
114	Keke Rosberg	(FIN)
	Patrick Tambay	(FRA)

CONSTRUCTORS

831	Ferrari
704	McLaren
623	Williams
492	Lotus
449	Toro Rosso (nee Minardi)
418	Tyrrell
409	Prost (nee Ligier)
394	Brabham
383	Arrows
358	Force India (née Jordan, then Midland, then Spyker)
325	Sauber (including BMW Sauber)
317	Benetton
301	Renault
261	Red Bull (née Stewart, then Jaguar Racing)
230	March
197	BRM
188	Mercedes GP (née BAR, then Honda Racing, then Brawn GP)
132	Osella

Barrichello raced for Jordan in the 1990s.

Driving for Williams in 2011, Barrichello is listened to by his former boss Sir Jackie Stewart.

Alberto Ascari powers his way to second place for Ferrari in the 1951 French GP at Reims, racing past crowds protected only by straw bales.

MOST GRAND PRIX WINS

DRIVERS

91	Michael Schumacher	(GER)	17	Lewis Hamilton	(GBR)	10	Gerhard Berger	(AUT)
51	Alain Prost	(FRA)	16	Stirling Moss	(GBR)		James Hunt	(GBR)
41	Ayrton Senna	(BRA)	14	Jack Brabham	(AUS)		Ronnie Peterson	(SWE)
31	Nigel Mansell	(GBR)		Emerson Fittipaldi	(BRA)		Jody Scheckter	(RSA)
27	Fernando Alonso	(SPA)		Graham Hill	(GBR)	8	Denny Hulme	(NZL)
	Jackie Stewart	(GBR)	13	Alberto Ascari	(ITA)		Jacky Ickx	(BEL)
25	Jim Clark	(GBR)		David Coulthard	(GBR)	7	Rene Arnoux	(FRA)
	Niki Lauda	(AUT)	12	Mario Andretti	(USA)		Juan Pablo Montoya	(COL)
24	Juan Manuel Fangio	(ARG)		Jenson Button	(GBR)		Mark Webber	(AUS)
23	Nelson Piquet	(BRA)		Alan Jones	(AUS)			
22	Damon Hill	(GBR)		Carlos Reutemann	(ARG)			
21	Sebastian Vettel	(GER)	11	Rubens Barrichello	(BRA)			
20	Mika Hakkinen	(FIN)		Felipe Massa	(BRA)			
18	Kimi Raïkkönen	(FIN)		Jacques Villeneuve	(CDN)			

CONSTRUCTORS

216	Ferrari	16	Cooper	3	March	
174	McLaren	11	Brawn GP (née BAR,		Wolf	
113	Williams		then Honda Racing)	2	Honda	
79	Lotus	10	Alfa Romeo	1	BMW Sauber	
35	Brabham	9	Ligier		Eagle	
	Renault		Maserati		Hesketh	
28	Red Bull (née Stewart,		Matra		Penske	
	then Jaguar Racing)		Mercedes		Porsche	
27	Benetton		Vanwall		Scuderia Toro Rosso	
23	Tyrrell	4	Force India (née Jordan,		Shadow	
17	BRM		then Midland then Spyker)			

This victory leap became a Michael Schumacher trademark, as performed at Sepang in 2004.

DRIVERS

	Driver		Year
13	Michael Schumacher	(GER)	2004
11	Michael Schumacher	(GER)	2002
	Sebastian Vettel	(GER)	2011
9	Nigel Mansell	(GBR)	1992
	Michael Schumacher	(GER)	1995
	Michael Schumacher	(GER)	2000
	Michael Schumacher	(GER)	2001
8	Mika Hakkinen	(FIN)	1998
	Damon Hill	(GBR)	1996
	Michael Schumacher	(GER)	1994
	Ayrton Senna	(BRA)	1988
7	Fernando Alonso	(SPA)	2005
	Fernando Alonso	(SPA)	2006
	Jim Clark	(GBR)	1963
	Alain Prost	(FRA)	1984
	Alain Prost	(FRA)	1988
	Alain Prost	(FRA)	1993
	Kimi Raïkkönen	(FIN)	2005
	Ayrton Senna	(BRA)	1991
	Jacques Villeneuve	(CDN)	1997
6	Mario Andretti	(USA)	1978
	Alberto Ascari	(ITA)	1952
	Jim Clark	(GBR)	1965
	Juan Manuel Fangio	(ARG)	1954
	Damon Hill	(GBR)	1994
	James Hunt	(GBR)	1976
	Nigel Mansell	(GBR)	1987
	Felipe Massa	(BRA)	2008
	Kimi Raïkkönen	(FIN)	2007
	Michael Schumacher	(GER)	1998
	Michael Schumacher	(GER)	2003
	Michael Schumacher	(GER)	2006
	Ayrton Senna	(BRA)	1989
	Ayrton Senna	(BRA)	1990

CONSTRUCTORS

15	Ferrari	2004		Ferrari	2007	7	Ferrari	1952		Ferrari	1976
	Ferrari	2002		McLaren	1998		Ferrari	1953		Ferrari	1979
	McLaren	1988		Red Bull	2010		Ferrari	2008		Ferrari	1990
12	McLaren	1984		Williams	1986		Lotus	1963		Ferrari	1996
	Red Bull	2011		Williams	1987		Lotus	1973		Ferrari	1998
	Williams	1996	8	Benetton	1994		McLaren	1999		Ferrari	1999
11	Benetton	1995		Ferrari	2008		McLaren	2000		Lotus	1965
10	Ferrari	2000		Ferrari	2003		Tyrrell	1971		Lotus	1970
	McLaren	2005		Lotus	1978		Williams	1991		Matra	1969
	McLaren	1989		McLaren	1991		Williams	1994		McLaren	1976
	Williams	1992		McLaren	2007	6	Alfa Romeo	1950		McLaren	1985
	Williams	1993		Renault	2005		Alfa Romeo	1951		McLaren	1990
9	Ferrari	2001		Renault	2006		Cooper	1960		Vanwall	1958
	Ferrari	2006		Williams	1997		Ferrari	1975		Williams	1980

MOST POLE POSITIONS

DRIVERS

68	Michael Schumacher	(GER)
65	Ayrton Senna	(BRA)
33	Jim Clark	(GBR)
	Alain Prost	(FRA)
32	Nigel Mansell	(GBR)
30	Sebastian Vettel	(GER)
29	Juan Manuel Fangio	(ARG)
26	Mika Hakkinen	(FIN)
24	Niki Lauda	(AUT)
	Nelson Piquet	(BRA)
20	Fernando Alonso	(SPA)
	Damon Hill	(GBR)
19	Lewis Hamilton	(GBR)
18	Mario Andretti	(USA)
	Rene Arnoux	(FRA)
17	Jackie Stewart	(GBR)

16	Stirling Moss	(GBR)
	Kimi Raïkkönen	(FIN)
15	Felipe Massa	(BRA)
14	Alberto Ascari	(ITA)
	Rubens Barrichello	(BRA)
	James Hunt	(GBR)
	Ronnie Peterson	(SWE)
13	Jack Brabham	(AUS)
	Graham Hill	(GBR)
	Jacky Ickx	(BEL)
	Juan Pablo Montoya	(COL)
	Jacques Villeneuve	(CDN)
12	Gerhard Berger	(AUT)
	David Coulthard	(GBR)
10	Jochen Rindt	(AUT)
9	Mark Webber	(AUS)

CONSTRUCTORS

205	Ferrari
146	McLaren
126	Williams
107	Lotus
51	Renault
39	Brabham
	Red Bull (née Stewart, then Jaguar Racing)
16	Benetton
14	Tyrrell
12	Alfa Romeo
11	BRM
	Cooper
10	Maserati
9	Ligier
8	Brawn GP (née Honda Racing)
	Shadow
	Mercedes
7	Vanwall
5	March
4	Matra
3	Force India (née Jordan, then Midland, then Spyker)
	Shadow
	Toyota
2	Lancia
1	BAR
	BMW Sauber
	Scuderia Toro Rosso

Ayrton Senna, Alain Prost and Keke Rosberg share the steps of the podium at Monaco in 1986 after the French ace's victory.

FASTEST LAPS

DRIVERS

75	Michael Schumacher	(GER)	17	Rubens Barrichello	(BRA)
41	Alain Prost	(FRA)	15	Felipe Massa (BRA)	
35	Kimi Raïkkönen	(FIN)		Clay Regazzoni (SUI)	
30	Nigel Mansell	(GBR)		Jackie Stewart	(GBR)
28	Jim Clark	(GBR)	14	Jacky Ickx	(BEL)
25	Mika Hakkinen	(FIN)	13	Alberto Ascari	(ITA)
24	Niki Lauda	(AUT)		Alan Jones	(AUS)
23	Juan Manuel Fangio	(ARG)		Riccardo Patrese	(ITA)
	Nelson Piquet	(BRA)		Mark Webber	(AUS)
21	Gerhard Berger	(AUT)	12	Rene Arnoux	(FRA)
19	Fernando Alonso	(SPA)		Jack Brabham	(AUS)
	Damon Hill	(GBR)		Juan Pablo Montoya	(COL)
	Stirling Moss	(GBR)	11	Lewis Hamilton	(GBR)
	Ayrton Senna	(BRA)		John Surtees	(GBR)
18	David Coulthard	(GBR)			

CONSTRUCTORS

226	Ferrari
148	McLaren
130	Williams
71	Lotus
40	Brabham
35	Benetton
31	Renault
22	Red Bull
	Tyrrell
15	BRM
	Maserati
14	Alfa Romeo
13	Cooper
12	Matra
11	Prost (née Ligier)
9	Mercedes
8	Brawn GP (née BAR)

MOST POINTS (THIS FIGURE IS GROSS TALLY, I.E. INCLUDING SCORES THAT WERE LATER DROPPED)

DRIVERS

1517	Michael Schumacher	(GER)	420.5	Niki Lauda	(AUT)
1086	Fernando Alonso	(SPA)	420	Mika Hakkinen	(FIN)
811	Jenson Button	(GBR)	385	Gerhard Berger	(AUT)
798.5	Alain Prost	(FRA)	360	Damon Hill	(GBR)
773	Sebastian Vettel	(GER)		Jackie Stewart	(GBR)
723	Lewis Hamilton	(GBR)	329	Ralf Schumacher	(GER)
669.5	Mark Webber	(AUS)	310	Carlos Reutemann	(ARG)
658	Rubens Barrichello	(BRA)	307	Juan Pablo Montoya	(COL)
614	Ayrton Senna	(BRA)	306.5	Nico Rosberg	(GER)
582	Felipe Massa	(BRA)	289	Graham Hill	(GBR)
579	Kimi Raïkkönen	(FIN)	281	Emerson Fittipaldi	(BRA)
535	David Coulthard	(GBR)		Riccardo Patrese	(ITA)
485.5	Nelson Piquet	(BRA)	277.5	Juan Manuel Fangio	(ARG)
482	Nigel Mansell	(GBR)	275	Giancarlo Fisichella	(ITA)

CONSTRUCTORS

4848.5	Ferrari
4313.5	McLaren
2680	Williams
1492.5	Red Bull (née Stewart, then Jaguar Racing)
1382	Renault
1352	Lotus
884	Mercedes GP (née BAR then Honda Racing, then Brawn GP)
877.5	Benetton
854	Brabham
617	Tyrrell
585	Sauber (including BMW Sauber)
442	Force India (née Jordan, then Midland, then Spyker)
439	BRM
424	Prost (née Ligier)
333	Cooper
326	Honda Racing (néeBAR)
278.5	Toyota
171.5	March
167	Arrows
155	Matra
148	Scuderia Toro Rosso

Jim Clark, shown at speed in his Lotus 25 in 1964, set 28 fastest laps in his F1 career.

Sebastian Vettel became the first winner of the Indian GP at Buddh International Circuit in 2011 for Red Bull Racing.

MOST DRIVERS' TITLES

7	Michael Schumacher	(GER)		Emerson Fittipaldi	(BRA)	Denis Hulme	(NZL)
5	Juan Manuel Fangio	(ARG)		Mika Hakkinen	(FIN)	James Hunt	(GBR)
4	Alain Prost	(FRA)		Graham Hill	(GBR)	Alan Jones	(AUS)
3	Jack Brabham	(AUS)		Sebastian Vettel	(GER)	Nigel Mansell	(GBR)
	Niki Lauda	(AUT)	**1**	Mario Andretti	(USA)	Kimi Raïkkönen	(FIN)
	Nelson Piquet	(BRA)		Jenson Buttopn	(GBR)	Jochen Rindt	(AUT)
	Ayrton Senna	(BRA)		Giuseppe Farina	(ITA)	Keke Rosberg	(FIN)
	Jackie Stewart	(GBR)		Lewis Hamilton	(GBR)	Jody Scheckter	(RSA)
2	Fernando Alonso	(SPA)		Mike Hawthorn	(GBR)	John Surtees	(GBR)
	Alberto Ascari	(ITA)		Damon Hill	(GBR)	Jacques Villeneuve	(CDN)
	Jim Clark	(GBR)		Phil Hill	(USA)		

MOST CONSTRUCTORS' TITLES

16	Ferrari	**2**	Brabham	**1**	Benetton
9	Williams		Cooper		BRM
8	McLaren		Red Bull		Matra
7	Lotus		Renault		Tyrrell
					Vanwall

NB TO AVOID CONFUSION, THE RENAULT STATS LISTED ARE BASED ON THE TEAM THAT EVOLVED FROM BENETTON IN 2002 AND INCLUDE THOSE STATS THAT HAVE HAPPENED SINCE PLUS THOSE FROM RENAULT'S FIRST SPELL IN F1 BETWEEN 1977 AND 1985. THE FIGURES FOR BENETTON AND TOLEMAN FROM WHICH IT METAMORPHOSED IN 1986 ARE LISTED AS BENETTON. CONVERSELY, THE STATS FOR RED BULL INCLUDE THOSE OF THE STEWART AND JAGUAR RACING TEAMS FROM WHICH IT EVOLVED. LIKEWISE, FORCE INDIA'S STATS INCLUDE THOSE OF JORDAN, MIDLAND SPYKER AND SCUDERIA TORO ROSSO THOSE OF MINARDI.

2012 FILL-IN CHART

DRIVER	TEAM	Round 1 – 18 Mar AUSTRALIAN GP	Round 2 – 25 Mar MALAYSIAN GP	Round 3 – 15 Apr CHINESE GP	Round 4 – 22 Apr BAHRAIN GP	Round 5 – 13 May SPANISH GP	Round 6 – 27 May MONACO GP	Round 7 – 10 Jun CANADIAN GP	Round 8 – 24 Jun EUROPEAN GP
1 SEBASTIAN VETTEL	Red Bull								
2 MARK WEBBER	Red Bull								
3 JENSON BUTTON	McLaren								
4 LEWIS HAMILTON	McLaren								
5 FERNANDO ALONSO	Ferrari								
6 FELIPE MASSA	Ferrari								
7 MICHAEL SCHUMACHER	Mercedes								
8 NICO ROSBERG	Mercedes								
9 KIMI RAÏKKÖNEN	Lotus								
10 ROMAIN GROSJEAN	Lotus								
11 PAUL DI RESTA	Force India								
12 NICO HULKENBERG	Force India								
14 KAMUI KOBAYASHI	Sauber								
15 SERGIO PÉREZ	Sauber								
16 DANIEL RICCIARDO	Toro Rosso								
17 JEAN-ERIC VERGNE	Toro Rosso								
18 PASTOR MALDONADO	Williams								
19 BRUNO SENNA	Williams								
20 HEIKKI KOVALAINEN	Caterham								
21 JARNO TRULLI	Caterham								
22 PEDRO DE LA ROSA	HRT								
23 JAIME ALGUERSUARI*	HRT								
24 TIMO GLOCK	Marussia								
25 CHARLES PIC	Marussia								

SCORING SYSTEM: 25, 20, 15, 10, 8, 6, 4, 3, 2, 1 POINTS
FOR THE FIRST 10 FINISHERS IN EACH GRAND PRIX
* Leading candidate at the time of going to press.

	Round 9 – 8 Jul BRITISH GP	Round 10 – 22 Jul GERMAN GP	Round 11 – 29 Jul HUNGARIAN GP	Round 12 – 2 Sep BELGIAN GP	Round 13 – 9 Sep ITALIAN GP	Round 14 – 23 Sep SINGAPORE GP	Round 15 – 7 Oct JAPANESE GP	Round 16 – 14 Oct KOREAN GP	Round 17 – 28 Oct INDIAN GP	Round 18 – 4 Nov ABU DHABI GP	Round 19 – 18 Nov UNITED STATES GP	Round 20 – 25 Nov BRAZILIAN GP	POINTS TOTAL

Sepang's wide main straight offers plenty of space for lining up a passing manoeuvre on the run down toward the first corner.

The Ferraris looked as spectacular as ever in 2011, but will be hoping for more than one win in the year ahead.

The publishers would like to thank the following sources for their kind permission to reproduce the pictures in this book.

Getty Images: /Alexander Nemenov/AFP: 63C

LAT Photographic: 4, 6-7, 19, 29, 54, 55, 61TL, 61R, 66-67, 90-91, 118L, 119, 121, 122; /Charles Coates: 11, 13, 17, 20, 22, 24, 27, 30, 32, 33, 34, 37, 38, 40, 41, 42, 47, 48, 49, 51, 53, 93, 104, 114-115, 118R; /Glenn Dunbar: 8-9, 18, 26, 31, 35, 43, 45, 46, 52, 56, 63B, 88-89, 92, 96, 103, 105, 110, 112; /Steve Etherington: 23, 25, 94, 95, 111, 120, 123, 126-127; /FOTA: 61B; /Andrew Ferraro: 14, 15, 39, 44, 58-59, 63TL, 98, 99, 102, 108; /Andy Hone: 10, 12, 36, 50, 100-101, 106, 107, 109, 113; /Nigel Kinrade: 28; /Alastair Staley: 57; /Steven Tee: 2-3, 16, 21, 64-65, 97, 128

Every effort has been made to acknowledge correctly and contact the source and/or copyright holder of each picture and Carlton Books Limited apologises for any unintentional errors or omissions that will be corrected in future editions of this book.